SILENCING THE OPPOSITION

THE HISTORY OF COMMUNICATION

Robert W. McChesney and
John C. Nerone, editors

*A list of books in the series appears at the end of this book.*

# SILENCING THE OPPOSITION

## Antinuclear Movements and the Media in the Cold War

Andrew Rojecki

University of Illinois Press
Urbana and Chicago

Manufactured in the United States of America
∞ This book is printed on acid-free paper.

Library of Congress Cataloging-in-Publication Data
Rojecki, Andrew, 1946–
Silencing the opposition : antinuclear movements and the media in the Cold War / Andrew Rojecki.
p. cm. — (History of communication)
Includes bibliographical references and index.
ISBN 0-252-02510-5 (cloth : acid-free paper)
ISBN 0-252-06824-6 (paper : acid-free paper)
1. Antinuclear movement—United States—History—20th century. 2. Antinuclear movement—Press coverage—United States—History—20th century. I. Title. II. Series.
JZ5577.5.R65 1999
070.4'493271747'0973—dc21 99-6180
CIP

1 2 3 4 5 C P 5 4 3 2 1

For Susan and my parents

# CONTENTS

# ACKNOWLEDGMENTS

I have been very fortunate during this project for the generous advice and support of colleagues and friends. Throughout this project, from its inception in a course paper through to the final manuscript, Bob Entman has been a generous adviser and friend. His urgings to improve, revise, and rethink and, above all, his passion for politics gave me a wonderful model for committed scholarship. At Northwestern University Ben Page offered invaluable commentaries and boundless enthusiasm that gave me the confidence to press on. My gratitude also to Jim Ettema, who opened my eyes to the multiple meanings in text and the subtle relationship between constraint and creativity, and to Tom Goodnight, Susan Herbst, and Jane Mansbridge for their intellectual generosity and guidance.

My thanks also to David Meyer and Tom Rochon for their expertise on the nuclear freeze; their guidance helped to shape chapters 6 and 7. David Meyer also offered detailed critiques of the work as a whole and pushed the analysis at critical times during its revisions. At Indiana University David Nord suggested invaluable historical references for chapter 1 and gave it a close thoughtful reading. Whatever errors remain there or elsewhere are mine alone.

The editorial staff at the University of Illinois Press was uniformly professional, kind, and hard working; my warm regards to Bruce Bethell, Laurie Matheson, Terry Sears, and especially Karen Hewitt, who had the faith to bring this project to fruition.

Throughout the tempests of this project, my wife, Susan, provided a calm island of intelligent support. I dedicate this book to her and to my parents, Walter and Kazimiera, who set me out on the waters.

# SILENCING THE OPPOSITION

# 1 Collective Deliberation and the Common Defense

Twice during the cold war Americans joined in mass public protest because they felt they were being held hostage to an elusive quest for nuclear security and the fabulous expense of national resources it consumed. By the end of the cold war the weapons stockpile had nonetheless grown to over 30,000 warheads, and estimates of its potential destructive power exceeded human scale. Today these weapons remain largely intact. This book examines the actions of two participants in this story: the political movements that attempted to stop or slow the buildup of these weapons stores and the news media that reported their efforts. The general question that drives the study is whether the news media provided these groups with a secure forum for their ideas, whether citizens had the ready access to the media that their government enjoyed.

In this study I examine the news media's treatment of two political movements: the test ban movement, which spanned the second Eisenhower and the Kennedy presidencies, and the nuclear freeze movement, which coincided with the first Reagan administration. Though separated by a generation, these movements shared similar constituencies and goals. Both sought to slow the nuclear arms race by mobilizing mainstream citizens to influence defense policy. Each thus came to depend on the news media for bringing its message to a wider public.

What varied and thus what makes these cases theoretically interesting was the degree of official support for the movements' aims. During the Eisenhower years, support for a test ban depended on various policy initiatives and patterns of administration dissent. By contrast, Kennedy generally sympathized with the movement's aims, for its goal dovetailed with his long-term plans for a shift in military strategy. Finally, the Reagan administration opposed a weapons freeze to the last.

These movements provide historical case studies that serve as fascinating miniatures of deliberative democracy in action. The news media stand at the center of these miniatures and of this study because they provide the link among dissident movements, citizens, and government. The patterns of their reporting provide a rich store of historical evidence that suggests answers to a number of questions: How dependable a forum do the news media provide for citizen-driven politics? To what degree does the availability of this forum depend on the state of official or editorial policy? Finally, to what extent do the news media influence the debate on national security?

As I sought answers for these specific questions, I discovered larger patterns that I had not anticipated but that began to make sense when contextualized historically. One such finding was a subtle change in the way the news media have appraised the political world. For example, who do the media regard as more credible and persuasive, specific individuals or the mass of a faceless public, a dignitary lending his or her reputation to an idea or a symbolically significant mass of people attending a rally or registering an anonymous opinion on a sample survey? Findings on this and related matters indicate a shift in the political culture that suggests important implications for political movements and thus for an understanding of participatory democracy.

Before beginning a detailed exploration of these miniatures, I need to set up a framework for establishing the significance of political movements in democracy and of the mass media's role in our deliberations as citizens. To do this, I begin with a traditional metaphor for understanding the shape and operation of our political system. I then examine the mass media's role in political deliberation and the pressures that influence their effectiveness. The chapter concludes with an overview of political movements and their importance for our system of governance.

## A Marketplace Metaphor for Politics

Any study of political movements requires a model of the way American democracy works, at least in some idealized way. The formal model set out in the Constitution suggests a delicately counterbalanced device that cushions and disperses applied forces. No individual, no group, and no branch of government is to exert such force unilaterally. The famous checks and balances discourage accumulation of power in any one branch, while representative democracy preserves the rights of the least organized.

The Constitution's framers rejected direct popular democracy as impractical and potentially harmful to the rights of minorities. In *The Federalist* no. 10, Madison reasoned that an unequal distribution of human faculties would eventually result in an unequal distribution of property. This would tend to obstruct the public good through expansion of self-interest. By entrusting the reins of power to those "whose wisdom may best discern the true interest of their country, and whose patriotism and love of justice will be least likely to sacrifice it to temporary or partial considerations," representative democracy would diminish the passions of self-interest, secure the public good, and advance private interest (Madison [1788] 1981, 93). Government would draw its authority and legitimacy from the consent of the people as equal representatives engaged in a process absent of manipulation and directed at the common good, not the interests of the few or the best organized.

As this system bridles organized power, it also pits incompatible political ideals against one another. The philosophy underlying the Declaration of Independence and the Constitution includes a measure of social contract theory that seeks to secure the common good through altruistic deliberation. At the same time, however, it champions a notion of liberty that equates the common good with the traffic of individual self-interest.

Though the founding documents are informed by both values, American values and political institutions are animated largely by liberty as a political ideal. McClosky and Zaller's (1984) survey of political values, for example, revealed that Americans revere liberty over equality by better than three to one. (Europeans are about evenly divided when asked to choose.) The propensity for liberty has profound consequences for our political culture.

Benjamin Barber (1984) argues that Americans' circumscribed views of individualism and liberty promote political institutions that restrict the development of a civic-minded culture. Conceived chiefly as means to individual and private ends, these values lead us toward a "negative" view of liberty (see Berlin 1969) that, though celebrating individual choice, deters the development of robust theories of participation, public goods, or civic virtue.

This individualized view of political transactions encourages a marketplace metaphor for a political system in which conflict is resolved by bargaining and exchange among free and equal groups and individuals who pursue their self-interests (Barber 1984, 143). The common good is defined by legislation that stems from the simple product of the multiple interactions and bargains involved. Extended, this marketplace metaphor suggests that if government fails to produce an outcome acceptable to all parties, citizens can organize and pressure government to produce it (Truman 1951). From this viewpoint, a citizen-led movement may be seen as a correction to a failed market and thus as a safety valve for maintaining the legitimacy of the political system.

### *The Market for Ideas*

To regard movements as correctives to failures in the political marketplace is to use the marketplace metaphor in a more familiar venue, the realm of information and ideas. The "marketplace of ideas" is a normative metaphor whose suitability depends on the truth of several controversial assumptions, including the self-righting principle (the truth always wins in a battle with falsehood) that John Milton developed in his tract *Areopagitica* as grounds for abolishing English censorship laws. Another relevant assumption comes from John Stuart Mill, namely, the claim that a vigorous, deliberative democracy depends on the "collision" of opinions. Mill ([1859] 1974) applies a kind of survival-of-the-fittest analogy to the evolution of right opinion: the longer the adversarial process, the greater the fitness of the surviving opinion. In this sense, a popular movement challenges received opinion and forces it to defend itself. According to this theory, the result is a muscular, defensible policy or one exposed as flabby and insupportable.

Markets, however, are rarely spontaneous or unregulated. The First Amendment created a theoretical space for a marketplace of ideas, but its practical boundaries have developed by tradition and legal precedent. There is even some controversy about the framers' intent in guaranteeing press freedom. Leonard Levy argues, for example, that the framers took English common law as the basis for their understanding of press freedom. Since common law neither prevented the state from suing newspapers for libel nor even regarded truth as a defense, Levy argues that the framers believed everyone to be accountable under criminal law for abuses of the right to speak or publish freely. Indeed, Jefferson's view, like that of his generation, was that "government could be criminally assaulted merely by lowering it in the public's esteem" (Levy 1988, 200).

As many critics point out, however (see Smith 1986; Baldasty 1976; Teeter 1968), colonial governors restrained themselves from prosecutions for fear of failing in the court of public opinion, which might have looked suspiciously on government that imprisoned its critics.

A libertarian theory of the press emerged in the early 1800s after the debate on the Sedition Act of 1798. This theory holds that free government cannot exist without freedom of discourse. In this view the press acts as a de facto fourth branch of government—and thus as a check on the other three—by exposing corruption, fragmenting power, and thus ensuring public accountability (Levy 1988, 213).

Even with an ideological marketplace guaranteed by law, precedent, and tradition, suppliers will emerge only when there is demand. This also came early on, when the Radical Whig authorities recognized the desirability of an informed citizenry. Historian Richard D. Brown writes that the catalyst for this idea came between 1763 and 1775, when a series of British parliamentary acts affecting trade, imports, and a number of other issues angered the American gentry. They soon realized that an effective protest would require the mobilization of popular opposition using public meetings, newspapers, and pamphlets. Foreshadowing later political movements, the Whigs unwittingly set in motion a series of precedents from which there would be no return:

> The Radical Whig gentlemen who led Boston politics were discovering in 1764 what leaders in other colonies would soon recognize: that by engaging the citizenry at large in their protests, their opposition became formidable to the royal administrations in their colonies and perhaps even to the ministry and Parliament. The recognition of this political reality, more than any other single factor, convinced revolutionary leaders, who had not previously devoted much attention to the subject, that an informed citizenry was a vital matter of practical politics. (Brown 1996, 53–54)

Public access to legislative galleries and newspapers provided the earliest venue for this marketplace. Citizens had the means for keeping abreast of political debate and, through the press, for developing an awareness of one another's discontent. As legal scholar Stephen Holmes has noted, "Independently operated newspapers paralyze a potential oppressor because they make disgruntled citizens aware of each other's disgruntlement and of their collective strength. As an open channel of communication, a free press can coordinate popular resistance" (Holmes 1990, 7).

In this model of collective deliberation, even a widely dispersed population can contribute to a national debate using the news media as a common forum (Page and Shapiro 1992; Page 1996). Provided that no systematic biases exist in the news sources tapped for this forum, citizens have, over time, the means for developing enlightened policy preferences (Mansbridge 1980, 25; see also Elster 1983). As an example, let's say the CIA has revealed the presence of a new weapons system in Iran that threatens the military balance in the Middle East. The president argues that this imbalance obliges the United States to sell advanced military equipment to Iran's neighbors, a measure that requires congressional approval. Let's also say that the media publicize two interpretations of this situation. One asserts that what appears to be a new weapons system constitutes merely an incremental improvement to an existing one and that the introduction of new U.S. weapons would begin a truly destabilizing arms race. The other interpretation claims that the Iranian advance was a response to a United States–supported hostile regime in Iraq and that a proper response would be to cut off sales of advanced weapons. The presence of such alternative interpretations, supported by credible sources, will foster enlightened opinion that can legitimately guide government action. Here the quality of policy reflects the enlightened preferences developed through the process.

## Market Failures

The ideal submits to the real, however, so now I turn my attention to the shortcomings of this model by focusing on the concept of "unenlightened preferences." These are traceable to real-world pressures on the news media and citizens themselves.

Unenlightened policy preferences result from two principal causes, limited flows of information and inattentive citizens. Unfortunately, as Entman (1989) has pointed out, these two factors stand in a reciprocal relationship that makes it difficult to assign causal priority: are citizens unenlightened because they prefer to be entertained rather than informed, or are they ill served because, as commercial organizations, the media seek large audiences they can sell to advertisers (Entman and Wildman 1992)?

Put simply, the news media's goals for profitability may conflict with the normative ideal of protecting the public interest. This is especially true now, for the absorption of networks and newspapers into media conglomerates has eroded the wall between the editorial and the business sides of the news media. CEOs now regard news media not as prestigious "loss leaders" but as profit centers that must do their part in adding to the corporate bottom line. In 1997, for example, the Times Mirror Company assigned a business executive to each of the editorial departments of the *Los Angeles Times*. The mission of these executives was to help plan the contents of the respective sections in an effort to stanch circulation losses, presumably to the electronic media. Although each new editor reassured the staff that advertisers would not influence content, the creation of new sections would depend in part on their ability to draw advertisers (*New York Times*, October 13, 1997, sec. D, p. 1). Since there are no advertisers for public goods, these economic pressures will likely highlight the identities of the public as consumers rather than as civic-minded citizens.

Mitigating these business pressures, however, is the professional ideology of journalists, which traces its origins to the libertarian theory of the press. In this view reporters are tacitly committed to the public interest, scrutinizing government officials so as to ensure citizens' rights. Here too, however, is a cross-current of pressure that comes from reporters' pragmatic needs to develop friendly but potentially co-opting relationships with their sources. The efficient organization of journalism redounds to the benefit of elected officials, who already enjoy the advantages of office and who thus regard the media as only one of several resources for wielding power (Kingdon 1984).

Politicians enlist the media strategically to gain support for their policies, especially when they are losing a fight. The goal is to attract public attention, which the losers hope to enlist in their favor (Schattschneider 1960). Ordinarily, if there is no significant disagreement, if a deal can be struck, there will be little or no media attention and therefore no issue for the public to contemplate. On balance this arrangement works well, but occasionally it breaks down, with enormous consequences for the public interest. During the 1988 presidential campaign, for example, both Democrats and Republicans tacitly agreed to ignore the embarrassing issue of savings and loan failures that resulted from the deregulation of the industry during the Reagan presidency. Because politicians did not make it an issue, the press largely ignored it, thereby prolonging and aggravating a crisis whose ultimate cost to taxpayers has been estimated between $500 billion and $1 trillion.

### *Political Movements*

Here then is one important source of citizen-centered politics: the issue/agenda advantage enjoyed by government officials may result in a gap between citizen preferences and policies. The gap becomes a potential source for a political movement.

In general, movements begin in the efforts of organized groups to make the larger public aware of an issue and a preferred solution. When and if the public responds, if it finds the appeal persuasive, a movement occurs. The term *movement* has been applied to diverse phenomena ranging from public-interest lobbies (e.g., Green Peace) to political revolutions (McAdam, McCarthy, and Zald 1988, 695). Although the concept embraces a potentially wide range of events, most recent research has focused on reform movements, such as the civil rights, women's rights, and antiwar movements.

Unlike earlier theoretical perspectives on movements that focused on societal breakdown and alienation, current theories assume that conflict is normal and constant but that what vary are the resources available to movement organizers and the "structure of political opportunities," the political system's receptivity or vulnerability to organized protest.[1] These dimensions include the formal political structure, climate of government responsiveness, absence of coherent policy, and large-scale demographic trends. Taken individually or collectively these factors obstruct or facilitate citizen action in pursuit of political goals (Eisinger 1973). For example, McAdam (1982) argued that the growing political power of blacks in the 1950s increased southern fears of federal intervention, which in turn reduced oppression. These trends combined to open a window of opportunity for the civil rights movement.

The media's receptivity to movement messages is an important dimension in this opportunity structure because citizens do not have (or may not wish to spend) the time or money needed to gather information independently. A key problem for the media—and thus for deliberative and pluralist democracy—is how to weigh the importance of political actors in an environment where there are more calls for attention than there appears to be space to accommodate them.

### *Weighing Issue Importance*

Bennett (1990) has suggested a partial normative solution to this problem of balance: the news media should index their selection of viewpoints to stable and majority public opinion. That is, the quality and quantity of views in the news ought to reflect the distribution of public opinion. If a majority of the public is at odds with a policy, and political leaders do not address it, the media ought to include adversarial voices from nonelite sources, such as movement representatives, experts, and academicians. Bennett's solution has a pragmatic appeal and the advantage of being empirically grounded, but it fails to address how the public is to establish a "stable" (or enlightened) opinion in the first place. If, as Bennett demonstrates, the voices of opposition are often drowned out, if their cases and arguments do not receive wide coverage, divergent public opinion is unlikely to develop the tenacity necessary to stand up to received wisdom. The danger here is less a "spiral of silence" (Noelle-Neumann 1974) than a straw man in the guise of an energetic, well-informed opponent.

Absent the fullest circulation of information and coherent, well-articulated policy proposals, public opinion is unenlightened and remains so because news organizations tend to behave as rational economic actors. Reporters maintain routine contact with politicians in the system of news beats that efficiently disburses organizational resources. This situation leads to information biases and shortages in mass-circulated outlets.

Because pressure groups, such as political movements, do not ordinarily merit a beat assignment, they must use creative tactics to gain media attention. Martin Luther King Jr., for example, formulated a successful plan that would expose southern police brutality to a horrified national press (Garrow 1978). Benefiting from her own academic training in media theory and her experience as a union organizer, Charlotte Ryan (1991) has written an analysis of media practices for movement activists interested in enlisting mass media resources for their cause. Discussing such issues as standards of newsworthiness, the structural components of news stories, and the organization of the media, Ryan's sophisticated guide is for activists who realize the mobilizing potential of the media but need to understand their inner workings for harnessing their power.

But even if a citizen-led movement gains our attention, what of the issue of legitimacy? Movements are, after all, defined by their unconventionality. What claim do they have on our attention? By definition movements will weaken unless they find some resonant chord among those outside their boundaries. To gain legitimacy and strength, they must tap public frustration and convert new awareness or changed opinion into a source of political pressure on an unresponsive political system. Because they tap firsthand experience, movements that aim for changes in domestic policy, such as the civil rights movement, enjoy an immense advantage over those that aim to change foreign policy. The absence of felt experience may reduce urgency and interest.

### *An Uninformed, Mercurial Public?*

Already hampered by their unconventionality, movements with foreign policy aims face an additional burden: the elite belief that citizen opinion on foreign policy is ill informed and volatile (Almond 1960; Cohen 1973). Political leaders challenged by movements with foreign policy goals may rationalize away such opposition by claiming that they are better informed and need to act decisively in a world populated by nondemocratic nations less encumbered by accountability to public will. These arguments are sometimes based on a legitimate need to act decisively or to prevent enemies from gaining access to sensitive information. As I will show, however, these arguments may also be enlisted to usurp the authority of the popular will.

The media play a role in the apprehensiveness citizens feel about taking positions on foreign policy and defense by neglecting foreign issues except during crises, when they often defer to official interpretations of events (Paletz and Entman 1981). In a practice variously named "rallying round the flag" and "supporting the president in crisis," the news media tend to defer or to grant wide latitude to the president in emergency situations and, more subtly, to permit government to define the terms and limits of debate (Entman and Page 1992). Nourished by a steady diet of these messages, people may come to feel ill equipped to make stable, rational judgments or even to develop passionate feelings about foreign policy. Thus a movement with foreign policy aims adds another burden to its already difficult task: overcoming the presumption of a public with an impaired ability to make reasoned judgments.

Why then entrust the nation's security to a presumably uninformed and capricious public opinion? The counterarguments come from two different directions. First, despite their presumed wisdom, elected officials are themselves susceptible to lapses in judgment. Examples include the Bay of Pigs invasion, the Tonkin Gulf incidents, the Iran-Contra affair, and the "tilt" toward Iraq during its war with Iran. There is no reason to believe that a group of isolated experts are inherently better equipped to develop wise policy. In fact, there is documented evidence that such isolation promotes a bunker mentality likely to limit the range of policy options (Janis 1972).

A second counterargument comes from recent studies of public opinion. Public opinion is a controversial concept, especially as it is currently conceived and measured by the modern sample survey. Some scholars reject it as fundamentally undemocratic because it reduces the cost of holding an opinion, thereby burying those who are well informed and passionate among those in a "silent majority," who may be uninformed or merely indifferent (Ginsberg 1986). Others question the value of opinions gathered by surveys that constrain the range of both questions and answers and thus can conceal an agenda for building support for a policy favored by the sponsoring organization (Bourdieu 1979).

In contrast, still other scholars argue that analysis of long-run trends suggests a sensible, rational public. In their study of national surveys conducted between 1935 and 1990 on over one thousand repeated survey questions, political scientists Benjamin Page and Robert Shapiro (1992) found that Americans in the aggregate held firm opinions on foreign policy grounded in a set of stable values. They argue that public opinion responds appropriately to changing circumstances and new information. Contrary to Gabriel Almond's claims as to the fickleness of the public's mood, the distribution of opinion on issues moves deliberately and "sensibly." For example, on foreign policy issues, fewer than half changed as much as six percentage points. On the majority of issues Page and Shapiro found a modest rate of change that they termed "reasonable response" to interpretations of world events provided by political leaders and the news media.[2]

My own view is that the value of public opinion must be considered in the light of the interest people have on a given issue as well as the quality of information available. Although it would be folly to be guided by the results of opinion surveys on obscure issues such as, for example, the desirability of reducing government supports for the sugar beet industry, it would be equally foolish to dismiss public opinion on issues that deeply engage the public, such as declaring a war and reinstating the military draft. Here, too, we need to evaluate the scope of debate and the quality of information available for developing enlightened preferences. These preferences in a very important way depend on the attention the media pay to an issue. In short, the value of opinion as measured by these sample surveys depends on the vigor and quality of public debate.

A second reason for paying at least some attention to public opinion is that surveys provide us with the most reliable method for determining what *everyone* is thinking. As imperfect a guide as public opinion offers, it is in the absence of better measures the best way to discover what the nation as a whole thinks. Naturally, some opinions are better informed than others, but by carefully designing surveys that include knowledge questions, we can distinguish uninformed from informed attitudes and determine whether it makes a difference on the issue in question.

A final reason for considering public opinion is that together with the content of the media, it provides an intermediate channel of communication between policymakers and movements. As I demonstrate in the analysis to come, both movement leaders and government officials regard public opinion as an important political resource. When politicians refer to the "average American" or the "American public," they use the symbolic political resources made available by measuring public opinion. Public opinion is a valuable rhetorical resource, independent of its status as an indicator of the state of the public mind, however volatile or informed. Beyond these normative reasons to value public opinion, moreover, there is an empirical one: public opinion has a reciprocal impact on government officials' talk and action and thus on policy outcomes.

But even if we give public opinion some credence as a guide to elected politicians, what of the presumably highly secret and complex technical issues surrounding nuclear arms? Here, too, there are empirical and normative arguments for legitimating public participation. Empirical evidence shows that citizens have "functional" knowledge of issues regarding nuclear war and arms negotiations that far outstrips their knowledge of technical jargon (Graham 1988, 328).

Technical expertise may lend dubious credence, however, for what makes arms control movements (especially nuclear arms peace movements) interesting is a unique quality they share: whereas the success of other kinds of movements can be gauged by some tangible result, few such indicators of success exist for arms control. In the civil rights movement, for example, participants could see how the passage of state and federal laws made voting easier, provided wider entrance to higher education, or reduced poverty. No similarly decisive indicator exists for arms control. With nuclear issues it is difficult if not impossible to claim that a certain course of action prevented nuclear war. We can, however, observe movement influence on changes in arms control policy and on treaties that lead to decreases in military spending (Doty 1984, 11).

Robert Dahl (1985) provides us with perhaps the most important normative argument for legitimating the role of citizen activism in highly technical issues. Dahl argues that anyone who delegates authority to a politician or an expert appointed by a politician does this with two expectations: that the expert is better qualified to make a decision and that continued delegation is conditional on adequate performance. The individual's authority is *alienated* when such delegation takes place involuntarily or when no clear path exists for recapturing it—say, through a vigorous public debate (Dahl 1985, 6–7).

A vigorous debate requires public adversaries, a neutral mass media, and citizen interest in the issues debated, hence the importance of the antinuclear movements for arousing public interest on what has traditionally been a highly sequestered set of issues. In some ways these movements provide us with the clearest (and perhaps most difficult) test for the media's immunity from opinion-distorting government influence, for citizens depend heavily on both for their information and thus for their preferences.

How the media convey their messages and arguments bears heavily not only on the distribution of public opinion but also on the passion with which citizens hold on to their beliefs and on the way they come to make tradeoffs among preferences and policies. For example, on the issues of peace and defense, Americans favor bargaining only from strength if they feel that there is at least parity in force levels between the United States and its foes (Russett 1990). The issue is not whether there is a preference for peace and accommodation but how we come to believe that we are adequately defended. It is on the latter point that the notion of a rational public fails to address the more relevant question of how well the media inform it.

Combining abstract and remote cause with immediate personal effect, the issues of nuclear war represent the extreme case of policy proposals made by a small group of highly specialized technical and diplomatic elites that might affect the lives of people not only in the United States but across the entire planet. As Hans Morgenthau has noted, "The great issues of nuclear strategy . . . cannot even be the subject of meaningful debate because there can be no competent judgment without meaningful knowledge. Thus the great national decisions of life and death are rendered by technological elites, and both the Congress and the people at large retain little more than the illusion of making the decisions which the theory of democracy supposes them to make" (in Boyer 1984, 833). These effects are not limited to the possibility of sudden incineration in a nuclear war but include redirected societal priorities and the resulting hardships caused by increased taxation and spending on weapons and weapons research. Consider, for example, a Brookings Institution estimate that the nuclear arms program cost the nation $5.4 trillion (in constant 1996 dollars), an amount equal to the national debt (Schwartz 1998).

## Why Movements Matter

To the extent that foreign and defense policy movements question received wisdom and call on elected officials to justify policy, they provide a valuable source of political education. The subject of their involvement throws light on issues on which the public has traditionally had little information. Increased public engagement sharpens the focus of debate and (one hopes) smokes out a reasoned defense of current policy. Beyond the achievement of wise policy, there is the long-term goal of enlarging the public sphere and enriching the political culture to a point beyond the need for defending the legitimacy of citizen influence on the political process. Initial favorable reception is insufficient for a movement to have a real effect on policy, however; it must stay in the public eye long enough to make its influence felt. To the extent that a movement remains immune to administration cues that question the legitimacy of its politics or its supporters' loyalty to the state, it has a fair shot at achieving some of its goals. And although the movement may fail to get all its favored policies accepted or to have immediate impact, it is severely hampered if its diagnoses and remedies do not become part of the national communicative discourse. In this sense a failed movement is a wasted opportunity to enrich a political culture that better nourishes deliberative democracy.

By what mechanism do the mass media affect the dynamics of opinion formation? I now turn to a closer examination of the opponents in this contest. To focus my discussion, I ask a commonsensical question: how can we tell whether the news media are presenting us with a fair picture of these opponents? The next chapter suggests some ways we might assess this.

## Notes

1. Lowi (1971, 53–54) argues that the numerous social movements in U.S. history result from the extreme difficulty of mounting an effective challenge to the status quo just because of the intricacies of the institutional checks and balances.

2. Page and Shapiro also argue for a rational public opinion "in the aggregate" by treating uninformed opinions as random measurement errors that cancel one another and leave informed opinions as the true central tendencies. For an interesting counterargument, see Althaus 1998.

# 2 The Origins of Common Sense

Issues of national defense and security, peace and war, and life and death often turn on perception: beliefs as to whether we are well armed, whether we have a credible deterrent force, or whether our foes believe what we believe. Public perceptions of the relative balance between American and enemy forces confine and guide the range of political options for decision makers, even though these perceptions may themselves be the product of official information (Garthoff 1985, 19). Indeed, some of the most important strategic decisions of our time can be traced to compelling official fictions, such as the notion of a missile gap, first used by John F. Kennedy to maneuver Richard Nixon into an obligatory defense of the outgoing Eisenhower administration (Giglio 1991, 17), and the idea of a window of vulnerability, used by Ronald Reagan to pave the way for large increases in the defense budget.

Because citizens often consider themselves incapable of understanding the complexities of defense policy, many relinquish their control to government officials (Dahl 1985). At times, however, a large number of Americans have joined with a core of peace activists to recover their place in the debate. Because their ideas are usually unrepresented or resisted by elected officials, they depend on pressure tactics to get their message across to others, to mobilize new followers, and to influence public opinion. Personal contacts, meetings, telephone networks, press releases, and specialized publications provide a base of communicative channels for this goal, but the mass media offer an indispensable forum for recruitment and influence.

## Media and Common Sense

Communication scholars have described the mass media as the "site on which various social groups, institutions, and ideologies struggle over the definition and construction of reality" (Gurevitch and Levy 1985). Political movements enter this contest at somewhat of a disadvantage because elected officials enjoy a presumption of legitimacy, especially on the ostensibly complex issues of defense. To overcome this disadvantage, movements need to engage a wide base of popular support that rests on the plausibility of their case, the persuasiveness of their appeal, and the dependability of the news for conveying their message.

Contemporary political movements regard the mass media as a tempting but risky resource (Gitlin 1980; Ryan 1991). On the positive side, they offer the widest communicative channel to potential converts, provide movement participants with the rewards of recognition, and certify movement legitimacy in the eyes of influential politicians. Attention by newspapers such as the *New York Times,* the major television networks, and the news weeklies legitimate political actors, anointing the key players on a given issue (Gamson and Meyer 1996, 287). On the negative side, newsgathering routines open reporters to entangling relationships with government news sources who may have a considerable stake in policy outcomes. These relationships and the conventional standards of newsworthiness that draw reporters' attention to the distractions of conflict, drama, and novelty can fractionate the delicate coalitions that make up movements. To gauge a movement's success in avoiding these hazards and achieving ongoing political success requires determining whether its message gets into the morning newspaper and the evening television news without significant distortion. In this chapter I consider how to measure such success.

## The Power of News Frames

The news derives its credibility and power from a presumption of objectivity among the news audience. Although we may be skeptical of perfect press neutrality, most people ordinarily give the news the benefit of the doubt. This is not to say that news audiences are incapable of being critical, but most people have neither the time, training, nor independent knowledge to challenge the sense of a news story (Fowler 1991, 10–11). Nonetheless, the news necessarily selects facts that support a particular view of the world; that is, it provides us with a (perhaps unconscious) bounded view of the world, a "frame."

The frame concept finds its roots in a central assumption of the philosophy of pragmatism: that we experience our everyday reality as something to be acted on rather than contemplated and understood (Schutz 1962). According to this view, we inherit the world in an organized form, as an unquestioned given, and act on it accordingly. The alternative—for example, questioning whether the ground will support our next step—would require a heavy and burdensome investment in critical reflection. For some on the left—Marx, Gramsci, and the critical theorists of the Frankfurt school—this lack of reflective thinking privileges a set of power relations, a rationalization of privileged class interest. Seen from the right, it is a less sinister (but no more conscious) expression of shared cultural values.

In this pragmatist view of the media, news stories are not so much reported as made, the world not chronicled but selectively constructed from facts and interpretations collected from a "news net" cast on the world (Tuchman 1972). The range of this net is the subject of much media theory that seeks explanations in the values of individual journalists, patterns of journalistic routine, organizational pressure, and ideology (see Shoemaker and Reese 1996). Before attempting an explanation for what this net contains, however, I must first consider the significance of those contents.

For the media, framing is essential to the work of producing stories. The need for economy and for satisfying the demands of reducing a complex set of events to a coherent and interesting summary requires adherence to story conventions that minimally answer (or seem to answer) the familiar questions of who, what, where, when, and why. These are, of course, questions that require reporters to select and highlight facts that comply with their sense of the event's larger meaning. Psychologists have found that we tend to recall events more readily if they are part of a familiar script (Bower, Black, and Turner 1979). Such scripts at a higher level of abstraction guide a reporter's reconstruction of a set of events that makes sense of them in a formal way. But as pragmatism has taught us, the significance of a set of facts depends on one's perspective.

Given a newsworthy event—say, a political demonstration—a reporter selects and emphasizes some facts over others so as to conform to the requirements of the kind of story he or she has decided to tell. The facts that it was a warm and sunny day, that participants released balloons into a gentle breeze, and that the atmosphere was festive and the songs cheerful comply with a familiar news formula, the human interest story. Here the political significance of an event recedes while those elements that highlight the festivity of the event come to the fore. The facts that participants walked many miles, sacrificed time away from family or job, and were determined to let the president know of their serious purpose describe a different kind of story with more potent political impact. Finally, the facts that the protesters were predominantly young and naïve, wore unusual garb or facial hair, chanted provocative slogans, and got into trouble with the cops follow the shape of a police story that discredits and perhaps damages the political viability of the issue promoted. If narrative may be considered a solution to the problem of converting knowing into telling (White 1987, 1), the choice of frame used in reporting affects the political impact of news coverage.

My first concern is in what the news frame contains, just as one considers what to include in a camera viewfinder, the object or person on which to focus. There is much to notice in a news frame, but I will limit my attention to the politically significant elements, the ones that affect the allocation of political space for those competing for public support. I use this metaphor because it combines the two most important dimensions of the problem all political movements face, finding a place on the media agenda and filling it with a credible and persuasive message.

To compete effectively in the political marketplace, a movement must call public attention to a problem and propose a plausible policy solution on an ongoing basis. Accordingly a news frame includes a statement of a problem (the issue), a diagnosis and moral evaluation of its cause, and a solution (Entman 1993). For example, the large number of nuclear weapons has resulted from a fruitless and wasteful contest for strategic superiority that has succeeded only in making the weapons more powerful and dangerous. The solution is to fix the weapons at their current levels and begin a good-faith effort at reducing their numbers. (This was, in the main, the proposal of the nuclear freeze movement.)

Because news reports are not medical diagnoses or political tracts, they may include the figurative language—catchphrases, slogans, and metaphors—thought necessary to attract the attention of the news audience. These are often the product of movements themselves (Gamson and Modigliani 1989). The test ban movement, for example, coined the phrase "no radiation without representation," an economical summary of its position that shrewdly anticipated and preempted an attack on its supporters' patriotism.

## *Framing the Message*

The political implications of news frames derive from the principle that the way one defines an issue affects its outcome. E. E. Schattschneider (1960) calls this the mobilization of bias, the process of selecting and highlighting those elements that make the strongest case for one's position, much as a prosecutor and trial lawyer grapple with different subsets of facts to make the strongest case for their sides. Here the members of the jury are conscious of the struggle for their hearts and minds. In other words, they are conscious that the issue is being framed. Our presumption of news objectivity or (even if we doubt objectivity) the lack of practical attentiveness and need for cognitive economy may allow such mobilization to take place with little or no struggle.

As political movements lock horns with government officials, each tries to gain the upper hand in defining the situation, doing so by deploying arguments that seek to persuade and justify. The core of the message, whether stated explicitly or suggested figuratively, usually remains constant: the problem, diagnosis, and moral evaluation of its causes and some preferred set of policies for solving it. But there is much more that movements need to consider.

Because movements evolve beyond the perimeter of conventional politics, their leaders must deal with issues of legitimacy and motivation. They need to engage a primarily voluntary force, one whose participation will depend on some estimate that its involvement will do some good and ideally on some moral imperative that engages a sense of obligation and responsibility (McAdam, McCarthy, and Zald 1988, 723; Tyler and McGraw 1983). The motivational property of movement messages is important because participation in this activity is often frustrating, daunting, and nearly always unpaid. At the early stages of such a campaign, knowledge that others are joining may serve as a catalyst for an individual's involvement (Klandermans 1984). At later stages small successes are essential for maintaining individual commitment and the integrity of the coalitions that make up peace movements. More radically minded groups usually must settle on a lesser issue to widen the movement's base and increase its chances of success. Disappointment at the lack of progress on this reduced unifying issue thus often drives a wedge between groups. Although movement success depends on maintaining group commitment to a coalition, the battle is often fought in the media eye at the individual level.

### *Framing the Messenger*

Media scholars have noted that the news tends to focus on the actions and achievements of individuals (Gans 1979; Iyengar 1991). This tendency is due in part to American political culture, which prizes liberty and thus narratives that put the individual at the center of action. A news story on rising unemployment, for example, is more likely to illustrate its effects on a particular working family than to discuss the structural factors driving the business cycle. This keying on individuals interacts interestingly with political movements' needs to establish legitimacy.

Because they challenge state authority and expertise, political movements must establish the legitimacy of their own, either by claiming their own substantive expertise on the issue in question or by claiming moral authority. For substantive expertise, the antinuclear movements could draw on the support of scientists such as Linus Pauling and sympathetic arms controllers. For the moral case, the movements drew on the authority of church leaders and intellectuals who offered compelling arguments for the rightness of their cause. The movements also mobilized ordinary citizens whose demonstrations presented the news media and government authorities with symbolic evidence of the authority of an informed and aroused public opinion.

Reliance on these individual-centered resources renders movements chronically vulnerable to ongoing judgments regarding the sufficiency of their members' expertise, loyalty, and representativeness to the political mainstream. This is especially heightened in the individual-centered format of newswriting because of its susceptibility to stereotyped judgment by reporters, perhaps influenced by self-interested news sources: after all, by making an effective ad hominem argument, one might be spared the difficulty of addressing the core of the opponent's position. In shifting attention to the messenger's character or expertise, suggesting he or she is reckless or naive, the reporter unwittingly can raise doubts in the minds of potential converts (Chong 1991). Conversely, calling attention to the praiseworthy qualities of the people involved either enhances their credibility or obviates the issue.

There is a practical psychological reason for the power of news framing, especially as it relates to stereotypes. Social psychologists argue that frames, or as they call them, *schemas,* help us to manage what would otherwise be an unruly cognitive world (Fiske and Taylor 1991, 14). Schemas provide order for incoming information. They thus structure memory and associate cognitions with affective valences (Hastie 1987; Lodge and McGraw 1991). These associations are stored in long-term memory after repeated mental connections. Social psychologists have amassed a large body of research on schemas and a number of generalizations on how they are invoked. I will summarize those findings that bear most directly on my study:

1. People appear less variable when categorized as outsiders—for example, as deviants or minorities—and thus cue less complex conceptualizations. Characterized as "sixties protesters," for example, movement participants may become associated in the public mind with a generic stripe of ineffectual and marginalized cultural protest.
2. People's perceptions are polarized on members of these *out-groups:* the best are seen in some ways as better than the best in the in-group, but the worst are seen as worse than comparable insiders. This may explain the alternation

between the saintly portrayal of movement participants, especially during early stages of media coverage, and the disapproving focus on cultural and social deviants during moments of acute political conflict engendered by the movement.

3. When schemas are weak or first developing, we notice complicating inconsistencies provided we are *continually* presented with this information. That is, we can develop suitably complex representations of the world—we are capable of getting beyond stereotypes—provided there is some basis for it. Such information is most critical in early stages.
4. People *consistently* presented with credible, persuasive schema-inconsistent information abandon the schema in favor of the incoming information (Fiske and Taylor 1991, 135–36). This is a corollary to the finding in the previous point. A continuous stream of news coverage that shows variety and complexity among movement participants is thus less likely to produce stereotyped thinking in the public mind.

I am not arguing here for definitive effects. Other possibilities exist. There is a body of scholarly literature, for example, that argues for an active media audience that critically processes and challenges the content and assumptions of news stories (though this seems implausible on issues with which the audience has little firsthand experience). Rather, I want to sensitize my analysis to ongoing news judgments, to the ways that reporters characterize participants in movements, and correlate the quality of these accounts with external events and pressures—for example, the reactions of those in power.

## The Rhetoric of Reaction

As political movements seek to challenge authority, government officials quite naturally seek to preserve it. Albert Hirschman (1991) has analyzed the patterns both of the arguments used by conservative critics and of the counterarguments used by their progressive foes. Although these arguments mainly speak to the substance of a message, they also imply ways of discrediting the messenger.

Hirschman identifies three principal species of counterarguments that he terms the rhetoric of reaction. In this study I view these as blocking actions on the progressive argumentation that characterizes the rhetoric of peace movements in general:

1. Perversity: the action will result in an outcome precisely opposite to the intended one. Hirschman cites as an example the conservative argument that the welfare state actually nurtures poverty by rewarding people for not work-

ing, rendering them even more dependent on the state. This appeal finds its origins in antiquity, in the Greek myth of Nemesis, the goddess of retribution who was said to bring down the proud and insolent.

2. Jeopardy: the action endangers some important good. In the *Road to Serfdom*, for example, Friedrich Hayek (1944) writes that the welfare state threatens liberty and democracy because it empowers bureaucrats to make coercive policy intended to enhance economic equality.
3. Futility: the action and effort are wasted because reality is governed by immutable laws or is so abstruse that it can be fathomed only by experts. Hirschman cites the world-weary French epigram *plus ça change, plus c'est la même chose* as an example of this position. The argument underlies Tocqueville's position that the main reforms credited to the French Revolution were already well underway, thereby rendering the blood spilled to achieve them a frightful and unnecessary waste. In some ways the rhetoric of futility is the most insulting of the three, for it calls into doubt the intellectual capacity of anyone sufficiently naive to suggest reforming the inevitabilities of power politics or of human nature itself.

Hirschman hastens to explain that such arguments are neither inherently illogical nor necessarily wrong but that they sometimes are advanced as received truths rather than as propositions requiring evidence for support. Sometimes mere repetition of the argument becomes evidence of its truth.

General rhetorical strategy must be applied to specific policy proposals, so I now turn to the issues involved in modern arms policy as seen from the viewpoint of the defense establishment.

### *Peace as the Sturdy Child of Terror*

Much of the theory regarding nuclear weapons is an extension of strategy developed as modern warfare evolved to include noncombatants. Military strategists came to understand that the murderous stalemate of World War I resulted from the union of traditional battlefield engagement with the productive wealth of modern industrial development. For the first time in history, an entire nation's industrial capacity could be thrown into the service of a protracted war of attrition whose outcome would depend on which nation yielded first to a debilitating struggle (Freedman 1989, 3–4). Military strategists came to regard industrial centers and the people who ran its machinery as strategic targets. Tanks and aircraft would bring the war to the heart of the adversary's industrial centers, putting the civilian population at risk. The invention of nuclear weapons made this application of force all the more efficient and decisive but also formidably complex.

The theory of nuclear strategy has evolved since the late 1940s to accommodate breakthroughs in technology that have made these weapons more deadly and more easily delivered. Lawrence Freedman writes that its development has followed three courses:

1. to use the destructive power of nuclear weapons as a way of making total war appear as folly;
2. to build a defense that renders an enemy's first strike harmless; and
3. to develop small tactical weapons capable of being delivered precisely to military targets with minimal risk to civilian society (Freedman 1989, 427).

None of these has proven decisive, for each side has devised plans that counter the other's best strategies for ensuring a credible risk of "unendurable destruction." As Winston Churchill put it, the peace that resulted from deterrence would be "the sturdy child of terror" (in Freedman 1989, 83).

Since the end of World War II U.S. foreign policy has been profoundly affected by the rapid evolution of nuclear weapons. In the chapters that follow, I will include a running commentary on the evolution of these strategies as experts, the military, and government officials responded to advances in weapons technology and its spread to other powers. Here I necessarily simplify the analysis of the arguments used to justify U.S. arms policy so as to explain more clearly the state of mind of leaders as they groped with the uncertainties inherent in guessing their adversaries' intentions. Such assessments become part of the public discourse in news coverage and thus either aid or challenge popular movements. Even if these technical analyses do not enter the popular discourse, however, administration officials need to defend their more general policy.

## *Cold War Models of Foreign Policy*

Although foreign policy may call for subtle judgment, historical erudition, and precise understanding of the complex interactions of policy and events, limited intellectual capacity and the need for quick summary judgments lead national leaders to construct simplified "cognitive maps" of the international scene. Philip Tetlock (1983) analyzed these coping strategies and discerned two principal models used to justify shifts in cold war policy (see also Russett 1990, 52–54).

The *deterrence model* paints a high-contrast portrait of a radically simplified world in which a remorseless aggressor relentlessly tests the resolve of a free and just adversary. A natural and inevitable antipathy between the two prevents any serious détente. Thus either party may view the other's move to negotiate as showing a lack of resolve. This argument is an example of the rhetoric of perversity. As Freedman writes of the view of nuclear strategists of the midfifties, "Diplomatic means to solve the cold war were considered impractical and dangerous, in that they involved concessions to Soviet demands. The result of this, it was supposed, would be only to add to the Kremlin's appetite" (Freedman 1989, 95). From this view, a responsible government would parry increases in Soviet arms with its own increase or, better, a new generation of weapons. Munich and the appeasement of Hitler provide the telling object lesson for this model.

In contrast, the *conflict* (or *spiral*) *model* portrays nation-states as mutual victims of an anarchic state of international relations that disposes them to build alliances and arms caches. These result in an excessive buildup of arms, with stockpiles eventually much larger than those needed to kill all potential victims. The inescapable uncertainty of all schemes used to gauge the effectiveness of arms rationalizes the development and accumulation of even more weapons. All this increases the chances of a dangerous sequence of misperception and miscalculation that could lead to accidental war. A solution, therefore, is to be found in an atmosphere of mutual trust brought by conciliatory gestures coupled to pronouncements of peaceful intentions. During the early sixties this strategy was formalized as GRIT: "gradual reduction of international tensions" (Osgood 1962). The idea that World War I resulted from a spiral of miscalculations is often used to illustrate this model.[1] (Popular culture offers its own examples in *Fail-Safe* and its satirical cousin *Dr. Strangelove,* movies released during the tensest periods of the cold war.)

These models closely correspond to the numerous distinctions made between hawks and doves, conservatives and liberals, and realists and idealists. As such, they simplify and falsely delimit political options and thus achieve their power by excluding other paths of action from consideration. As an administration seeks to justify its foreign policy, its model of the international scene changes to comply with that policy; a previously mistrusted aggressor the administration once sought to deter becomes a fellow victim of a dangerous arms race. The 1962 Cuban missile crisis and its effects on Americans' perspectives on U.S.-Soviet relations provide one example of such a transformation.

## Opening Space for Political Opportunity

Gamson and Meyer (1996) use the metaphor of political space to analyze the way movements create opportunities for influence. As I showed in chapter 1, the political system—institutions and policy-making—is subject to periods of instability that offer movements opportunities for influence. Some elements of the system, such as the legitimacy of Congress and the presidency, are usually stable and offer few opportunities for challenge. Others, such as policy itself and the degree of elite consensus on it, are more fluid and typically offer greater possibility for influence. Such influence may not be forthcoming, however, if the news media fail to convey movement messages or if state power distorts them.

To answer my first question, whether the news media provide a durable space for oppositional politics, I must perform two tasks. First I need to examine the historical record to assess both the official state policy and the degree to which it was supported within the executive branch. My working hypothesis will be that the media offer greater space to oppositional politics under two circumstances: when official policy is open to movement goals or when internal dissent impedes consensus on policy. On the latter point, for example, Daniel Hallin (1986) found that the American news media established the legitimacy of the antiwar movement's opposition to the Vietnam War on the degree to which political leaders supported it. Lance Bennett (1990) termed this phenomenon "indexing" and found it in the *New York Times*'s coverage of the Nicaragua debate in Congress.

Second, I need to consider the quality of the news coverage itself. How does the news describe and characterize movement arguments, activities, and the participants themselves? In table 1 I list the arguments one might expect from each side given its political goals. Movements, which depend on the increasing participation of bystanders, obtain that participation by stressing the people's right to influence government policy, the optimistic odds in favor of success, and the moral compulsion to get involved. Conservative adversaries are likely to rely on one or more of the principle blocking arguments outlined by Hirschman.

As I pointed out earlier, it is sometimes necessary to infer issue positions from the presence of certain themes, catchphrases, and emphasis on certain categories of facts (Gamson and Modigliani 1989). For example, mention of Munich calls to mind the perverse effects of a search for peace at any cost. Similarly, references to the complexities of negotiation and the arcane language of nuclear deterrence suggest the futility of a presumably simple-minded call for peace.

If we judge a messenger as naive, reckless, or unrepresentative of mainstream thinking, we will tend to discount the message. Table 2 lists depic-

*Table 1.* Movement Claims and Their Counterarguments

| Movement Position | Blocking Argument |
|---|---|
| Citizens and government can work together to prevent war. | a. The complex issues of defense and nuclear deterrence are best left in the hands of experts; citizens are not well enough informed (F).<br>b. The USSR is not pressured by its citizens; action by Americans citizens is futile (F).<br>c. Though peace is desirable, it is an unworkable utopian ideal in a world of power politics (F). |
| If we stick together, there is potential for bringing about some good. | a. Protest weakens the hand of American negotiators (J).<br>b. A weakened defense will actually promote a war (the Munich argument) (P).<br>c. Technological advance is the key to military security (J).<br>d. A weakened defense will jeopardize American security (J). |
| There is a moral obligation to get involved. | a. Peace demonstrations undermine the morale of our troops (J).<br>b. Protest is unpatriotic (J) or strengthens the hand of the enemy (P).<br>c. Morality has no place in realpolitik (F). |

*Key:* P = rhetoric of perversity; J = rhetoric of jeopardy; F = rhetoric of futility.

*Table 2.* Characterizations of Movement Participants

| Positive | Negative |
|---|---|
| 1. Participants are serious and rational. | Participants are emotional or flighty. |
| 2. Participants are knowledgeable and mature. | Participants are ignorant of complexities of foreign policy, well-meaning but simple-minded, or utopian. |
| 3. Participants are motivated by justice, morality, or other high-minded purpose. | Motivation is whimsical, selfish, partisan, or unwittingly seditious. |
| 4. Participants are unified. | Participants are wrought by division, infighting, or incompatible goals. |
| 5. Participants are mainstream, average Americans. | Participants are extremist in appearance or belief or otherwise set apart from the mainstream. |
| 6. Public opinion favors the movement. | Movement is not supported by public, or public opinion is irrelevant to proper policy-making. |
| 7. Participants are likely to be successful. | Participants are unlikely to influence policy; their action is merely symbolic. |

tions of movement participants that indirectly support or undermine the integrity of their political message (Entman and Rojecki 1993).

The power of the news lies not so much in individual stories but in the patterns they create. It is the sameness of these patterns, their regularity, that often permits them to escape attention. As Gitlin puts it, "Media frames, largely unspoken and unacknowledged, organize the world both for journalists who report it and, in some important degree, for us who rely on the reports" (Gitlin 1980, 7). These frames may not necessarily force news audiences to judge the political world through imposed standards of appraisal, but they do at least contribute reliable evidence of the reporters' own views. This is why, in the hunt for news frames, I will be especially alert to those circumstances that define what Chilton (1987) calls "critical discourse moments," instances when these routine patterns are disrupted and thus become visible as patterns. Such disruption occurs when external events draw attention to administration policy, significant dissent and policy disarray emerge within the administration, or a change in policy becomes imminent. My strategy will be to observe all changes in the news media's framing of the antinuclear movement—its ideas and supporters—and see whether they correspond to those moments.

## The Plan of the Book

The remainder of the book is organized into three parts. The first examines the principal actors involved in the antinuclear movement during the Eisenhower and Kennedy presidencies and the coalition of groups making up the test ban movement. I also summarize the overall patterns of media coverage. These broad strokes frame the more detailed analysis of the development of policy in the Eisenhower administration, which is followed by an analysis of news frames in each identified policy stage. A similarly structured chapter follows for the Kennedy administration.

The second part focuses on the nuclear freeze movement of the 1980s. It begins with a historical overview of policy after the test ban treaty and the circumstances that led to the freeze. The following chapter traces the development of defense policy during the Reagan administration and correlates it with media coverage.

The book concludes with a summary of the patterns found during these two movements, an analysis of the differences between the two historical periods, and some remarks on what all this means for participatory and deliberative democracy.

## Note

1. Some analysts argue that the extraordinarily suspicious and hostile relationship between the two superpowers made deterrence the only realistic model to follow (see Freedman 1989, 205).

# 3 The Politics of Terror: The Test Ban

During World War II science and the nation-state cooperated to create the atomic bomb, a device that in an instant could obliterate both from the face of the earth. Whether this was seen as good or bad depended on one's political perspective and sense of optimism. Those who thought it to be good credited the atomic bomb with ending World War II and preventing a major war in Europe over the following fifty years (see Newhouse 1989). Those who considered it to be bad pointed out that anyone cheered by these years of peace was like the man who fell off the Empire State Building and, after passing the fiftieth floor, remarked, "So far, so good" (Betts 1987, 1–2). Beyond decrying the dangers of accidental war, pessimists voiced what would prove to be realistic concerns about the spread of atomic weapons to other nations. The first movement for the control of nuclear arms warned of this eventuality but was thwarted by the mutual suspicions and politics of the cold war, which equated peace with increased numbers and varieties of these weapons, as well as swifter and more accurate means of raining them down on the enemy.

This chapter provides a historical context and an overview of the key actors in the test ban movement. It begins with a synopsis of the Eisenhower and Kennedy administrations' diplomatic efforts to conclude the first arms control agreement with the Soviet Union. It continues with a short history of the coalition making up the peace movement that pressured the two administrations toward this goal and concludes with an overview of the broad patterns of news coverage through this period. My intent here is to present a wide view of the patterns and thus to create a context for interpreting the media's coverage of the antinuclear movement as it correlates with policy changes during the Eisenhower and Kennedy administrations, which I do in the two following chapters.

## The Path to the Test Ban

The path to the test ban meandered through the force fields of domestic and international politics as an invigorated peace movement pressured the Eisenhower and Kennedy administrations to scale back the arms race. Each administration responded in ways that characterized its formal policies and feelings on nuclear weapons. Of the two presidents' responses, Eisenhower's were the more complex because they were the most conflicted.

### *Eisenhower: From Atoms for Peace to the New Look*

Eisenhower viewed nuclear weapons as a mixed blessing. His military background lent him considerable insight into their strategic value, which he regarded as dubious. For example, his decision on a Korean armistice was based on his insight that nuclear weapons made total war unthinkable and limited war unwinnable (Ambrose 1984, 107). As a political leader directly responsible for the lives of all Americans and indirectly responsible for the lives of all others who would be harmed in an all-out war with the Soviet Union, he was horrified by their destructive potential. As a fiscal conservative, however, Eisenhower saw nuclear weapons as a relatively cheap means of containing Soviet expansion.

Early in his first administration, Eisenhower acted on his cautionary impulse and proposed "Atoms for Peace," a plan for redirecting the use of nuclear energy to peaceful purposes (Pach and Richardson 1991, 83). The three nuclear powers—the United States, United Kingdom, and Soviet Union—would make small contributions from their nuclear stockpiles to an international agency under UN control. This agency would direct these to other agencies and groups conducting research for such constructive purposes as "providing abundant electrical energy in the power-starved areas of the world" (in Ambrose 1984, 148). The proposal was bold and generous (the United States would contribute five times the material expected of the Soviet Union), but the Soviets could not completely overcome their fear that they would be unable to match, much less exceed, the numbers of atomic bombs that the United States possessed. The American demand for a clear advantage and the Soviet desire to thwart it fueled an arms race that would continue over thirty years.

Soviet rejection of Atoms for Peace hardened Eisenhower's attitude and made him all the more determined to maintain an American advantage, a posture facilitated by his fiscal restraint and its effects on military strategy; this approach came to be known as the "New Look." Eisenhower believed that the best means for containing the Soviet Union was a strong dollar, not an expanding military (Pach and Richardson 1991, 80). Known by economists as "strategic monism" and by weapons scientists as "infinite containment," the policy called for the ability to apply a sudden and massive destructive force. As Richard Nixon put it, "Rather than let Communists nibble us to death all over the world in little wars, we would rely in the future primarily on our massive mobile retaliatory power" (in Freedman 1989, 86). The New Look would reduce the numbers of conventional forces on land and sea while greatly increasing the numbers of nuclear weapons. Cheaper and more powerful than conventional military forces, nuclear weapons offered an efficient solution but incurred a multitude of unforeseen political costs that would nag Eisenhower during the remainder of his term in office by preying on his profound ambivalence.

The increase in weapons whose dreadful power had twice been vividly demonstrated on civilian populations aroused a general anxiety among citizens and an increasing moral outrage among scientists, intellectuals, and religious leaders. This discontent began to manifest itself during Eisenhower's second term when he came under increased and conflicting pressures to cease atmospheric testing. The sources of this pressure included a heated debate among scientists on the hazards of radiation and the feasibility of remote detection of underground nuclear explosions. Eisenhower also felt cross-pressures from Great Britain, itself faced by an energetic peace movement, and France, which resisted a ban while it sought to develop its own nuclear arsenal.

Throughout the period journalists and policy experts perceived the Soviet Union as winning propaganda points at U.S. expense by offering a variety of well-timed arms proposals. The result of these cross-pressures and Soviet initiatives was a pattern of proposal, counterproposal, stalemate, withdrawal, and retrenchment. Toward the end of Eisenhower's term, the United States and the Soviet Union appeared to be on the brink of an agreement, but the Soviets downed a U.S. U2 spy plane on the eve of the summit where the treaty was to be discussed, and the affair spoiled the agreement's chances of success. The issue would not be resolved until the Kennedy administration.

### *Kennedy and Flexible Response*

Kennedy regarded the New Look as a hindrance to his foreign policy options. He believed its all-or-nothing application of force had handcuffed the United States in its range of responses to past crises in Korea, Indochina, Hungary, the Isthmus of Suez, and Lebanon. The growing number of peripheral and guerrilla wars then taking place in the Third World suggested that massive retaliation actually facilitated the "nibbling" that Nixon and John Foster Dulles argued it would prevent, a claim exemplifying the rhetoric of perversity used to justify a change in military policy. If massive retaliation had failed in the past when the United States enjoyed a clear advantage, it would surely fail in the future when the Soviets caught up. As Kennedy put it: "Their missile power will be the shield from behind which they will slowly, but surely advance—through Sputnik diplomacy, limited brush-fire wars, indirect non-overt aggression, intimidation, and subversion. . . . The periphery of the Free World will slowly be nibbled away. . . . Each such Soviet move will weaken the West; but none will seem sufficiently significant by itself to justify our initiating a nuclear war which might destroy us" (in Freedman 1989, 230). Apart from recognizing its growing feebleness as a diplomatic tool, Kennedy also felt that the New Look put the United States in a morally disreputable position of nuclear blackmail that had won it little sympathy from the nonaligned nations, especially India. He also feared the bomb would spread to other nations (Newhouse 1989, 193).

To lessen dependence on this encumbering and morally distasteful weapon, Kennedy's defense secretary, Robert McNamara, adopted a policy of "flexible response," a graduated system of military action that called for development of new technologies and an expansion of conventional forces. Nuclear conflict would thus become the last of many options in a ladder of escalating military replies. For example, one such reply was McNamara's concept of "counterforce," the nuclear targeting of military bases rather than civilian populations in cities, a policy that rendered nuclear arms less distinguishable from conventional weapons (Meyer 1990, 33).

To put this ambitious policy in motion, Kennedy requested a 15 percent boost in military spending, thereby doubling the number of combat-ready army divisions and expanding the number of combat-ready naval and marine units (Giglio 1991, 46). The success of flexible response was demonstrated in a Brookings study that found the Kennedy administration to have been the most belligerent of the modern presidencies in its application of political military force (Paterson 1989, 5).[1] Kennedy's step back from nuclear brinkmanship increased the use of conventional forces, making his the most combative presidency of the modern era.

With nuclear weapons no longer an exclusively American trump card, Kennedy became sympathetic to an arms control treaty with the Soviet Union. He had been a longtime supporter of a test ban treaty, notwithstanding his having won the presidency in part by going to the right of the Republicans, who he claimed had created a missile gap.[2] A gap did exist, but the Soviets, not the Americans, suffered by it: in early 1961 the United States had a six-to-one advantage in intercontinental ballistic missiles (ICBMs) and enjoyed a twenty-to-one advantage in nuclear warheads (Page and Shapiro 1992, 367; Beschloss 1991, 65).[3]

Despite a clear lead, Kennedy increased nuclear forces (committing to 1,000 new ICBMs) to give himself increased political leverage over the Soviets. Predictably this magnified the Soviets' perceptions of the missile gap and only increased their desire to catch up (Giglio 1991, 47).

As the presumed missile gap rendered the strategy of massive retaliation moot, a test ban treaty with the Soviets became politically practical and even attractive.[4] As evidence of his support for such a treaty, Kennedy appointed Glenn Seaborg as chairman of the Atomic Energy Commission (AEC), the first scientist to occupy this sensitive position. Unlike his predecessors, Seaborg was sympathetic to an agreement, but he saw his role as balancing his preferences against the "technical and security realities" raised by the other commissioners. He also recognized the institutional reasons for the traditional AEC opposition to the ban: had such a ban gone into effect, the organization could not attract the top-flight scientists it needed to do its work. Such candidates would be reluctant to join the organization if they were unable to verify their theories and calculations through real-world experiments in the form of nuclear explosions (Seaborg 1981, 33–35).

As was largely true during Eisenhower's administration, international forces exerted cross-pressures on the United States during Kennedy's as well. The Campaign for Nuclear Disarmament (CND) continued its activities in Britain even as Charles DeGaulle sought a nuclear capability for France. Khrushchev, however, was torn between, one the one hand, expanding the Soviet domestic economy and vying for international prestige and, on the other, competing with the Chinese for leadership of the "socialist" nations, which would leave him increasingly vulnerable to U.S. foreign policy. With the U2 incident having effectively ended a period of rapprochement, Khrushchev was anxious to explore new possibilities but also to test and possibly exploit an inexperienced, younger man (he remarked that Kennedy was younger than his own son). The confluence of these forces, coupled with Kennedy's attempt to shore up support among conservatives by significantly expanding the military, put in place the structural elements that led to a dangerously volatile period in U.S.-Soviet affairs.

Throughout the multiple crises in Berlin and Cuba, however, Kennedy remained committed to a test ban agreement with the Soviets. In contrast to the Eisenhower administration, which was riddled with dissent and second-guessing, the Kennedy era saw a unified search for a treaty, albeit one interrupted by a series of international crises.

## Strands of the Peace Movement

Throughout the Eisenhower and Kennedy years, a rejuvenated peace movement kept up the pressure for arms control. A unique set of circumstances had reconstituted its disparate elements. The historian Lawrence Wittner (1969) has used the metaphor of an onion to describe the structure of the American peace movement—a core of devoted absolutists holding fast to the center with less committed groups building up the outer layers. As war fever develops, the outer layers peel off, only to rejoin when distaste for war returns. This explains a peace movement's paradoxical weakness yet tenacity during times of international crisis. It is also another manifestation of the phenomenon recorded in public opinion data that indicate a preference for negotiation only during those times when Americans feel they are adequately defended.[5]

This, then, is the central dilemma facing all peace movements—bridging the gap between an ideal of peace and a realistic need for an adequate defense against an anarchic world order. Pacifists regard this as a false dilemma, arguing that even though peace may be an unrealistic objective in the short run, the long-run consequences of an arms race are almost always disastrous (Wittner 1969, ix–x). If these positions sound familiar, it is because they represent the frames of reference foreign policy experts use to justify either weapons development or arms reduction: peace from strength versus the spiraling arms race that leads to a war no one wants.

The peace movement did not engage many Americans until the end of World War I. The aftermath of the war to end all wars brought disillusionment, weariness, and cynicism (see Fussell 1975). The core constituents of the peace movement included predominantly middle-class ranks of professional women, clerics, and students (Wittner 1969, 4–7). A variety of organizations sprang up to press the cause for peace, although the groups they represented drew on different motivations and tactics. Some early examples include the Women's International League for Peace and Freedom, or WILPF (women), the Fellowship of Reconciliation (Protestant churches), the War Resister's League (a secular version of the Fellowship of Reconciliation that attracted socialists, radicals, and anarchists), and the National Council for the Prevention of War (NCPW). The NCPW, a Quaker group, was the first to serve as an umbrella group for a number of other organizations whose common goal secured their unity despite their varying agendas and tactics. This set a pattern for future coalitions: a common, lesser goal secured for unifying the movement, which would eventually fracture along the fault lines of its ideological divisions.

World War II reduced the movement to its core of pacifist absolutists. Conscientious objectors adapted the nonviolent resistance tactics of Mohandas Gandhi to express their opposition to war, which they viewed as a symptom of greater problems of injustice. This wing of the movement would later inspire several generations of nonviolent resisters, including Ralph Abernathy and Martin Luther King Jr.

Atomic weapons temporarily revived the movement, now led by the scientists who had worked to produce them (Wittner 1993). This did not last long, however, for the Korean War and the cold war inspired army-McCarthy hearings cleaved the movement once again along fault lines that this time separated devoted pacifists from liberal internationalists. Wittner notes that in 1950, nearly eight in ten Americans approved the use of nuclear weapons in a future world war and that "proponents of disarmament in Western nations also labored under the heavy burden of being identified with Communism" (Wittner 1993, 313, 319).

The end of the Korean War and Stalin's death improved U.S.-Soviet relations and thus weakened the forces cleaving the movement (DeBenedetti 1980, 157). By the spring of 1957 a number of influential Americans—notably Norman Cousins—had convinced Albert Schweitzer to announce his opposition to nuclear testing. On April 24, 1957, Schweitzer broadcast a radio message to fifty nations in which he expressed the hope that "world opinion" would pressure the atomic powers to cease nuclear testing, thus preventing the spread of such arms to other countries and removing the threat of radioactivity through the air and water. His speech and the radiation issue were the catalysts that would once again interlace the divergent strands of the peace movement.

Given the disparate groups and appeals that made up the changing peace coalition, I have decided to reduce these to two major strands, each made up of several separate groups. There is no avoiding the issue of leadership because the news media tend to embody a number of ideas and positions in the personality of a single individual who comes to symbolize what they misconstrue as a monolithic policy position. The Women's Strike for Peace (WSP), for example, encouraged all its members to participate by refusing to appoint a leadership hierarchy; despite this, the media nonetheless regarded Dagmar Wilson as its head (Swerdlow 1993, 52).

The manner in which the media characterize individual leaders becomes a convenient shorthand for their estimation of organization politics in general. Nevertheless, it would be a mistake to assume that these groups are either mutually exclusive in terms of goals or membership or fixed in number. Several factions (the scientists, for example) joined with a larger umbrella organization, the National Committee for a Sane Nuclear Policy (SANE), and then split off for strategic or ideological reasons, and in the early 1960s SANE lost its younger constituency to the Student Peace Union and the Students for a Democratic Society (SDS). At about the same time the WSP emerged in Washington, D.C., and spread quickly to other major cities. With these cautions in place, I will examine the major peace groups as they were constituted during the second Eisenhower administration:

1. Liberal pacifists and internationalists. This group had three major constituents: proponents of world government and other cold war liberal groups, scientists, and religious organizations.

Groups in the "internationalist" camp included Americans for Democratic Action (ADA), World Federalists, and the WILPF. Their common bond was a tolerance of or an apathy to cold war politics (DeBenedetti 1980, 154–55). Figures such as Norman Thomas, Dwight MacDonald, and Norman Cousins were most closely identified with this group.

Several groups of scientists, including the Federation of American Scientists (FAS), became active in the test ban movement. Although they included a number of spokespersons (including Ralph Lapp, Eugene Rabinovitch, and Hans Bethe), by virtue of his publicity-conscious work in organizing and petition gathering, California Institute of Technology chemist Linus Pauling came to represent the scientists.

The religious front against testing included the World Council of Churches and the American Friends Service Committee (AFSC). However, not all members of the AFSC used conservative tactics. Some crossed over to the more aggressive wing of the movement.

2. Radical pacifists. Using the tactics of direct and bold action—such as scaling the fences around AEC testing sites and leaping aboard nuclear submarines—these groups repudiated negotiation and compromise for active resistance to what they considered wrongheaded ways of thinking that promoted war and injustice. Most conspicuous was the Committee for Non-Violent Action (CNVA), led by A. J. Muste, David Dellinger, and Robert Gilmore (Wittner 1969, 247).

The CNVA developed a political analysis that eschewed both conventional Marxist radicalism and liberalism. Neither had effectively addressed the issues of peace, war, and social justice. An outline of its philosophy appeared in the first issue of *Liberation,* a monthly CNVA publication established in 1956 by Lawrence Scott and A. J. Muste:

> We do not conceive the problem of revolution or the building of a better society as one of accumulating power, whether by legislative or other methods to "capture the State," and then, presumably to transform society and human beings as well. The national, sovereign, militarized and bureaucratic State and a bureaucratic collectivist economy are themselves to be avoided. Seizure of the war-making and repressive machinery of the State cannot be a step in toward transforming society into a free and humanly satisfying pattern. It is the transformation of society by human decisions and action that we seek. (*Liberation* 1956, 5)

Unlike the mass media, movement publications address highly specialized and generally sympathetic audiences. They provide movement figures ("issue entrepreneurs") a forum for developing and articulating positions, for stimulating discourse intended to broaden the base of support and reinforce confidence in their beliefs (Strodthoff, Hawkins, and Schoenfeld 1985). (This base need not be especially large; for example, *Liberation* had a circulation of only 6,000 in 1962.) As issue positions are vetted, refined, and strengthened, they begin to percolate into the mass culture, where they enter a more contested arena (see Gamson and Modigliani 1989). This is where access and treatment—framing—influence the scope and vigor of public discourse. Later in this and other chapters I will have occasion to follow the development of issue positions, strategies, and internal disagreements among movement influentials as they were articulated in *Liberation.*

In the late fifties and early sixties, students began to join the movement. An organization called the National Student Committee for a Sane Nuclear Policy (Student SANE) came into being on the campus of Swarthmore College. By March 1959 the organization had spread to twenty-five colleges and had collected 10,000 signatures on petitions intended for the Geneva peace conference. This became the base for the student movement of the sixties, which would later peel off to form the Student Peace Union and the SDS.

The radical pacifists and internationalists united under SANE, a coalition umbrella that saw in the radiation issue a means of unifying the disparate groups. The coalition held together until May 1960, when, at the height of its influence and prestige, an old-style cold war attack by Senator Thomas J. Dodd of Connecticut split the movement (Katz 1986, 43, 60). By the spring of 1963 the two wings were publicly at odds, the more conservative SANE blaming "unilateralists" and pacifists for shifting the image of the movement in the direction of the "pacifist, radical pacifist, anarchist, and Soviet apologist positions" and the CNVA tweaking SANE for its conservatism.

## Media Strategy

Movement strategy for dealing with the media developed reactively, especially after the Dodd incident, and reflected the philosophical differences between the two wings. SANE strained to maintain the air of respectability that its leaders felt was required to sustain its influence with government leaders. In the spring of 1963 the national board issued a document instructing local and regional SANE committees to avoid contact with peace marchers and demonstrations that might associate SANE with radical causes. At one Easter demonstration sponsored by Turn Toward Peace, a leaflet had been distributed giving the impression that all involved shared a "radical pacifist position," which several rally speakers had advocated. Henceforth SANE would not join ad hoc demonstrations that included all "elements of the peace spectrum." SANE membership would join only those organizations sharing SANE's multilateralist perspective—"conceivably W.I.L.P.F., S.P.U., and W.S.P." (*Liberation* 1963a, 11).

The document included the following observation on media behavior, which anticipates Gitlin's (1980) analysis of the media's role in radicalizing the New Left movement of the mid- and late sixties: "After a few years, march-type demonstrations tend to go to seed, to lose spontaneity, and to lead to emergence of the more radical, less responsible views among the participants. Demonstrations tend to take on, or to be interpreted as, negative responses to problems and to attract as participants persons who have habitually supported unpopular causes. [The tendency of the press] is to distort demonstrations and to present to the public the most unfortunate aspects" (*Liberation* 1963a, 11).

Less concerned with currying a favorable image and coddling the media, the CNVA and allied organizations took their lead from the more militant civil rights movement and characterized the cautious tactics of the internationalists as "Uncle Tom-ism." In an editorial David Dellinger of the CNVA expressed his admiration for the tough-mindedness of the civil rights movement, once in the hands of the "high-minded but non-revolutionary leaders of the NAACP" but then running at full speed to catch up with their more radical followers, and his contempt for what he regarded as the "Madison Avenue" mentality of the peace movement's more timorous wing. His full-throated exhortation to action previewed the New Left's position on the draft, Vietnam, and social justice in general:

> When pacifists awake from the anesthetizing effects of soft-selling public relations campaigns, let themselves go a little, and experience the full pain and horror of the annihilative economy, perhaps they will be as ready as black people have become to disrupt the surface calm of a corrupt and decadent society, rather than limit themselves to minor demands that can be considered respectable by—and therefore are not even challenging to—those who support the economic and political *status quo*. . . . It is time that those of us who are in the peace movement aspired to be to be equal to the children of Birmingham, whose vision of human dignity made it possible for them to rise above their natural human fear and face, unarmed, the clubs and dogs of Bull Connor's police force. . . . Whatever the material costs may be, can we evade the "unrespectable" direct-action tactics of economic boycott, massive social disruption, and civil disobedience which have made the nonviolent movement for integration a powerful force for revolutionary change? (*Liberation* 1963b, 3)

The media strategy of the WSP, a protofeminist peace movement that emerged during the Kennedy years, followed a more pragmatic course. I will turn to its case in the course of the media analysis to follow.

## Media Coverage: A Bird's-Eye View

For the first of these two case studies, I selected coverage in two sources. The *New York Times* is the self-styled newspaper of record that devotes considerable resources to national political news coverage and, by its prestigious standing, influences the news agendas of many other news outlets, print and electronic. Its reputation for favoring liberal causes (the paper often piqued Eisenhower's ire [Beschloss 1986, 2]) suggests that it would grant greater than average access to oppositional politics and contain relatively balanced coverage.

In addition, I decided to look at a similarly prestigious but more widely distributed and popular national source. Ideally this would have been some form of television, but coverage for this period is scattered and incomplete. Thus I selected *Time* magazine. During this period the magazine enjoyed influence far greater than any other national publication's, and its circulation was the largest among news weeklies (Halberstam 1979, 352).

*Time* provided little direct coverage of the protest movement itself. Instead the news magazine widened its view beyond the day-to-day activities of protest to the underlying issues—for example, the fallout controversy—and the political and scientific elites who took conflicting positions on them. This wider perspective was the product of a lengthier news cycle and an editorial policy that permitted judgment on the merits of the issues themselves. Often these stories included direct references to the peace movement and, occasionally, short pieces on the demonstrators.

With both sources, I searched yearly indexes for stories on the antinuclear movement. (In the *New York Times* these stories were indexed under the heading "Arms Control"; in *Time* they fell under two headings, "Atomic Bomb" and "Radioactivity.") With its shorter news cycle, the *New York Times* provides a large number of data points that allows an inspection of the broad patterns of news coverage. During the course of the seventy-six months of coverage of the test ban issue (forty-eight months for Eisenhower's administration and twenty-eight for Kennedy's), the *Times* published 190 stories on the antinuclear movement. Figure 1 illustrates a month-by-month tally of story counts. During the second Eisenhower presidency, coverage peaked dramatically in the spring of 1958. There was an unusually large number of stories in April and May that year, followed by a dip that did not recover until Kennedy came to office. Smaller yearly peaks also occur around Easter, the traditional start to yearly peace demonstrations, and in August, the anniversary month of the Hiroshima and Nagasaki explosions.

During the Kennedy administration the paper increased coverage to a point that matched the 1958 peak, with the coverage being especially heavy in the latter part of 1961 and the first half of 1962. This surface measure shows an overall increase in coverage during the Kennedy administration, a pattern verified in table 3.

During Kennedy's term the *New York Times* increased its overall coverage by nearly 50 percent and almost doubled its average monthly front-page coverage. Front-page stories peaked in 1958, five of the year's nine coming in April, on the eve of a major change in Eisenhower policy. Yet another peak occurred in 1962, when seven stories made it to the front page. Average visibility, the last entry in the table, combines the number of stories in a given period with their placement in the paper.[6] The pattern repeats here as well: the movement enjoyed twice the visibility in the *New York Times* during Kennedy's presidency than in Eisenhower's. This measure will help focus my more detailed content analysis in the two chapters to follow. Following the general model set out in chapter 2, this analysis will be organized by changes in policy set against a backdrop of external events and internal dissent.

Figure 2 plots movement visibility in the *New York Times* set against arms policy development during Eisenhower's second term in office, beginning in February 1957 and ending with the inauguration of John

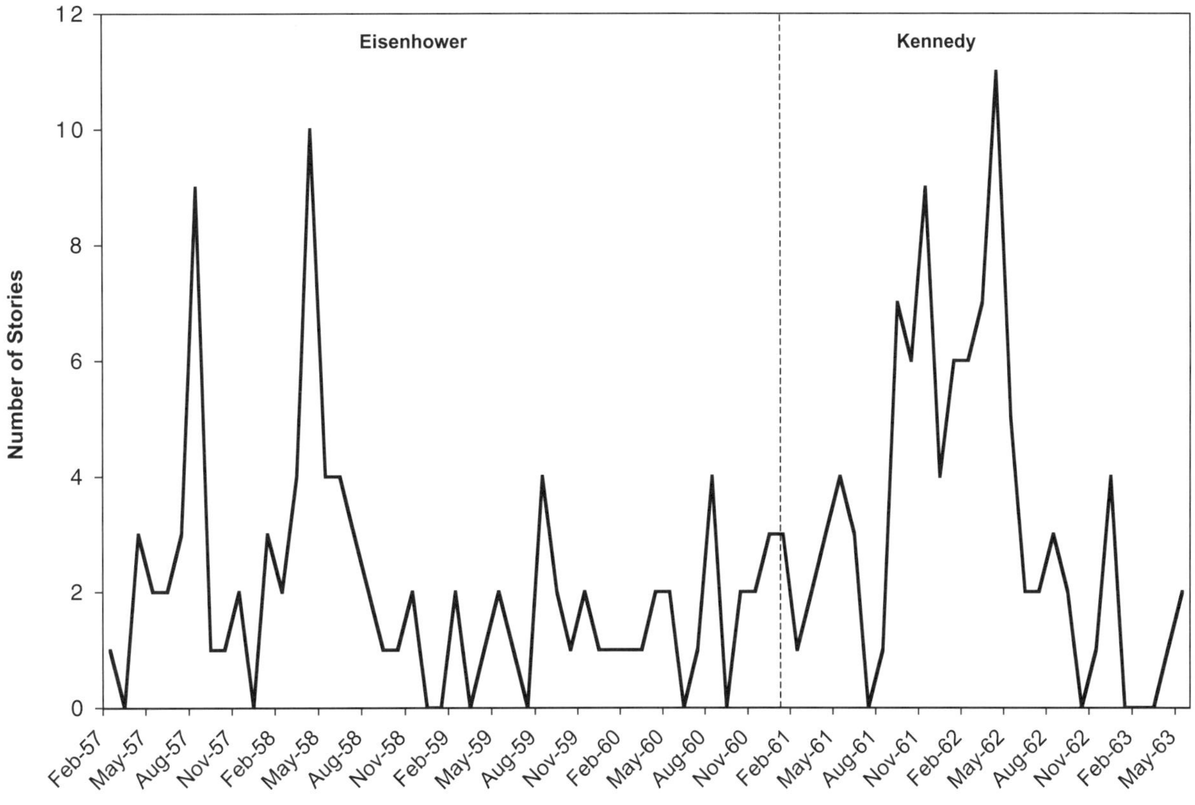


Figure 1. *New York Times* coverage of the test ban movement, 1957–63.

*Table 3.* Movement Visibility in the *New York Times*

| | Eisenhower administration | Kennedy administration |
|---|---|---|
| Total stories | 98 | 92 |
| Average/month | 2.31 | 3.39 |
| Front-page stories | 12 | 12 |
| Average/month | 0.25 | 0.43 |
| Average visibility | 0.16 | 0.32 |

Kennedy in January 1961. The following chapter discusses these changes in greater detail, but table 4 summarizes the broad outlines of the policies in force in each of the five periods. This summary illustrates Eisenhower's ambivalence as he made tentative moves toward arms control in period 1 before retreating, advancing decisively in period 2, then backtracking somewhat because of technical complications in period 3, and advancing on a more modest goal before finally retreating after the U2 incident wrecked the chances for a test ban during his presidency.

The gross patterns of movement visibility in the *Times* correlate with the tentative opening in period 1 and then the decisive move toward a test

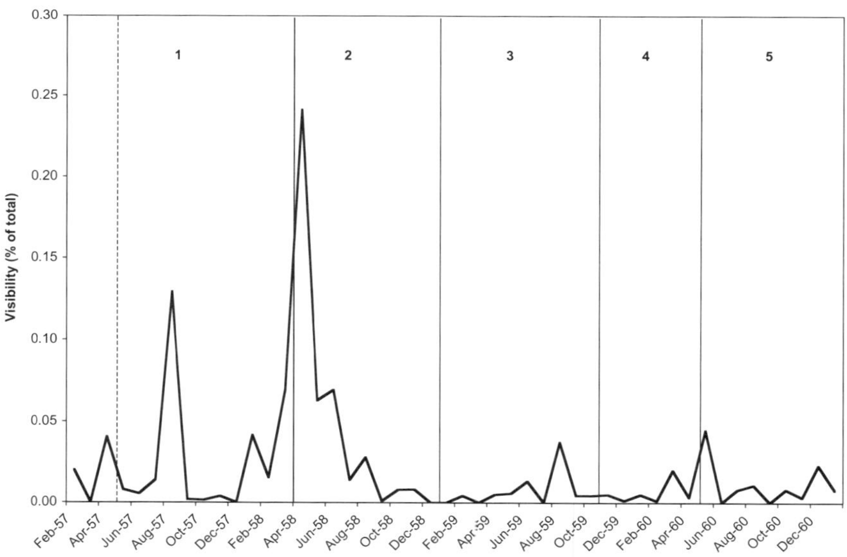


Figure 2. Presidential policy and movement visibility in the *New York Times:* Eisenhower administration. The numbers represent policy periods summarized in table 4.

moratorium in period 2. Table 5 shows average visibility for each of the five periods. This summary masks some of the irregularities evident in the chart, but it reveals the peak of coverage in period 2 when, following a unilateral Soviet moratorium, Eisenhower moved toward an American ban. Subsequent coverage drops, with a slight increase preceding the Vienna summit.

*Table 4.* Summary of Eisenhower's Nuclear Testing Policy

| Period | Policy |
|---|---|
| 1. January 1957–March 1958 | Amid a worldwide debate on the dangers of radiation, Eisenhower appoints Harold Stassen as special assistant on disarmament. Stassen commits a political gaffe in Geneva that irritates U.S. allies, and Eisenhower backs off from a dialogue with the Soviets on a possible test ban. The Soviets launch Sputnik on October 4, 1957, making Americans feel vulnerable to a Soviet missile attack. |
| 2. April–December 1958 | The USSR unilaterally ceases testing, driving Eisenhower to reconsider U.S. policy. With scientists' assurance that remote detection of nuclear tests is possible, the administration moves toward a test moratorium. The United States ceases testing on October 31 and begins negotiations in Geneva. |
| 3. January–October 1959 | Negotiations stall as scientists discover flaws in their remote detection studies. Administration dissent increases, but Eisenhower continues the test moratorium nonetheless. |
| 4. November 1959–May 1960 | With remote detection possible only for tests of a certain threshold, scientists settle on a compromise for a partial test ban. Final negotiations for an agreement are scheduled for a Soviet-American summit in Paris. |
| 5. June 1960–January 1961 | The Soviets shoot down an American U2 in their air space. Khrushchev uses the incident to embarrass Eisenhower at the summit, spoiling the chances for an arms control agreement. Eisenhower urges Kennedy to resume U.S. tests. |

*Table 5.* Movement Visibility in the *New York Times*

| Period | Visibility |
|---|---|
| 1. January 1957–March 1958 | 0.16 |
| 2. April–December 1958 | 0.27 |
| 3. January–October 1959 | 0.16 |
| 4. November 1959–May 1960 | 0.18 |
| 5. June 1960–January 1961 | 0.17 |
| Average | 0.16 |

Kennedy sought a treaty throughout his term, despite foreign policy reversals and crises. A look at the coverage pattern for movement activity (figure 3) shows a dramatic break from that during the Eisenhower administration. The pattern here is more constant, and unlike the downward trend of the Eisenhower era, the trend moves upward before falling precipitously at the onset of the Cuban missile crisis and then, after the crisis abates, rising to its previous level. Table 6 briefly describes the policy in force during each of the five periods marked in figure 3. Table 7 shows average visibility for each policy period. Here there is also a rise in visibility, which, except for the short two-month period in 1961, was sustained at a higher and more consistent level than during the Eisenhower years. Unlike the Eisenhower administration, with its shifting attitudes, the Kennedy administration was bent on changing its fundamental defensive posture from all-out retaliation to flexible response. One might expect it to have been, if not more favorable, at least less opposed to a policy that sought less reliance on a strictly nuclear policy.

In summary, the historical record shows the Eisenhower administration moving uncertainly toward an arms control position, approaching and backing away in response to Soviet initiatives, world opinion, and techni-

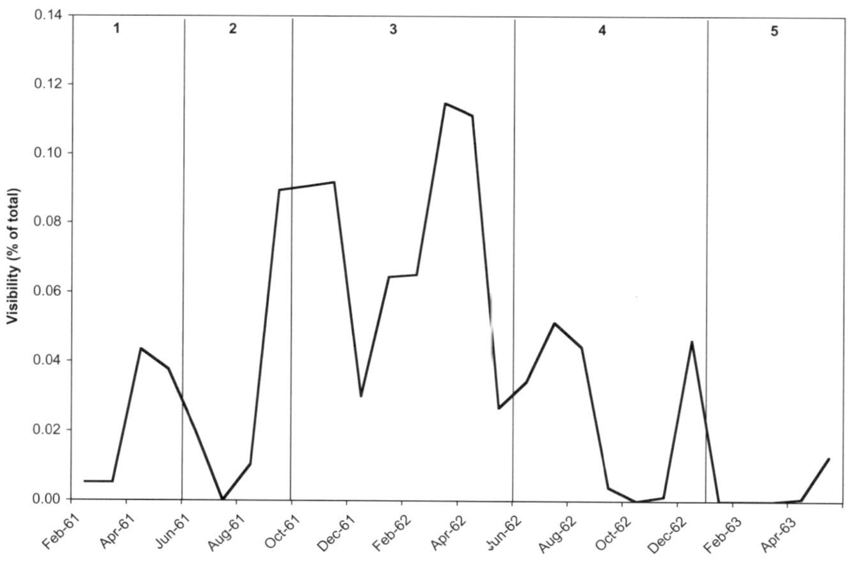


Figure 3. Presidential policy and movement visibility in the *New York Times:* Kennedy administration. The numbers represent policy periods summarized in table 5.

*Table 6.* Summary of Kennedy's Nuclear Testing Policy

| Period | Policy |
|---|---|
| 1. February–May 1961 | Kennedy forms a White House group to study the prospects for a test ban. With the only issue remaining the number of on-site inspections, Kennedy looks forward to negotiating an agreement with Khrushchev at a June summit in Vienna. |
| 2-3. June 1961–April 1962[a] | The summit fails. Khrushchev then tests U.S. resolve by forcing the issue of East German autonomy and Allied access to Berlin. The Soviets resume atmospheric tests, and Kennedy reluctantly begins preparations for resumption of U.S. tests. |
| 4. May–November 1962 | The United States resumes atmospheric testing. That fall the Soviets begin building missile sites in Cuba and precipitate a crisis in late October that nearly leads to nuclear war. |
| 5. December 1962–May 1963 | The end of the crisis leads to a period of rapprochement. Kennedy and Khrushchev exchange conciliatory messages, preparing the way for the Limited Test Ban Treaty signed in August 1963 and ratified by the Senate one month later. |

a. The two-month period following the Vienna summit and the resumption of Soviet tests is here combined with the succeeding period when Kennedy contemplated resuming U.S. tests.

*Table 7.* Movement Visibility in the *New York Times*

| Period | Visibility |
|---|---|
| 1. February–May 1961 | 0.24 |
| 2. June–August 1961 | 0.12 |
| 3. September 1961–April 1962 | 0.53 |
| 4. May–November 1962 | 0.33 |
| 5. December 1962–May 1963 | 0.18 |
| Average | 0.32 |

cal issues. By contrast, Kennedy moved with greater assurance. Overall coverage patterns show the movement enjoying twice the visibility in the *New York Times* during the Kennedy administration than during the Eisenhower. Moreover, peaks in coverage correlate with major policy initiatives in both administrations. I now turn to a closer look at the news coverage, beginning with the second Eisenhower administration.

## Notes

1. *Belligerence* is defined here as the application of military force to some political end "without engaging in a continuing contest of violence" (Blechman and Kaplan 1978, 12). Examples in Kennedy's term included the Bay of Pigs invasion, the assassination of Trujillo, and the quarantine on Cuban during the missile crisis.

2. Actually Senator Stuart Symington was the first to use the issue against the Eisenhower administration's defense posture, doing so as early as 1956. It would not stick until Kennedy made it an issue in the 1960 campaign (Ambrose 1984, 313).

3. Evidence from Khrushchev's memoirs indicate that Soviet reluctance to accept U.S. demands for up to twenty inspections per year as a condition for a comprehensive test ban was based less on fears of espionage than on the discovery of their weak position (Divine 1978, 288).

4. Some cynics in the administration said that the push for a test ban would quiet fears about fallout (Newhouse 1989, 193).

5. There are inconclusive data on American preferences for a test ban in this era. Rosi (1965) points to wide fluctuations in aggregate levels of support depending on question phrasing and international events (e.g., the Sputnik launch). Graham (1989), however, concludes that there was consistent support for a multilateral test ban. My own examination of the data supports Graham's position somewhat, but a significant reframing of survey questions during much of the Kennedy administration makes it difficult to be certain about this. Four major surveys conducted during the resumption of Soviet testing and U.S. restraint—June 1961 to March 1962—asked about preferences not for a multilateral agreement but for resumption of U.S. testing. For example, after the Vienna summit, Gallup prompted survey respondents with the reminder that no arms control agreement with the Soviet Union had been reached since the test moratorium in November 1958; in the light of that fact, the survey asked, should the United States now resume testing? Presumably the international climate had changed such that this question seemed reasonable, but its wording invited a response grounded in frustration with the negotiating process rather than a preference for a multilateral ban. One could, after all, hold both attitudes simultaneously.

6. For each month I calculated the average page position of the stories and converted each to its reciprocal, such that a front-page story has the greatest value. These were summed and then divided by total visibility for the entire Eisenhower administration. Thus the data point for any given month represents the percentage of total movement visibility between February 1957 and January 1961.

# 4 The Dawn of Protest: The Eisenhower Administration

In 1957 the inventor of the H-bomb could command the courteous attention of *Time*'s editors when he presented his plan for surviving nuclear war. Edward Teller assured his readers that, with foresight and adequate provision—including underground shelters and caches of surplus food—the nation's infrastructure could be rebuilt quickly. The road system would stand up, except for bridges, which could be speedily repaired as long as repair equipment was stored near vulnerable points: "We can be back in business within a few hours of attack" (*Time*, January 21, 1957, p. 17).

In the fifties the needs of the national security state were such that a credible willingness to use nuclear weapons was part of an overall defense strategy. Poll results reveal that the public was willing to risk the effects of radiation for the perceived benefits of building a credible nuclear arsenal that most saw as coming into use in a conflict with the Soviet Union (Graham 1989).

This chapter analyzes news coverage of the test ban movement set against the making of arms policy in the second Eisenhower administration. Here and in the following chapter (a similar analysis of coverage in the Kennedy administration), I will be alert to stories that define "critical discourse moments," those points when there are shifts in the news media's treatment of the antinuclear movement and its messages. My working hypothesis is that these correspond closely to the making of arms control policy in the executive branch of government.

I now take a closer look at each of the five policy periods identified in chapter 3, during which there were significant changes in the balance of forces for and against arms control. Since these changes were formally approved by the president himself, I looked specifically for changes in the president's directives to his subordinates, especially to his secretaries of state and defense and to the chairman of the AEC. Following the work of Bennett, Hallin, and others (see Wolfsfeld 1997), I also take note of significant differences of opinion among members of the president's cabinet and his principal advisers. These policy changes and differences of opinion offered antinuclear movements opportunities for taking significantly greater control of the political agenda and thus for gaining favorable media coverage.

## Ambivalence and Retrenchment, January 1957–March 1958

In 1955 Eisenhower appointed Harold Stassen as special assistant on disarmament. In so doing he substituted the more modest but practical goal of arms control for his ideal: eliminating all nuclear weapons (Ambrose 1984, 246). Granted a cabinet-level position, Stassen drew the displeasure of Eisenhower's secretary of state, John Foster Dulles, who keenly resented an intrusion into what he regarded as his private sphere. Eisenhower intended the new position to broaden the range of policy discussion for disarmament measures (Divine 1978, 60), but it also created friction within the administration as Stassen vied with Dulles and Lewis Strauss, chairman of the AEC, for dominance. Stassen persevered and in March 1957—amid a growing worldwide debate about the effects of radiation—convinced Eisenhower that a change in policy was politically necessary. Eisenhower instructed Stassen to sound out the Soviets on a temporary test ban, a first step toward a comprehensive arms proposal (Divine 1978, 143–45).

In May 1957 Stassen went to Geneva and at once committed a diplomatic gaffe. Letting his enthusiasm get the best of him, he showed his "talking papers" to the Soviets without first briefing the British and French delegations. Secretly pleased by the affront and the opportunity to rein him in, Dulles reassured the Allies that no change in U.S. policy was imminent and that in any case, all Western powers would be consulted before any change was contemplated. The opening to a test ban that had seemed so promising that spring had closed. (The broken line in fig. 2 represents this reversal.)

Despite his change of heart, Eisenhower continued to be troubled by the health hazards of radioactive fallout, the lingering residue of atmospheric nuclear explosions. Earlier tests had aroused public fears, and now Linus Pauling's well-publicized campaign on the genetic dangers of fallout began to concern him. Privately Eisenhower quizzed Strauss on the need for further tests, but publicly he supported the concept of a "clean bomb" promoted by Edward Teller. Briefed by Strauss on Eisenhower's continuing concern for transforming nuclear energy into peaceful uses, Teller pleaded for the additional tests needed for producing a fallout-free tactical weapon. Confused, or believing what he wanted to believe, Eisenhower approved further testing in June (Ambrose 1984, 398–400).

Beyond the presumed need for a clean bomb, other factors retarding the chances for a Soviet-American agreement included contrary views on the relative importance of ceasing to test and produce nuclear weapons. The latter program was an American precondition known to be unacceptable to the Soviets, who, because of their inferior position, feared a permanent American advantage. Talks in Geneva stalled, and the Soviet Union began its own series of H-bomb tests.

Then on October 4, 1957, the Russians launched Sputnik, the first artificial satellite, and all but eliminated what hopes remained for an agreement. The successful launch alarmed Americans, who had become accustomed to feeling that theirs was the richest, most powerful, and most technologically sophisticated nation on earth (Ambrose 1984, 427). Although they may not have appreciated the intricacies of defense policy, Americans trusted in the advantage their nation held in science and technology, expertise they believed the Soviet Union could achieve only second-hand through espionage (Pach and Richardson 1991, 170). Sputnik shook this confidence, for it suggested not only a surprisingly superior Soviet technology but one that made Americans feel vulnerable to a missile attack, even though the Soviets were far from offering a credible threat to the vastly superior American nuclear forces. In fact, they would not have their first ICBM until 1961, but for several reasons to be outlined later, their inferior position was known only to a small group in the White House.

Eisenhower resisted domestic pressures to respond to this ostensible Soviet lead in military technology. He rejected, for example, the recommendations of the Gaither Report—a top-secret assessment of nuclear security—for a 25 percent defense budget increase, a substantial portion of which would finance a program to build a fallout shelter for every single American. Eisenhower knew the panic stirred by Sputnik would probably facilitate congressional approval of this extravagant program. Reassured by intelligence reports that indicated an American lead in the capacity to wage a war with nuclear-tipped missiles, he rejected every recommendation of the report and remained committed to his middle way (Pach and Richardson 1991, 173).

In a final bid to challenge Dulles, Stassen proposed that the United States uncouple the test ban from a halt in arms production. Although the proposal found some support among his advisers, Eisenhower rejected the plan in the face of strong opposition from Strauss and the Pentagon. Stassen resigned a few weeks later, in February 1958.

In summary, during this period the Eisenhower administration took tentative steps toward arms control but quickly retreated to its restrained policy of military deterrence.

### *The Media: Wavering between Politics and Science*

The peace movement made its first prominent appearance in the *New York Times* during this period of official wavering. By the early spring of 1957, Norman Cousins and others in the antinuclear movement had convinced Albert Schweitzer to make a public appeal for an international test ban. He did so in April 1957 when he addressed an international radio audience. The *Times* did position Schweitzer's appeal on its front page, but below the fold, yielding column 1 to a New York City Council scandal. Excerpts of Schweitzer's remarks on the potential dangers to genetic material and of proliferation to other nations appeared on an interior page (*New York Times* [*NYT*], April 24, 1957, p. 1).

While the newspaper approached the antinuclear movement with caution and uncertainty, *Time* magazine stood foursquare in unyielding ideological opposition to accommodation with the Soviets. This chapter opened with one such story, Edward Teller's plans for surviving all-out nuclear war, a component of a war-fighting strategy (*Time,* January 21, 1957, p. 17). The newsmagazine was also given to a pattern of reporting in which comments of U.S. and Soviet officials were paired to contrive a sort of Manichaean wrestling match. In one example, the U.S. Air Force secretary's veiled threat of nuclear retaliation—"We will resist aggression with our quality weapons from the outset"—was paired with a similar bravado from the Soviet defense minister: "The Soviet air force is capable of delivering crushing blows against any adversary, wherever he might be or hide" (*Time,* April 1, 1957, p. 23).

Given its ideological commitment, *Time* tended to blunt the force of the antinuclear movement. For example, the magazine used the Schweitzer speech as a foil for the remarks of Dr. Willard Libby, an AEC commissioner who minimized the dangers of fallout, saying the average person had more to fear from the natural radiation discharged by concrete and bricks. The report referred respectfully to Schweitzer as the "illustrious missionary-physician" but, using a jeopardy objection, questioned rhetorically whether it was not worth enduring the small risk from fallout to avert the far greater one of "slackening our defenses" against totalitarian forces until some method of safeguarded disarmament had been achieved (*Time,* May 6, 1957, p. 24). Whatever the true dangers of the fallout risk, however, it became a pivotal issue for the test ban movement.

*Fallout and the Scientists' Debate* — A key element of the movement's case rested on the health effects of fallout. This proved to be an effective issue for the movement and thus stimulated a counterattack from its foes, who used a number of ripostes in what became a frame contest for mobilizing public support (see Ryan 1991).

Linus Pauling, a professor of chemistry at the California Institute of Technology, led the movement's campaign on the dangers of radiation. At this early stage of the movement, he had been circulating a petition among fellow scientists calling for an international moratorium on nuclear testing. Reflecting its continuing ambivalence, the *New York Times* positioned the story in its interior pages under a qualifying subhead, "Other Scientists Dispute Radiation Views." The story sowed doubt on Pauling's scientific views in two ways, by reference to dissenting views among fellow scientists ("He has made repeated statements that nuclear tests were causing widespread disposition to such ailments as leukemia. These contentions have been contradicted by other scientists of equal standing") and by characterizing his politics as "left of center" (*NYT,* June 4, 1957, p. 17).

Noteworthy here is the linkage of Pauling's views on radiation not strictly to contested scientific theory but to a political agenda and the representation of his position as controversial not by virtue of its scientific merit but on his right to claim that merit. To bolster the case against him, the *Times* mentioned Pauling's colleagues who shrank from his views: "Many prominent scientists were conspicuous by their absence from the list, even one from Cal Tech: 'I feel that scientists ought to confine their public statements to their own fields, or to make it clear that they are speaking not as experts but are expressing private opinions.'" Here, then, is a clear example of how a news frame deflects attention from the issue at hand by questioning the credibility of the messenger.

A week later, on the same day the *New York Times* reported the Stassen talking papers incident, a story covered Pauling's departure for Paris, where he was to begin a lecture tour to press his case for an atomic test ban. The full text of his statement followed a quotation where he made this appeal: "I just feel strongly that scientists have a moral duty to give their fellow citizens the benefit of their general understanding of these [radiation] questions." Almost as an afterthought the story included this gratuitous remark:

"Dr. Pauling, who is left of center politically, said he would like to add the names of Russian scientists for his appeal, but was not sure just how he could go about this" (*NYT*, June 12, 1957, p. 6).

Pauling's self-appointed and media-anointed status hampered the movement because his politics came to be associated with a legitimate, albeit controversial, scientific position. Pauling's counterpart on the right was Edward Teller. Although Teller's politics were arguably as off-center as Pauling's, the *Times* referred to him in somewhat gentler (though perhaps dubious) terms as "Father of the H-bomb."

To this point the radiation controversy had stayed out of the political fray and in fact had been covered only in the back pages of *Time* magazine, in its science section, where the controversy was awash with scientific jargon. Ordinary citizens had no place amid a highly technical discourse studded with references to the exotic assortment of radioactive isotopes—strontium 90, cobalt 60, cesium 137, manganese 54, and iodine 131—that spew from nuclear explosions. It followed, then, that scientists would lead the debate. Early coverage focused on education, describing, for example, the progress of strontium 90 through the food chain and the human body's tolerance for the isotope.

Then the narrow opening to a ban offered by the Eisenhower administration (flubbed by Stassen) created an unusually large scientific forum for the testing issue. A two-page article in *Time* magazine's science section polled a number of American and foreign scientists on the dangers of testing. Coverage characterized Libby's "calm" position but also made a case against testing, especially from geneticists who warned of the potential for large numbers of mutations. The story also opened space for Pauling but, because of the forum's scientific nature, made no reference to his politics. (This omission would change when the venue shifted to the magazine's political pages.)

In general, biologists and physicists disagreed over the risks involved, and it was clear even at this early stage of the controversy that a univocal scientific estimate of risk would not be forthcoming. After noting that physicists were less concerned about the potential for somatic and genetic harm,[1] the article astutely concluded that scientists would contribute only a "minor part of the wordage" in the controversy as they realized the decision to stop testing would be moral and political rather than scientific (*Time,* June 3, 1957, pp. 64–65).

In fact, both sides in the debate had merit. Those who minimized the risks—the Teller position—pointed out that fallout from atomic testing emitted only tiny amounts of radiation, far less, for example, than the average person absorbed in diagnostic X rays. Those who maximized the risk—the Pauling position—argued that even a tiny increase in the incidence of cancer or in the rate of birth defects would result in a small but not insignificant increase in the mortality rate.

Which argument would hold the day depended on the answer to the more general question of whether the body has some threshold limit on the amount of radiation it can tolerate during a specific time period. Amounts below that limit would thus have no discernible effect. Teller held that the existence of such a threshold would render harmless the tiny amount added by testing fallout. Pauling argued that no such threshold exists and thus that any additional radiation, no matter how small, will increase the risks for the population. Some forty years into this controversy, science has yet to resolve the threshold issue (Weart 1988, 207–9). Although this may be an unsatisfactory result for anyone keen on a solution, it serves my interest in assessing the quality of news coverage: given the irresolvable controversy, how did the editors treat Pauling, Teller, and others sharing their views when the issue entered the political arena?

*Denaturing the Fallout Issue: The Clean Bomb* — After the Stassen incident, the *New York Times* dropped stories on Pauling's petition gathering and other general aspects of the peace movement to its interior pages, yielding the front page to arguments by Teller and his colleagues Ernest Lawrence and Mark Mills for developing a miniature hydrogen bomb that would leave minimal fallout (the subhead read, "3 Scientists Tell President Radioactivity Can Be 'Essentially Negligible'"). The scientists lauded the clean bomb by promoting its versatility as a battlefield tactical weapon and as a "city buster" that would spare the lives of tens of millions by minimizing radioactive debris. Instead of melding the scientific views with a political agenda, as it had done with Pauling, the *Times* avoided tainting Teller's scientific credibility with his equally politically inflected view that a test ban would hinder development of the clean bomb: "If such a suspension is agreed on, it is doubtful that the weapons could be developed" (*NYT*, June 25, 1957, pp. 1, 3).

*Time* magazine was also sanguine about the prospects for the device. Under a group photo of Strauss, Lawrence, Mills, and Teller, a caption asked rhetorically, "Why stop at the verge of success?" The idea of a clean bomb simultaneously defused the radiation issue and yielded bonus benefits as promising an unlimited source of fusion energy: "Give us four or five more years . . . and We'll produce an absolutely clean bomb (*Time*, July 8, 1957, p. 8)."

Headlined "Atoms for Peace," *Time*'s lead story the following week described how the administration's hard line had softened. Eisenhower offered to suspend tests if the Soviets would agree to stop their production of nuclear weapons (a red herring, for this was known to be unacceptable) but argued that further tests would be necessary anyway to build the clean bomb (*Time,* July 15, 1957, pp. 15–16). Libby bolstered the case for the "little fellow," reporting the effects of an underground blast by a small atomic bomb that had hollowed a fifty-foot tunnel inside a Nevada mesa. Libby surmised that one or more similar explosions could carve out a harbor on the Peruvian coast or bring oil to the surface from underground formations (*Time,* March 24, 1958, p. 64). Thus the movement momentarily lost its momentum as the press accepted the jeopardy argument implicit in its opponents' frame of reference. The clean bomb rendered moot the radiation issue and deftly recast the test ban as an impediment to its development. For the moment administration allies had won the frame contest, but the competition had diverted the two sides from a common rhetorical ground and thus disengaged the opponents from a single focal argument. The press finally selected the clean bomb argument, in part because it resonated with the American value of scientific progress (see Gamson and Modigliani 1989).

August 1957, the anniversary month of the Hiroshima and Nagasaki bombings, marked the first peak of coverage of movement visibility in the *New York Times.* A closer look at the stories, however, reveals a flurry of short pieces in the interior pages and a single front-page story, a summary of an appeal by the World Council of Churches to the nuclear powers to stop testing. Typical of coverage of such church-related stories, the *Times* printed the full text of the council appeal without comment or qualification, leaving the organization's moral authority undisturbed (*NYT,* August 6, 1957, p. 1). Despite the story's apolitical flavor, its appearance on the front page signaled the paper's legitimization of the issue on its most formidable appeal, the moral cause.

Other shorter stories included the first on the CNVA and included this quotation from Lawrence Scott: "This will be civil disobedience against the laws of the U.S. We are doing this in a spirit of prayer and conscience" (*NYT,* August 6, 1957, p. 2). This and a few brief stories indicated a holding position on the part of the *Times*'s editors: they acknowledged the moral legitimacy of the issue but seemed reluctant at this point to lavish it with prominent coverage. Thus although the first peak in coverage appeared in August 1957, the stories it comprised were short, largely empirical (facts only), and (excepting the World Council of Churches story) off the front page.

Six months passed before the next front-page story appeared, an account of Pauling's presentation to the United Nations of a petition with 9,000 scientists' signatures that he had gathered abroad. The story made no mention of Pauling's politics, but it included this subtle qualification: "The petition did not refer to the Soviet campaign for suspension of nuclear bomb tests without regard to other phases of disarmament," a reference to Eisenhower's objection to the Soviet refusal to link the moratorium on testing to a halt on the production of weapons (*NYT,* January 14, 1958, p. 1). This unevenly balanced coverage continued until the administration signaled a major policy change the following spring, a move that coincided with the next peak in movement visibility.

## Breakthrough, April–December 1958

After completing a series of tests, on March 31, 1958, the Soviets announced a unilateral moratorium on testing, adroitly anticipating and thus preempting a new series of American tests and scoring a public relations coup.[2] The flanking maneuver coincided with the results of an investigation by Hans Bethe that suggested the possibility of remote detection of underground tests. Bethe had been brought into the President's Scientific Advisory Committee (PSAC), a panel created by Eisenhower's science adviser James Killian after the Sputnik launch.[3] The possibility of remote detection and Bethe's assessment of vastly superior nuclear forces on the American side finally pushed Eisenhower toward the test ban. Although Strauss objected, he was by now a lame duck (due to resign in June) with waning influence.

In early April Eisenhower instructed Dulles to propose a technical conference that would include a feasibility study of test detection. Later that month Eisenhower also accepted Stassen's proposal to uncouple the production issue from the test ban. On April 8 Dulles sent a letter to the Soviets proposing a technical conference on a test ban inspection system, and on April 28 he offered the Stassen proposal to separate the test ban from production issues (Divine 1978, 207–11).

With the Soviets having outflanked the United States, Eisenhower and Dulles concluded that further opposition to a ban would leave the country morally isolated in world opinion. In August, after the technical conference had established an inspection model, Eisenhower proposed a moratorium on testing, and on October 31 the United States joined the Soviet Union in a temporary stoppage. Just prior to the moratorium, the United States conducted a last-minute series of atmospheric tests known as Project

Argus. The tests would remain secret until the following year, when the *New York Times* conceded advance knowledge of the project. Administration policy remained consistent until late November, when the Geneva talks once again foundered.

In summary, between April and December 1958 the Eisenhower administration consolidated its views on a negotiating policy.

### *Media Coverage: Opening the Doors*

Whereas up to this point the *New York Times* had limited its coverage of the movement to occasional facts-only stories and to qualified reportage of the Pauling campaign, the first days of spring 1958 brought increasingly morally impassioned stories to its front page. They included reports on SANE-sponsored "peace walks" and a CNVA-sponsored attempt by Albert Bigelow and a partner to sail a boat, the *Golden Rule,* into an AEC test zone in the central Pacific. (The first *Golden Rule* story had appeared in the *Times* several months earlier, buried deep in an obscure section of the paper next to a schedule of New York ship arrivals.) A U.S. Navy lieutenant, Bigelow had been arrested at an AEC Nevada test site the previous August and now intended to sail into the test zone (*NYT,* January 13, 1958, p. 48).

By the end of February the story of the *Golden Rule* had crept to page 13 and was accompanied by a two-column photo that showed Bigelow at the prow of his boat ready to sail again (a storm had interrupted the first journey). "A spokesman said the group could not believe that the tests would proceed with lethal hydrogen-bomb explosions in the face of four people who mean no harm" (*NYT,* February 27, 1958, p. 13).

Whether alarmed by the increasing publicity accorded to this symbolic protest or genuinely concerned for the safety of the crew, the AEC passed a regulation that barred U.S. citizens from entering the Pacific proving grounds. One would expect this story to have garnered little attention, for it concerned a bureaucratic proclamation no more newsworthy than a regulation barring people from leaping to their deaths in the Senate chamber to protest a bill under consideration, but an imminent change in American foreign policy thrust the story onto the front page. A quotation from A. J. Muste reinforced the moral dimension of the protest: "We shall continue to sail to the testing area, come what may. We hope that our act will remind our fellow citizens that the United States does not have to go through these tests. We do have a choice" (*NYT,* April 12, 1958, p. 1).

Three weeks later the *Times* reported the arrest of the crew of the *Golden Rule* as it sailed into Honolulu harbor. The front-page story told of the morally impassioned protesters' intention to violate the AEC regulation "come what may" and their subsequent arrest by the U.S. Coast Guard. The prominence of the story and the symbolism of the men caught in legal machinery signaled an important change in the paper's sympathy to their cause. That such sympathy was in line with the administration's intent to proceed with a moratorium was not a coincidence, for the paper had given only one short page 2 story to similar acts by the CNVA the previous summer (scaling a fence at a Nevada test site). Further evidence establishes that the story's newsworthiness depended on more than simple facts.

During the same period stories of SANE-sponsored "Walks for Peace" emerged more prominently and for the first time were accompanied by pictures that depicted ordinary citizens taking part in the movement. One short piece heralded the arrival of 115 peace marchers by doing a close-up of four of the middle-class participants. One of the group—a seventy-one-year-old veteran of the women's suffrage movement—remarked that the women's movement did not get off the ground until it left the meeting halls for parades and street demonstrations (*NYT*, April 4, 1958, p. 6).

The next day the movement broke onto the front page with a three-column head, "Peace Walkers Score Nuclear Arms," over a photo of the marchers with picket signs in full view headed for the United Nations. The story drew a parallel between the protesters who had walked from "as far away as Philadelphia" and Gandhi's antitax march to the sea.[4] The march through Manhattan gathered several hundred more demonstrators, "swelling" its ranks to seven hundred, a "courteous and respectful" group of children, teenagers, and elderly who sang pacifist parodies of popular songs and hillbilly tunes to banjo and guitar accompaniment. The piece concluded with a friendly swipe at the Wobblies: "The Industrial Workers of the World was represented in the march. The delegation consisted of a leather-jacketed youth on a motorcycle with a teen-age girl on the rump seat" (*NYT*, April 5, 1958 p. 1).

A similarly respectful, if not bemused, front-page story followed the next day. It related how leaders of the SANE-sponsored peace protest had permitted some Hungarian counterdemonstrators to speak to a midtown "crowd" of 150. Characterizing the incident as a friendly exchange between two groups exercising their right to free speech and assembly, the account concluded on this decorous note: "With handshakes and an exchange of mailing addresses among the two groups, the meeting soon dispersed in an atmosphere of harmony" (*NYT*, April 6, 1958, p. 1). Once again the *Times* provided sympathetic coverage, considering the small numbers of demonstrators involved and, to the fifties mind, their comparatively exotic nature.

On the same day as the peace-walk coverage, Pauling, Muste, and Bertrand Russell also made it to the front page, in an account of a suit they had brought against the AEC to enjoin it from further development of nuclear weapons (*NYT,* April, 5, 1958, p. 1). A small takeout described Pauling as a "left of center man who has frequently been caught in the middle" mentioning his disagreement with a colleague on the scientific evidence for the existence of God, his view that the problem of atomic war "must not be confused by minor problems such as communism versus capitalism," his willingness to lend his voice to "leftist groups," and, despite his declarations under oath that he was no communist, his insistence "on the right to speak his mind and associate with anyone he pleases" (*NYT,* April 5, 1958, p. 3).

Prior articles on Pauling had deflected his scientific views by tying them to an underlying political agenda. With the movement now prominently featured, the paper subtly changed its characterization of Pauling from formulaic reproof to admiration of his pluckiness, his willingness to defend unconventional views and associates (a takeout revealed that Pauling had defied public sentiment by keeping a Japanese gardener during World War II). His view that radiation endangers health, however, would continue to be weighed down by unrelated political baggage.

*Project Argus* — To a casual observer, the *New York Times* seemed at this point willing to grant the antinuclear movement the legitimacy and publicity it needed to sustain pressure on the administration. Behind the scenes, however, the paper maintained unstated loyalty to the administration demonstrated in its complicity with a secret project that deprived the movement of a potentially productive issue. The Project Argus incident illustrates the importance of the media both to political movements (and government) and to modern democratic theory.

The surprise Soviet test moratorium in early spring of 1958 elicited from the Eisenhower administration a similar pledge to cease testing the following October. Prior to the moratorium the Defense Department scheduled Project Argus, a hastily arranged series of high-altitude tests over the South Atlantic. The following March the *Times* revealed it had learned of the plans for the project the previous summer but had refrained from publishing the information to avoid a flap: "The information was obtained without limitation on its use. Nevertheless, scientists associated with the Government said they feared that prior announcement of the experiment might lead to protests that would force its cancellation" (*NYT,* March 19, 1959, p. 16).

Angered, A. J. Muste, a member of *Liberation*'s editorial board, posted a letter to the *Times* in which he accused the editors of blocking the free flow of information out of what he regarded as misplaced loyalty: "The editors of the *Times* deliberately decided to withhold important news so that citizens who had shown that they were deeply concerned about nuclear testing and related matters might not have the opportunity to protest in time. Who gave them this authority? Who are these men? What becomes of the whole idea of a free press which keeps the people informed if this is the way such information is handled even in peace time?" (*Liberation* 1959a, 10).

The managing editor of the *Times*, Turner Catledge, offered a flat contradiction, but Walter Sullivan, a reporter, wrote in the *Times* house organ that the principal reason the paper had released the story in the first place was because both *Newsweek* and *Time* had gotten wind of it and might have scooped the paper. Sullivan reiterated the paper's stated reason for suppressing the story: "Virtually all [scientists] agreed that the only reason for withholding the story was political—to avoid embarrassment to the Government" (in *Liberation* 1959b, 3).

Muste also received a reply from the newspaper's military editor, Hanson Baldwin, who took responsibility for withholding the story. Baldwin's self-assured identification with state policy provides a revealing example of what Hallin (1992) has called the "high-modernism" of American journalism. Baldwin's self-assured justification took the following utilitarian course:

> You [Muste] speak of conscience, of responsibility and ideals. You have no monopoly on any of these. Freedom of the press means a great sense of responsibility to the good of the country and to the greatest good of the greatest number. Every newspaperman worth his salt faces the problem of whether or not to publish certain information and every newspaperman worth his salt does at some time or another withhold some information. Freedom can never mean license. Nor can it mean the kind of naivete you display. Your point of view, in my opinion, is the fuzzy, well intentioned but highly dangerous one which motivates far too many of our so-called Liberals. You are inaccurate in fact as well as in opinion. The Argus tests were of tremendous potential and actual military importance; the issue was not only political. Furthermore the question of fallout had virtually nothing to do with the issue; small-scale detonations at high altitude result in inconsequential fallout.
>
> It is precisely because I feel and the Times feels a high sense of responsibility to the greatest good of the greatest number and a sense of our responsibility to our country that the story was handled as it was. I repeat: you have no monopoly on conscience. (*Liberation* 1959b, 3)

The editors of *Liberation* prepared a collective response in which they pointed out that a handful of news-gathering agencies with a virtual monopoly on the flow of information had used their privileged position to support the chicanery of the nuclear powers pursuing military advantage even as they sought to capitalize on world peace sentiment (recall that the Soviet Union called a moratorium on its tests immediately after completing a test series). They accused the *Times* of following the "false god of military expediency" as it gave semblance of support for a free press: "Realistically, those who fail to face up to this schizophrenia—and its inevitable result—are the ones who are guilty of fuzzy, well-intentioned but highly dangerous naivete, and are adding to the rush toward world suicide" (*Liberation* 1959b, 4). This exchange appeared only within the pages of *Liberation,* whose circulation is estimated to have been somewhere under 6,000 at this point.

* * *

While the *New York Times* shifted its coverage, *Time* magazine stuck to its ideological guns. The news magazine regarded the Soviet test moratorium to be a "gimmick" (April 14, 1958, p. 19) and on the eve of the administration's contemplated policy change ran a prominent piece on the "world debate" concerning the continuation of testing. Unlike a similar article published in its science section the previous spring, this one appeared in the front of the magazine, in the prominent section devoted to politics. Once again scientists held the floor on the debate, but they were described in loaded terms—those in favor of testing characterized as "distinguished" (Libby) and those opposed as "left-leaning" (physicist Edward Condon). Teller held the lion's share of the debate, in which he opposed test cessation on the grounds that dangers of strontium 90 were exaggerated and that in any case the Soviets would evade any arms agreement (*Time,* April 7, 1958, p. 16). Paralleling earlier coverage in the *New York Times,* the news weekly appraised the validity of a scientific view on testing on its presumed political motivation.

By publishing a full-page ad for a ban in the *New York Times,* SANE provided a peg for an extended piece in *Time* that described SANE's "well-heeled and influential" membership. Under photos of an impressive array of intellectuals—Norman Cousins, David Riesman, Paul Tillich, Louis Mumford, and Bertrand Russell—a caption posed the following jeopardy question: "Defenders of the unborn or dupes of the enemies of liberty?" Whereas in the back pages the editors had referred to Pauling in neutral and even respectful terms that highlighted his achievements as a Nobel

Prize–winning scientist, here he was "Caltech's busy chemist and busy politician" and "longtime supporter of Communist-line fronts." The story referred glancingly to organizations in the peace coalition as "mutations" and concluded with this lesson in realpolitik (and perversity) for the Quakers on the sailing of the *Golden Rule:* "The folks who listened to the horror stories without listening to evidence on fallout, to say nothing of survival, the religious-minded who doubted that the ends of liberty and peace justified the means of nuclear deterrence, were all stepping up the pressure as the crucial Eniwetok tests drew nigh. It seemed to matter not at all that this was precisely what the sworn enemies of religion, liberty and peace itself were telling them to do" (*Time,* April 21, 1958, pp. 13–14).

*Time* magazine's coverage of the scientific controversy changed somewhat a month after the new Eisenhower initiatives. Summarizing a variety of thematically related events on the eve of a new series of weapons tests at Eniwetok, in the South Pacific, an article spared Pauling his customary political smear and reported a change of heart by Teller. Said to have "raised eyebrows" by his shift in views, Teller now recommended that dirtier bombs be tested underground (*Time,* May 12, 1958, p. 20). (In late 1957 a short, obscure article in the magazine's science section had reported the presence of highly radioactive fallout in Eniwetok following the testing of a clean bomb [November 25, 1957, p. 68].)

Reinforcing this view, a piece in the science section reported that a UN panel of scientists had concluded that radiation from natural and artificial sources had reached dangerous levels. Bomb tests were the "least" dangerous of these sources of radiation, but their addition to other natural sources now presented a real health problem. The scientists stopped short of recommending a moratorium on tests, but their report, which downplayed the risks to current generations, pointed to the dangers for future ones; even minor exposure to radiation could cause mutations and lower the average of human intelligence and life expectancy (*Time,* August 25, 1958, p. 37).

The UN report permitted *Time* to change its position on the radiation issue without undermining its larger political agenda, an example of the doublethink nature of its analysis. Articles in the science section conceded the dangers of radiation, but stories in the prominent politics section continued to defend testing on the grounds of national security. In late October 1958, for example, after Eisenhower's agreement to a moratorium, a commentary by "Harvard University's tough-minded political scientist and military theorist" Henry Kissinger opposed the moratorium on grounds that nuclear weapons offset the advantage enjoyed by the Soviets in conventional forces. Moreover, a ban on tests would stymie the nuclear arming of NATO[5] and development of low-fallout tactical weapons. Reinforcing *Time*'s conspiracy theory, the weekly reported Kissinger's concession that, "despite the perils of a nuclear-test ban, the U.S. has to bow to the Communist cultivated worldwide fear of fallout." Of all the perils to peace, the worst remained Western irresolution, which undermined the will to resist aggression (*Time,* October 6, 1958, p. 26).

## The Radiation Controversy and Technical Issues, January–October 1959

During this period the fallout controversy came to full bloom as scientists detected a sharp rise in background radiation levels. More ominously, tests on milk revealed the presence of strontium 90, a radioactive isotope that the human body mistakes for calcium. With their bodies needing significantly more calcium than adults, children are especially vulnerable to this poisonous substance. In the spring of 1959 the Holifield radiation subcommittee held a series of hearings in the House to settle several questions: how much of the radioactive byproducts of fission explosions can the human body tolerate, how much of this material had been injected into the air, and at what rate was it coming down? The commission produced a reassuring report that was intended to still public anxiety. (In 1955 the committee had conducted public hearings to discuss the effects of fallout radiation on health and global weather patterns and concluded with the AEC that fallout poses no hazards [Weart 1988, 187].)

By fall the fears of radiation had eased, although the publicity had the unintended effect of crippling any moves to resume atmospheric testing. The presidential campaign that year showed no difference by party affiliation for support of a continued moratorium, despite Nelson Rockefeller's call for resumption of tests and John McCone's public comment that the moratorium ought to be renewed on a weekly basis (Divine 1978, 291).

The Geneva talks stalled on the composition of a proposed inspection team and, more seriously, on the feasibility of long-distance detection. The Bethe panel had apparently miscalculated the size of the explosion that could be detected; it now seemed impossible to distinguish between minor earthquakes and explosions of less than twenty kilotons, a difficulty that would require increased inspections, which the Soviets saw as a pretext for espionage and confirmation of their weak military position.

In early January 1959 the American ambassador to the Geneva talks told his Soviet counterpart that the technical foundations supporting the negotiations were no longer valid. With negotiations at an impasse, an emboldened Pentagon and AEC—now led by McCone—pressed for resumption of the testing required for deploying the missiles thought necessary to counter the advantage the Soviets were presumed to have gained by launching two satellites (Divine 1978, 247). Although the Soviets apparently were unaware of it, the inner circle of the Eisenhower administration already knew about their continuing weak defense position. Since 1956 the U2, an aircraft specially designed to gather data using high-resolution photography, had provided American intelligence with an accurate picture of Soviet defenses. These established that the Soviet Union did not have anything resembling a credible missile program.[6] Knowing this and reassured by a new finding reestablishing feasibility of a remote detection system, on August 26, 1959, Eisenhower extended the moratorium through the end of the year (Divine 1978, 226).

Thus between January and October 1959 the administration was divided on the issue, although Eisenhower's views on continuing the moratorium prevailed.

### *Media Coverage: Fading from View*

Coverage of the movement dropped off precipitously in the *New York Times* during this period. Whereas in 1958 there had been fifty-one stories, nine of which had appeared on the front page, the period of troubles at the Geneva conference (largely between January and late October 1959) yielded only sixteen stories for the entire year, and none on the front page. I combed several sources for movement events during this period. During 1959 a number of newsworthy movement events took place: an "acts for peace" display in a Manhattan storefront dramatizing the effects of strontium 90 that drew forty thousand people in four weeks (Katz 1986); a week-long CNVA-sponsored vigil at the Omaha Strategic Air Command base, during which A. J. Muste (then seventy-four years old) was arrested for climbing a security fence; a SANE-sponsored rally in which Linus Pauling addressed a Carnegie Hall audience of three thousand; and a Muste-led CNVA protest onto the French proving grounds in the Sahara. None of these stories appeared in the *Times*.[7]

The peace movement had nevertheless built a substantial following, in part by pointing up the hazards of radiation in full-page ads in the *Times*. Sponsored by SANE, these ads first used Linus Pauling and then Benjamin Spock to lend scientific credibility to their appeals. That fall increased talk of resumed testing and the detection of elevated levels of radiation alarmed the nation and pressured Congress to reconvene the Holifield committee hearings.

Apparently mindful of the possibility of renewed testing, the committee chairman arranged to exclude testimony from movement activists such as Linus Pauling. The *Times* accommodated this agenda by carrying only brief stories on the hearings in its inside pages (Divine 1978, 276). The committee report concluded that existing radiation levels posed "relatively small" perils but warned of potential danger if "intensive" testing resumed (*NYT,* August 24, 1959, p. 1). Divine and others conclude that what seemed like an apparent whitewash had the unintended effect of preventing future tests by increasing the public's fear of strontium 90.

Contrary to this conclusion, however, analysis of public opinion data (Rosi 1965) shows an inverse relationship between education and the belief that radiation endangers one's health. That is, more informed individuals exhibited less fear toward the ill effects of radiation. Citing three surveys conducted in 1957, 1958, and 1961, Rosi found that individuals in the attentive public (see Rosenau 1961, 39–40) were much less concerned with the risks of radiation than were those who did not regularly follow the news. Although this led Rosi to conclude that informed Americans seemed willing to risk possible long-term effects of radiation for the sake of national security, a plausible counterexplanation may be traced to the way the press covered the fallout issue.

Recall that the *New York Times* associated Pauling's views on the health perils of radiation with his left-of-center politics but made no such attributions to Teller and other administration supporters in the scientific community, who enjoyed wide access to its front pages as politically disinterested researchers. That the *Times* downplayed the Holifield hearings until the committee presented its reassuring report squares with Rosi's findings that the attentive public was less concerned with the dangers of radiation. The attentive public, being better "informed," was thus less able to render critical judgment, whereas ironically the "ignorant" public was more able to do so. Another way of putting this is that the greater the clarity of received opinion, the greater the conformity to it (Gamson and Modigliani 1966).

In his analysis of public opinion data regarding the underlying dimensions of support for the test ban, Graham (1989) found that fears of radiation did not predict support for the test ban and concurs with Rosi on American willingness to trade short-term health risk for a secure national defense. The Eisenhower administration knew its forces were indomitable (it would not have entered negotiations with the Soviets without that assurance). Nevertheless, it suppressed information on Soviet force levels to keep its options open for further weapons development. The suppression of the radiation debate served the same political goal. Certainly Pauling must accept some of the responsibility for making exaggerated claims (Divine 1978, 321), but *New York Times* coverage of his position created reasonable doubt not only about his exaggerated claims but about radiation hazards and the "left-oriented" movement as a whole. Thus by Zaller's (1992) standard, the "attentive public," unless dismissive of the overall attack on Pauling, could not help but accept the views of the untainted experts, those who downplayed the dangers.

*Time* meanwhile continued to grouse about the testing moratorium, questioning Soviet sincerity and warning of the advantage the United States had relinquished by stopping its testing program, a puzzling and seemingly illogical objection since any advantage enjoyed at the time the testing had ceased would have been preserved as long as both sides adhered to the moratorium. In early February a boxed feature described a "nuclear test debate" between John McCone, chairman of the AEC, and Eisenhower's scientific adviser, physicist James Killian. Setting a context for the debate, between 1957 and 1958 the Soviets whipped up a storm of propaganda on fallout's hazards to health and wholesome genetics. Then they stopped their own tests, which earned them special plaudits from Asian and African neutralists and U.S. pacifists. The United States, in other words, was losing the propaganda war (a point also made by James Reston at the *New York Times*) (*Time,* February 2, 1959, p. 17).

In May 1959 *Time* reported on the Holifield hearings. The health issue remained an unknown because of the relatively short period (fifteen years) during which explosions had been taking place. The article repeated an oft-cited statistic, namely, that in regard to contracting leukemia, background radiation was no greater a threat than is smoking two cigarettes a year. The panel concluded that the strontium 90 then in the environment posed few health hazards but that serious damage, especially to genetic material, would be a strong possibility if atmospheric testing resumed. Like the *Times,* the news weekly downplayed the story (*Time,* May 18, 1959, pp. 59–60).

## Breakthrough, November 1959–May 1960

This short period revived hopes of an agreement, but one that fell well short of a comprehensive test ban. AEC chairman McCone proposed a way out of the technical and diplomatic deadlock. Known as the 4.75 solution, it would ban all tests that exceeded 4.75 on the Richter scale, the threshold of detection by existing instruments. McCone also saw this as a way of smoking out what he considered insincere Soviet overtures. If the Soviets refused, he suggested that the United States reevaluate the temporary ban on a daily basis after January 1, 1960. Warming to the proposal, the Soviets countered with a voluntary ban on subsurface tests below the 4.75 threshold. Divine argues this compromise signaled the end of a quest for a comprehensive test ban and, with France nearing its first atomic test, the end of hopes for preventing the spread of nuclear weapons (Divine 1978, 295–96).

With an apparent compromise in place, the Vienna summit scheduled for May seemed like the opportune place and time to sign a provisional agreement, but the U2 incident postponed a formal agreement well into the third year of the Kennedy administration.

### *Media Coverage*

In the fall the presidential campaign had politicized the testing issue. Nelson Rockefeller went to the right of Eisenhower by pressing for resumed testing after the expiration of the U.S. moratorium. The editors at *Time* sympathized with Rockefeller, saying the United States had bowed to the world outcry against radioactive fallout, thus jeopardizing its military position by preventing the development of nuclear antimissile missiles (*Time,* November 9, 1959, p. 22). In a later issue a lead article in the nation section took a dim view of the thaw in Soviet-American relations. It chided Christian Herter, successor to Dulles at the State Department, for believing in "something called co-survival." Readers were left to consider the wisdom of this policy against the backdrop of Nikita Khrushchev's ("Mr. Cold War") cartoonishly boastful claims: "We were born Communists. We live as Communists, and we shall not die but we will keep going ahead as Communists. . . . We are prepared to sink all rockets. But let me tell you and they take note of it abroad; I don't hide it—in one year a rocket factory has mass-produced 250 rockets with hydrogen warheads" (*Time,* November 30, 1959, p. 13).

By this time SANE's campaign had gained a wide following on the East Coast and in large cities elsewhere. In the spring of 1960 the movement, including its direct-action wing, was attracting thousands to New York City rallies and street marches and had garnered sympathetic news treatment.

In early May the CNVA sponsored a protest against "Operation Alert," a national Civil Defense drill that required everyone to head to the nearest shelter. Although this was the seventh such national alert and the sixth in which CNVA members refused to take part, it was the first to merit prominent treatment in the *New York Times.* On May 3, 1960, about five hundred protesters refused to leave City Hall Park during the drill. Because the police were underequipped for transporting this large number, they could arrest only twenty-six. Details of the incident appeared in a front-page *New York Times* story. Much of the story took up the orderly activities of those who obeyed, but a significant portion described the protest and included a photo of a protester being carried off by three police officers. One sign said, "After two weeks in a shelter, then what? No food, no water, just hot dust and death." A protester identified as a novelist said, "War is not possible if we all say no! Civil Defense is a way to say to the world: "Go ahead and drop your damn bombs!" The reporter followed the police wagons to court, where a magistrate sheepishly dealt with the protesters, and then on to local college campuses, where students demonstrated in a variety of ways. This lavish coverage seems all the more remarkable given that the protest involved a small number of people compared to the millions who had dutifully obeyed.

A few weeks later SANE organized the largest demonstration to date, a rally that drew seventeen thousand to Madison Square Garden and then continued as a march into midtown Manhattan. Front-page coverage of the rally and march divided evenly between a description of the march and reports on numerous speeches given by a variety of political celebrities, including Alf Landon, Eleanor Roosevelt, Norman Cousins, Adlai Stevenson, Norman Thomas, Michigan governor G. Mennon Williams, and union leader Walter Reuther: "None of the speakers spoke despairingly. All said they felt that if there was a swelling demand 'from the grassroots' for action, there would be action" (*NYT,* May 20, 1960, p. 1).

*Time* magazine's suspicion of Soviet gains continued through the decoupling controversy, the revelation that underground tests could not be detected if set off in caverns that absorbed the telling shockwaves. A number of articles detailed attempts to develop a solution to the problem; one accused the Soviets of gaining on the United States by secretly testing more weapons (see *Time,* February 2, 1960, p. 14), while another disparaged Christian Herter as "misty eyed" for subscribing to the spiral theory of international relations—the notion that accidental war would be caused by miscalculation of intentions and the spread of atomic weapons to lesser powers (*Time,* February 29, 1960, pp. 20–21).

Even the breakthrough in Geneva, where the Soviets accepted the principle of a ban on above-ground atomic tests and a voluntary ban on tests measuring less than 4.75 on the Richter scale, became a news peg for reiterating deterrence theory. A lead article warned the West that (1) weapons of war had been used for good as well as evil ends; (2) the horror of war had in the past undermined national morale, preparedness, and peace (a reference to the appeasement at Munich); and (3) aggression-minded nations had tried to use disarmament to weaken their enemies. Citing Czar Nicholas's urging of a European conference at The Hague in 1899 and Soviet advocacy of disarmament in the 1920s and 1930s as historical examples of the guile of competing nations that prosecute for peace when their rivals enjoy military superiority, the editors pressed their case against détente. If the analogy was meant to refer to the current state of negotiations, it was disingenuous, for just five months earlier the editors seemed to take as established fact Khrushchev's claims that the Soviets had built hundreds of missiles with hydrogen warheads (*Time,* April 4, 1960, p. 9).

There was little coverage of arms control in *Time* after this period. The only significant article (July 4, p. 53) described testimony Linus Pauling gave to a Senate subcommittee investigating his "suspicious" activities during his petition-gathering drive in 1957.

## U2 and Retrenchment, June 1960–January 1961

On the eve of the Paris summit, the Soviets shot down a U2 near Sverdlosk, 1,300 miles inside the Soviet Union. Soviet farmers captured pilot Francis Gary Powers and turned him over to the KGB (Beschloss 1986, 24–28). Eisenhower denied that the plane was on a spy mission and refused to apologize, dooming the summit. Khrushchev could not come to an accommodation now that his conservative opponents had seized on the incident as evidence of U.S. treachery. Both leaders were caught on the horns of the same dilemma: they favored an accommodation, but neither could afford to look weak, Khrushchev by a de facto acceptance of the overflights and Eisenhower by apologizing to the Soviets on the eve of a presidential campaign.[8] Coming as it did at the beginning of the campaign, the failure at Paris put an end to any meaningful negotiations at Geneva and any further policy initiatives by the administration. The issue would not be revived by Eisenhower, who by the end of his term of office was recommending that Kennedy resume testing to make up for lost time.

### *Movement Dissension*

At nearly the same moment, the antinuclear coalition itself was shaken by an incident that would cause it to fracture along its ideological division.

Senator Thomas J. Dodd, a Democrat from Connecticut who was temporary chair of the Senate Internal Security Subcommittee (and, ironically, a next-door neighbor of Norman Cousins), accused SANE of communist infiltration. Unwilling to risk the growing influence of his organization, Cousins acceded to Dodd's demand to purge SANE's ranks of communist influence and asked his New York City organizer Henry Abrams to resign (Abrams had invoked the Fifth Amendment at the Dodd hearings to avoid answering questions about his political past).

The Cousins decision split the movement, driving a wedge between the compromising moderates and its most idealistic elements. Many of its younger members would go on to join the more radical Student Peace Union and the SDS. Most immediately, the incident resulted in the resignations of A. J. Muste and Robert Gilmore, as well as those of Linus Pauling and Bertrand Russell. Despite this bloodletting, the movement would continue to flourish in its public aspect, nourished by the strategically motivated favor of the incoming Kennedy administration.

The most tangible effect of the schism was the movement's weakened political appeal. For example, before the accusations that SANE harbored communists among its ranks (later refuted by the House Un-American Activities Committee and the FBI), the considerable media power of Hollywood had been brought to bear on the movement. Among its supporters was comedian Steve Allen. After Dodd's accusations, however, the comedian was dogged by pickets that carried signs such as: STEVE WANTS TO CRAWL ON HIS KNEES TO THE KREMLIN; YOU CAN HAVE HIM, WE DO NOT WANT HIM (Deming 1961, 200).

*New York Times* coverage of movement activities was slightly greater during 1960 than during the previous year. Movement activities, however, continued at about the same pace. For example, in August three thousand SANE demonstrators rallied at the United Nations. A similar but much smaller demonstration in April 1958 garnered extensive coverage, including a front-page story accompanied by a photograph. This time the paper devoted two short stories to the rally, one on August 4 (page 7) and one on August 7 (page 31).

The single story later that year that garnered unusual coverage was a CNVA-sponsored event, a San Francisco to Moscow protest "march." Although there was no story per se, a three-column photo showing a group of marchers with CNVA pickets appeared on page 3. A long caption described the group as pacifists leaving Union Square on the first leg of their march to protest the buildup of nuclear weapons (*NYT,* December 2, 1960, p. 3). The newsworthiness of the CNVA activity in this case appears to have been warranted by the group's intent to protest Soviet actions, for up to this point, excepting the *Golden Rule* incident, this energetic wing of the peace movement had been covered in photoless short stories in the inner pages of the paper.

## Analysis

Two principles were at work in the two outlets' coverage of oppositional politics: apparent sympathy but damaging duplicity at the *New York Times* and ideological consistency but revealing doublethink at *Time*.

The *New York Times* shone its approving lights on movement politics more or less on schedule with official changes in policy, despite a steady stream of movement activity whose nature did not change significantly over the four-year period.The same story type would thus be first highlighted on the front page with a three-column photo (e.g., the peace walkers) and then later consigned to the inner pages. The editors at the *Times* seemed to harmonize their coverage of movement politics with imminent changes in official policy, as if the latter sounded a major new theme for which the former served as a decorative flourish. The prominent coverage given to the Quaker sailors and the peace walkers served as symbolic sanction and legitimization of a policy already accepted and, in a wider context, of the democratic process itself as evidenced by a government responsive to the concerns and wishes of "the people." Evidence for this interpretation comes from two sources.

When Eisenhower declared a testing moratorium, the *Times* attributed the political pressure behind the decision not to the movement or to domestic public opinion (which favored a bilateral ban by a margin of three to one) but to "world opinion," which it had mentioned in a Sunday week-in-perspective story a year earlier (*NYT,* May 19, 1957, sec. 4, p. 6). Only when a change in Soviet policy made an American response all but certain did the *Times* acknowledge ordinary citizens as legitimate actors in the debate and provide them with commendable moral motivation. Perhaps inadvertently, the *Times* had cooperated with a crucial movement goal, making the moral case for a test ban.

The second body of evidence is movement coverage when the detection issue undermined the stalled Geneva talks in 1959. As dissent within Eisenhower's cabinet began to increase and the resumption of tests seemed imminent, movement coverage tailed off, despite continuing activities by SANE and the CNVA. Throughout the period the paper seemed to hedge its bets by maintaining different patterns of coverage for the two branches of the movement, the more responsible SANE enjoying prominent coverage on the eve of policy changes. Apart from the *Golden Rule* and (indirectly) the civil defense incidents, the CNVA never achieved the same degree of visibility, despite its numerous activities at a variety of military and AEC sites.

Some might object to this interpretation by pointing out that much SANE activity took place in convenient proximity to New York City, but there is compelling evidence that this pattern of differential reporting had its origins in the *New York Times*'s institutional links to the state.[9] The Argus case underlines the paper's identification with state policy and its perverse effects on definitions of press freedom. The paper came into possession of information about a secret series of nuclear tests and justified hiding it from public scrutiny on the novel argument that it regarded freedom of the press as freedom to decide (with higher government authority) what the public should or should not know. In any case, by suppressing the information, the *Times* revealed where its loyalty lay and how that loyalty undermined the democratic process in the name of a greater good defined by a tiny (but powerful) elite.

Finally, the paper undermined the credibility of the movement's most visible and potentially most influential figure, Linus Pauling, while noting other movement leaders—Muste, Gilmore, Lawrence, and Cousins—only in passing. None received a fraction of the publicity lavished on Pauling, and all failed to capture the celebrity status presumably warranted by their representation of an issue supported by majority public opinion. In fact, the *Times* never mentioned public opinion in the context of movement politics, a striking contrast with coverage of the 1980s freeze movement.

Unlike the *New York Times,* whose stories display changing news frames and an ebb and flow in the prominence they give to the movement, the news magazine's coverage demonstrates a near-perfect relationship between policy preferences and transmission of oppositional political messages. Nonetheless, contrary to the hypothesis that a mass-market news weekly would provide a forum for a policy with a high degree of support among the population (i.e., approval for a multilateral test ban; see Graham 1989), *Time* denied the peace movement any forum whatsoever. In fact, the relevant policy preferences were those not of the administration but of the editors, who opposed any move from hard-line deterrence, an attitude that did not change through four years of coverage. The editors derided those within the Eisenhower administration who were open to negotiating with the Soviet Union, calling them misty-eyed idealists, while frontally attacking the leadership of the peace movement as dupes and communist sympathizers. The voices of ordinary people and participants in the peace movement, as well as public opinion itself, were absent from the issue discourse. This represented perhaps the most extreme example of the cold war mentality that saw in the arms control issue a transcendence from politics itself; that the world could be seen with such icy clarity and certitude may appear astonishing to our postmodern time, but it is a sobering reminder of how blind the press may become to its normative assumptions. Shut out of the discussion, the peace movement could not engage and challenge the assumptions of the mindset.

Despite the rigidity of its politics, however, *Time* did provide a forum for extensive and reasonably open discussion of the radiation issue. Linus Pauling received a good deal of coverage that in some ways was fairer than he received in the *New York Times*. Nevertheless, this may have been due to the different structure of the two sources. The news weekly divided its articles into topic categories that allow the segregation of politics and science. As long as Pauling stayed in the nonpolitical science section, his opinion received more or less impartial treatment. Once in a political context, however, he received the same diminishing treatment as did other movement leaders. Because the *Times* did not segregate its stories topically, Pauling's scientific status and his politics were conflated, with injury done to both.

By comparison, the overall coverage patterns of the *New York Times* seem tolerant and broad-minded indeed, even as they bear the marks of narrow-minded presumption when dealing with figures such as Pauling. During these moments of the cold war, both media outlets compromised the democratic process by appeals to a greater good, which their actions implied to be incapable of withstanding a free and open debate. Both accepted the jeopardy rhetoric of the conservative foes of the test ban movement and in so doing narrowed the scope of cold war political discourse.

There is one other notable feature of this coverage: its intimate scale, primarily because of its focus on celebrity and on small groups. Despite the habitual references to "left-of-center" politics, those who appear in these reports have a certain credibility and autonomy that derive from their commitment to moral causes, no matter how misguided those causes may have appeared to the reporters and editors who covered them. The captain of the *Golden Rule*, who risked sailing into the Pacific testing grounds; Linus Pauling, who willingly risked his reputation and name to sound an alarm on the potentially dangerous effects of radiation; or the peace walkers, who sacrificed time and effort to make their case against nuclear testing—all come across as morally committed individuals. Despite the cold war rhetoric that suffuses these reports, the stories take the protesters at their word, largely, I believe, because the reporters seem to share a view that moral commitment trumps self-interest. I raise this issue here because by the time of the freeze movement, this assumption seems no longer to have held sway. This important change in perspective first becomes evident during the Kennedy presidency.

## Notes

1. It follows that physicists untrained in biochemistry or cellular physiology, for example, would not have the requisite expertise to comment on the somatic or genetic effects of radiation. But this was not mentioned in this or any other report. Since physicists enjoyed greater prestige than any other group of scientists (perhaps because physicists had built the atomic bomb), a plausible interpretation of this framing is that their uninformed views were nevertheless held up as carrying the prestige of their profession and by that illogical reason outweighed the views of the biologists and geneticists, presumably because their views agreed with those of *Time*'s editors.

2. The *New York Times*'s influential columnist James Reston characterized it as a "propaganda tragedy" for the United States (*NYT*, April 1, 1958, p. 1).

3. Killian and Bethe represented the presence of the peace movement within Eisenhower's administration. Both had been members of the Federation of Atomic Scientists, a group that had unsuccessfully attempted to bring fissionable materials under international control after the war. Knopf (1991) argues that their entry into the Eisenhower cabinet upset the conservative advantage held by Dulles, Strauss, and the Joint Chiefs of Staff and resulted in a purchase on administration thinking that the movement could not exert through public opinion. Ambrose (1988) argues this was a standard Eisenhower move to keep his advisers off balance.

4. Newspaper coverage of the march and Gandhi's arrest enlarged his base of popular support (see Kertzer 1988).

5. There was no such obstacle; nuclear arming of West Germany, Italy, Greece, and Turkey began in April 1959 (see *NYT*, April 12, 1959, p. 1).

6. Although the Soviets were well aware of the flights, the U2 flew at an altitude that was out of reach of their defenses. As long as the flights continued unmolested, the Soviets could expose them only at the cost of a humiliating admission. Further, Eisenhower did not want to expose the thinness of Soviet forces because public knowledge of this would likely force the Soviet Union into an expensive and dangerous arms race (Ambrose 1988, 173).

7. The storefront display received quite a lot of coverage in the *New York Herald Tribune*, however (Katz 1986, 37–38).

8. It is not implausible that Khrushchev did not want an accommodation with the United States. Had he wanted an agreement, he could have delayed announcing news of the U2 or suppressed it altogether. From the other side, Eisenhower could have suppressed the overflights during this extremely sensitive period (Ambrose 1988, 173).

9. These links were so intimate as to allow James Reston, writing in his column, to threaten the Soviets with nuclear war if they did not back down in Berlin. The text of his wording had been approved by John Kennedy (Reston 1991, 469–70).

# 5 Flexible Response: The Kennedy Administration

As John Kennedy took office, the test ban movement appeared to have entered perilous waters. Its most illustrious leaders—Linus Pauling, A. J. Muste, Robert Gilmore, and Bertrand Russell—had resigned, and the two wings of the movement were at serious odds on strategy and tactics. The absence of centralized leadership left the moderates increasingly dependent on the kindness of elites and the press (though, as I will show, the latter depended on the former). Increased dependency left the movement vulnerable to the short-term political needs of elites and to the story demands of the press; these needs only exacerbated the tensions within the coalition. The stories featured potent rhetorical themes of futility that drew on a paradoxical set of circumstances: a leaderless, unraveling coalition, a seemingly sympathetic but militarily aggressive administration, and an influential newspaper taking its cues from Kennedy's "best and brightest."

Kennedy's sympathy for a test ban belied his aggressive arms policy. More ambitious than Eisenhower's, it provided for a 15 percent increase in defense spending that expanded the range of both conventional and nuclear weapons. These would provide a wider set of options from which an appropriate military response could be chosen. Yet Kennedy warily recalled that miscalculation was a principal cause of World War I, and he was shaken by expert estimates of the potentially staggering human losses in a nuclear exchange (Giglio 1991, 71). Thus, despite his aggressive posture on arms, he made the test ban a high priority, seeing it as a way of preventing nuclear proliferation. Kennedy's general support for a test ban makes the five policy periods identified here somewhat less distinct than those in the preceding administration. (See fig. 1, in chapter 3, showing the greater visibility of movement politics throughout much of the Kennedy presidency.) There were reversals, however, driven by external events such as the Berlin crisis, that were the product of tensions between the United States and the Soviet Union rather than dissent within the administration.

## Policy Review, February–May 1961

The Kennedy administration's involvement with the nuclear arms issue began on inauguration day with an overall review of test ban negotiation policy by John H. McCloy, Kennedy's special adviser on disarmament. An ad hoc committee that came to be known as the Fisk Panel reviewed the transcripts of over 250 negotiating sessions in Geneva. It concluded that existing means were adequate for detecting atmospheric and underwater explosions but that underground and outer space detection continued to pose problems (Seaborg 1981, 37). In mid-March 1961 the panel presented its report to a group known as the Committee of Principals, which consisted of the secretaries of defense and state, the director of the CIA, the chairs of the AEC and the Joint Chiefs of Staff, and the director of the U.S. Information Agency. (Later, after the establishment of the Arms Control and Disarmament Agency [ACDA], its director joined the committee.) The report sought a test ban treaty to be enforced by a number of on-site inspections. Provisions were made for the resumption of testing if the Soviets resumed, but the preference was for an informal adherence to the moratorium.

The U.S. negotiators in Geneva went to work on the treaty but soon met Soviet objections to the number of inspections requested. The Soviets regarded these as an attempt to gain more precise estimates of their defenses. Negotiations stalled once again, but Kennedy looked forward to resolving this and other problems with Khrushchev at the Vienna summit scheduled for June.

### *Media Coverage*

In a calculated effort to influence their coverage, Kennedy was careful to maintain good relations with *Time*'s editor and principal reporters (Nacos 1990, 17–20; Kern, Levering, and Levering 1983, 3–6). White House officials invited Henry Luce to lunch on a regular basis and granted the magazine's chief correspondent, Hugh Sidey, unusual deference and access. If the White House planned a speech for a Monday, the day following the magazine's close, Sidey got an advance copy. This began to change in 1963 when, sensing the greater political potential of television, Kennedy began to turn his favor on television reporters (Halberstam 1979, 358–62). The effort seems to have been rewarded, despite Luce's doctrinaire Republicanism, for even a wing of the peace movement began to receive favorable coverage in its latter phases.

I continue my analysis of the *New York Times* and *Time* magazine here but also take note of the improving fortunes of television news during this period. Several scholars (see Zelizer 1992) argue that the Kennedy assassination established the foundation for its authority and popularity.

On the eve of Kennedy's inauguration, *Time* reasserted its preference for a nuclear war-fighting strategy. It did this in two articles, one lauding an analysis of nuclear deterrence by Herman Kahn, RAND Corporation's senior staff physicist (*Time,* January 3, 1961, p. 16), and the other featuring the outgoing head of the AEC, John McCone, who made the case for resuming nuclear testing to counter a possible clandestine Soviet program. Just a "few further tests," he said, would triple the blast power of the Polaris and Minuteman missiles and speed development of the neutron bomb, a weapon that would kill people but leave buildings and other strategic infrastructure undisturbed. The temporary test ban—a political triumph for the Soviet Union won by its "propagandizing the terrors of fallout"—had stymied these improvements (*Time,* February 10, 1961, p. 16).

In this early phase of the Kennedy presidency, *Time* ignored the American peace movement, turning its scorn periodically on the "Ban the Bomb" demonstrations in the United Kingdom. One account of a Campaign for Nuclear Disarmament (CND) demonstration declared that protesters engaged in "outdoor sport" that snarled traffic and irritated Welsh villagers who depended on the American submarine fleet for their economic livelihood: "You'd have to search for a long time round here to winkle out anyone who doesn't want Americans to come" (*Time,* February 10, 1961, p. 31). Another account of a CND march on England's nuclear research facility at Aldermaston likened marchers walking through a London rain to a "damp crocodile, four fifths of them teen-agers living on sausages, posing for photographs" (*Time,* April 14, 1961, p. 35).

The swipes at the British peace movement foregrounded an analysis of the Geneva talks fairly characterized as "long and futile." The Soviets, who "claimed" they had quit testing, had proposed a three-member panel that would decide on the need for inspections following unidentifiable seismic disturbances. According to the magazine, the disingenuous part of this proposal was that any one of the panel's members (an American, a neutral, and a Soviet) could exercise a veto, making it a transparent scheme for closing the nuclear gap with the United States: "The Soviets can only close that gap by continuing with secret tests while U.S. tests stand suspended." Underground salt mines in central Russia could absorb the shock waves that would otherwise be detected by a seismograph, and a "top official" said that the West had recorded some "pretty big bangs," although no one knew whether they were nuclear. A year earlier *Time* had reported that a test ban would freeze a Soviet advantage. Now it claimed that the Soviets were testing secretly to correct a deficit (*Time*, February 29, 1961, pp. 20–21).

Unlike its policy in the Eisenhower years, when attention to the peace movement varied according to administration policy initiatives, during Kennedy's term the *New York Times* regularly opened its front page to the movement, doubling its visibility. The prominent coverage played an important role in attracting other traditional sources of strength to the movement.

April 1961 marked the beginning of a new peace campaign. The movement had planned a number of public demonstrations for both Easter and the anniversary of the Hiroshima explosion, the points defining the beginning and end of this first Kennedy peace initiative. The *Times* provided thorough coverage to all these activities but of necessity had shifted its attention from efforts by movement leaders to those of ordinary citizens.

On the first of April 1961, a three-column headline—"Quakers in Times Sq. Easter Vigil Pray for Peace"—appeared over a photo showing a row of contemplative women standing in Times Square. The comparatively long article, though treating the protest as largely symbolic and devoid of political significance ("the Quakers drew only passing notice from the holiday crowd in the square"), nevertheless depicted the participants as serious and dignified, bolstering the movement's moral case. The prominence of the story is all the more remarkable given the small numbers involved: "By the time the vigil began about 100 Quakers had registered for services on the line. They were divided into watches of two hours each until Sunday morning" (*NYT*, April 1, 1961, p. 1).

The Quakers were not the only ones participating in the Easter demonstrations. At about this time the *Times* also began providing the student movement with significant coverage, but in a pattern that would continue through the Kennedy presidency, the stories also made reference to their naïveté and caprice, contributing to an impression of fecklessness: "Despite the serious undertones of the slogans, many of the participants appeared to consider the event a frolic. There was a good deal of hi-jinks and bantering exchanges as the groups moved through the streets" (*NYT*, April 2, 1961, p. 66).

Also receiving prominent treatment for the first time was a CNVA-sponsored peace walk from San Francisco to Moscow. Whereas the CNVA's activities during the Eisenhower years had mainly been consigned to small interior articles (excepting the *Golden Rule*), the arrival of a contingent from San Francisco now appeared on page 3, accompanied by a three-column photo of the marchers with a large number of peace signs marching into the UN plaza. The story mentioned the group's plans for that night and even went so far as to provide the address of the church where a public meeting was to take place (*NYT,* May 29, 1961, p. 3).

These prominent stories made no challenges to the demonstrators' credibility but also made little connection to realistic political pressures on an administration already committed to some of their goals. From the standpoint of the *New York Times,* the issue remained the exclusive prerogative of the president, with the peace movement an interesting miniature of democracy in action.

## Vienna, Berlin, and Soviet Testing, June 1961–April 1962

Khrushchev chose the Vienna summit to test Kennedy's mettle, demanding a German peace treaty that would have effectively rescinded Western rights to Berlin. On the proposal for a test ban, he rejected more than three annual inspections and deprecated the value of a test ban without concomitant disarmament (Giglio 1991, 77; Schlesinger 1965, 369). Whether this constituted a genuine move for arms control or a disingenuous attempt to gain superiority by virtue of superior Soviet conventional forces, the failure of the summit began a spiral of gamble, escalation, and confrontation that led to the Berlin crisis in August and then to the resumption of Soviet testing.

Because of Soviet testing, Kennedy experienced increased pressure, especially from the military, to resume the U.S. program. He resisted for a time, but the Soviets continued to ratchet up the explosive yields of their bombs. Since Kennedy was doubtful of Soviet gains, there seemed no compelling military reason to resume testing, but he anticipated the need to convince the Senate of U.S. nuclear superiority should ratification of an arms control treaty come to pass (Knopf 1991, 235).[1] In November 1961 Kennedy ordered preparations for a new round of tests and announced their resumption the following March.

### *Media Coverage: The* New York Times

I have combined the relatively short period encompassing the failed Vienna summit and the end of the Soviet moratorium (roughly two months) with the eight-month period that ultimately led to the resumption of U.S. tests. I split my analysis of the two sources in this section because much of the coverage in the *New York Times* focused on the increasing numbers of women and students who joined the movement during this period. *Time* meanwhile drew mainly on the familiar themes of Soviet cheating and threats to American security to lobby for a more aggressive arms buildup, only occasionally using the peace movement as a naive foil.

During the period encompassing the resumption of Soviet testing, the *New York Times* gave movement activities the greatest visibility in its seven years of covering them. As coverage widened beyond movement celebrities, however, it also brought risk, for now the increasing presence of ordinary citizens—some politically naive and some culturally disaffected—changed the balance of power between reporters and the movement. Whereas once movement leaders could carefully fashion their rhetoric and message to hit a desired political target, power was now dissipated among the disparate groups in the movement whose heterogeneity provided a spectrum of elements that could be more easily selected to tell a variety of stories.

After a two-month hiatus—bridging the failed Vienna summit—coverage of the peace movement resumed on the anniversary of the Hiroshima explosion. Unlike the Easter coverage, which prominently portrayed the Quaker participants as moral paragons, here coverage slipped to an interior page (accompanied by the now customary photo that showed people sitting and listening to a speech) and highlighted the unsettling elements in the crowd and their disquieting behavior: "Some of the crowd advocated a general strike and attempted to sell the *Daily Worker,* the Communist Party newspaper. However, most were pacifists or student Socialists or members of the National Committee for a Sane Nuclear Policy, Inc." There was a moment of silence for the Japanese victims while church bells tolled, but "the bells could scarcely be heard over the folk singing and guitar strumming and strident arguments between Villagers and demonstrators around the fountain" (*NYT,* August 7, 1961, p. 4). This small story provides another telling example of a story frame that hinged the legitimacy of political action on the personal characteristics of the participants and their conduct.

Announcement of Soviet tests brought the first clear indication of celebrity's diminished role in the movement. There was a flurry of protest, but once-prominent movement figures received scant attention in a short article buried in a page of paragraph-long stories on reactions to the tests. Here Linus Pauling and Norman Cousins condemned Soviet testing and asked the United States to appeal to the UN to pressure the Soviets to stop. Edward Teller called for the United States to resume testing, but his article did not warrant a headline; it followed the short Pauling and Cousins story as a pickup from the Associated Press (*NYT,* September 1, 1961, p. 2). Contrasted with the highly visible coverage provided these leaders only three years earlier, this meager and perfunctory treatment confirms that the issue had escaped identification with an elite core. Now individual groups making up the body of the expanding movement would enjoy the prominent attention once given its leaders.

The peace movement achieved peak visibility when the CNVA arrived in Moscow, the culmination of its "walk" begun in San Francisco ten months earlier. A front-page story (accompanied by a four-column photo that showed the marchers in Red Square) noted the marchers had been forbidden from making speeches and highlighted the innocence of the protesters against a backdrop of cynical manipulation by the Soviets, who used the incident as grist for their propaganda mill. The marchers "had hoped to make speeches advocating unilateral disarmament and an end to nuclear testing. But the Soviets said no speeches would be permitted" (*NYT,* October 4, 1961, p. 1).

A few days later a follow-up story told of an encounter between ten of the marchers and Khrushchev's wife, Nina, whom they had met for tea. She tried to reassure the group that the Soviet Union was not preparing for war and offered as evidence the absence of a Soviet fallout shelter program (Kennedy had announced such a program in July). The story once again contrasted the openness of democratic society with the repressive Soviet system: "Mme. Khrushchev stared at her plate and sighed deeply as the visitors pleaded for an end to the Soviet tests." Later the reporter recalled a gathering at Moscow University in which Soviet students passed notes to the CNVA marchers saying "Do not pay attention to the official line, we are with you" and "They are talking nonsense, you are talking sense" (*NYT,* October 7, 1961, p. 1). The prominence of coverage here magnified an underlying theme of futility, for the story frames highlighted the uneven pressures exerted by popular movements in democratic and totalitarian society, thereby implicitly delegitimating whatever political influence the test ban movement might have seemed to have in the United States.[2]

*Two Constituencies Rejoin the Movement* — Near the end of the year, women began to rejoin the peace coalition without the prompting of an organized mobilizing effort. Frustrated by the heightening political tensions brought on by the Berlin crisis and resumption of the Soviet testing program, Dagmar Wilson, a children's book illustrator, called friends in other cities, who reacted favorably to her idea of a day of protest, the Women's Strike for Peace.

Because the WSP had no funding and lacked a political and institutional base, its leadership was obsessed with gaining sympathetic media coverage for attracting support. As important as this coverage was for reaching potential recruits, it also gave the membership a psychological lift: "After years of feeling themselves and their concerns ignored, coverage of a WSP action by the New York Times or the Washington Post brought a sense of power and influence to those who had participated, and spurred them on. A media blackout was viewed by the women as a failed action, even if thousands had participated and public officials heard their demands" (Swerdlow 1993, 72). Conscious of the need for friendly coverage, the organization strove to maintain a respectable "ladylike" image. *La Wisp,* the Los Angeles WSP newsletter, advised its members to wear flowered bonnets and white gloves to public organizing activities (Swerdlow 1993, 73), an image belying the mainly affluent backgrounds of most group members, many of whom had been "red-diaper babies" whose parents had taken part in the Old Left movement of the thirties.

The WSP's first public demonstrations took place in early November 1961 and injected a novel element into what by then had become a routine pattern of public events. The *New York Times* provided this wing of the movement friendly coverage, albeit focused on the novel elements of the protest (*NYT,* November 2, 1961, p. 5). As Swerdlow points out, "When women and dogs step out of their space and place, they make good copy." Continuing friendly press attention after the strike helped the WSP to continue its initiatives (Swerdlow 1993, 21, 23).

Reading this daily coverage, essentially snapshots of fast-moving events, it is easy to become inured to the patterns of minutiae that make up the substance of many of these stories. It is worth breaking the chronological pattern of the analysis here to make a point about the quality of this daily coverage, namely, its orderly ritualistic pattern and the way this cuts into a movement's political sinew. The contrasting example that brings some perspective on this is an in-depth *New York Times Sunday Magazine* analysis of the WSP. (By the time of publication the United States had resumed testing.) In this item, entitled "Close-up of a 'Peace Striker,'" the author drew a parallel between the WSP and the women's suffrage movement and related how Wilson had reacted to Bertrand Russell's jailing for his role in an antinuclear demonstration in London: "I thought it was a disgrace. He was speaking out for humanity. I called up a few friends and the next thing I knew we had this women's movement. They called their friends.

And they in turn called others. And they all wrote letters to friends in other cities." All this is quite remarkable given that this embryonic movement managed to draw 50,000 women to nationwide demonstrations at a time when public opinion had moved in favor of resumed testing (66 percent favored it in March 1962).

Wilson did not share the writer's criticism of the larger peace movement for its unwitting support of the Soviet line and underappreciation of the intricacies of foreign policy:

> It's all rather reminiscent of some of the games our 6–year-olds play. They make the rules as they go along and when they are not winning they change them. We can tolerate this with our 6–year-olds because we know they are going to be 8 in a couple of years and they will learn to stick to the objectives of the game and agree to abide by the decision of an umpire whether they like it or not. The men in Geneva are not 6–year-olds. They are grown men and are entrusted with the greatest responsibility—the destiny of the human race. (*NYT Sunday Magazine*, May 6, 1962, p. 68)

Wilson was also critical of Kennedy's position on inspections, which the Soviets had rejected:

> Frankly I believe inspection would expose their weaknesses rather than their strength. I think they are diffident to show us their marbles. And I think it is unfair for us to say we want to look at them. In short, I think that if we show signs of giving a little, the Russians will, too. I believe the Russians want to disarm. They really have everything to gain by disarming. They do not have the private money tied up in the armament industry so they don't have the vested interest profiting from the arms race. If they could, they would obviously would like to provide more for the material needs for their people. (Ibid., 66)

What stands out here is the refreshing clarity of what is an essential core of the movement message—the defining issues and supporting arguments—that rarely made its way into daily news coverage. Rarely did a movement participant get this kind of access to the media stage. Rarely did the articulation of issues rise above the ritualistic reportage of numbers, clipped summaries of speeches, and unusual elements in the crowd. Rather, the daily coverage indirectly, through the subtle shifts in the stock story elements, called attention to the admirable or the ridiculous, the patriotic or the disloyal, the polite or the strident, the sagacious or the naive. Here, then, is an illustration of the true power of what appears to be sympathetic daily coverage, the slow but persistent construction of an image whose weight is imperceptibly impressed on the audience. In little of this coverage did those involved in the movement get a chance to articulate their views as fully as Wilson did here, despite Kennedy's apparent sympathies for their efforts and their policy aims.

As an example, one *Times* story noted a WSP delegation's plan to present a petition to the stalled Geneva disarmament conference. The story referred to the text of the petition but lingered on the participants, some known by the reputation of their husbands (Mrs. Cyrus Eaton and Mrs. Martin Luther King Jr.), but most of whom it presented as self-described "unsophisticated" wives and mothers for whom the dominant issue of the day was that "a world cannot be improved if there is no world left to improve." The writer's concluding observation underscored the group's artlessness: "They were well-dressed, good natured and obviously proud of what they were doing" (*NYT,* April 2, 1962, p. 3). The WSP's image-conscious media strategy cut both ways, attracting prominent coverage and insinuating movement messages but with a thick sugar coating that, as this example shows, often distracted from the group's central message.[3]

*The Students* — By the end of November news of student protests had begun to appear with increasingly regularity. These reports were followed by an extended front-page analysis of the "small but active ferment on college campuses across the land." The Student Peace Union figured prominently in the planning of the protests, but most of the demonstrators represented an unaffiliated group of students from a core of elite eastern colleges and universities—Amherst, Mount Holyoke, Smith, Vassar, Cornell, and Columbia. The news peg for the analysis was a demonstration by students who had come to Washington to protest the Soviet tests and to caution the administration about following suit. The president's sympathies were such that Kennedy had even invited some of the students to speak with his disarmament advisers. The SPU and Student SANE had organized the students, and although they were not yet exerting much influence, "they [were] growing rapidly and making their presence known" (*NYT,* November 24, 1961, p. 1).

Nevertheless, and paradoxically, the *New York Times* reported, "The principal barrier to greater activity, most of the leaders of the student peace movement say, is apathy. Most undergraduates, now as in the past, seem more interested in their studies and sports than in the expression of ideological or moral concepts." This was underlined by an SPU leader at Princeton who was "profoundly disappointed" by the apathetic attitude of the students. The analysis summarized the feelings of many of the peace movement leaders, who allowed themselves few illusions about changing the world: "I don't really think that by itself, this is going to change policy. But at least we've gone on the record showing how we feel" (ibid.).

The *Times* continued to lavish attention on the students, but with an eye to proper social credentialing. In February 1962 another group picketed the White House. A large photo of the demonstration illustrated a front-page report that described the marchers as good-natured, orderly, and "interested in the issues of the day—disarmament and civil defense, as well as the basketball season and the latest exhibit at the National Gallery of Art." Once again demonstrating his open sympathy, Kennedy ordered his aides to deliver a five-gallon urn of coffee to the students, whom a large photo on the continuation page showed helping themselves to the refreshment. After the demonstration various subgroups of the students broke off to what had by then become customary visits to waiting delegations at the House, Senate, and State Department.

A brief story following the lengthy account of the protest suggested its true significance for the White House. A short pickup from the Associated Press (AP) headlined "Reception Stirs Anger" said that one student group was angered by their treatment at the hands of their State Department hosts, who had received them with a mixture of condescension and sarcasm. One student complained, "[They treated] us as if we were very, very young and totally in the dark about issues of the Cold War. . . . The general impression I got was that we were very much resented for daring to question the policies of the Government. Very little tact was used." A State Department official had pointedly asked one of the students why he did not picket in the Soviet Union and added that the student questions had been naive and "indicate they had the answers to world peace" (*NYT*, February 17, 1962, p. 1).

The next day a follow-up story of approximately equal length, but buried on page 51, described the continuing demonstration and the attempts by its leadership to create a respectable image: "We don't want to look just like a bunch of beatniks. That's why we told everybody no guitars, no folk-singing, and dress in regular suits and wear a tie" (*NYT*, February 18, 1962, p. 51). Indeed, their sobriety induced the reporter to observe that the students appeared sedate and solemn as they "plodded" along: "But for the placards, they might have been queuing to see a late-season football game at Harvard University." The enforced respectability—stimulated in part by the red-baiting of Dodd and others—became a wedge that continued to pull the movement apart at its ideological seams. The rhetorical themes of futility that threaded through the reporting would become political realities as the movement foundered.

*Schism* — In early March Kennedy announced his intent to resume atmospheric testing. This stimulated an antinuclear demonstration in Times Square that led to forty-two arrests when a group sat down in traffic to protest the actions of the police, who had pushed a demonstrator. The appearance of the malefactors seemed a relevant issue, for the writer observed that several of those arrested were bearded "beatniks." As if to underscore the violence of the event, the story continuation appeared on a page next to a vivid photo of a Japanese demonstrator grimacing as arresting police officers subdued him by pulling his arms behind him. A caption said the student belonged to a group in a Marxist federation of students protesting U.S. plans to resume testing. The pairing of the stories thus associated the peace movement with an obscure Marxist group at a time when U.S. policy had shifted (temporarily) away from the goals of the movement. In this instance the presence of violence at the demonstration did not make unreasonable a pairing with a foreign event, but the change to a story theme calling attention to the appearance of some of the demonstrators also suggested a change in sympathy and a corresponding shrinkage in the space afforded to oppositional politics, further restricting the boundaries of what the paper considered respectable protest.

After this incident subsequent stories picked up on the presence of beatniks, whom the police had come to view as visible symbols of disorder. Because the movement now depended increasingly on good press, it tacitly accepted the media's premise that responsible protest required adherence to conventional norms of dress and behavior. In one story a spokesperson for an organization called the Workers Defense League said, "One of the problems is that these groups have a number of beatniks and you can't control them" (*NYT,* March 6, 1962, p. 1).

Troubled by media coverage that called attention to the worrisome beatniks, the following year SANE's national board issued a directive to local chapters recommending that they avoid ad hoc marches in which "all elements of the peace spectrum [are] represented." The document concluded: "Since SANE, of the major activist organizations, has the policy and program geared to attract the widest American support and to be the most effective in securing world-wide disarmament under a strengthened UN, SANE cannot afford to compromise on sponsoring demonstrations" (in *Liberation* 1963a, 11). The singling out of beatniks as politically dangerous foreshadowed a parallel use of hippies in the sixties New Left movement. Both beatniks and hippies focused their protest on the conformist values of capitalist culture rather than on a sharply drawn political critique, but politicians and the press nevertheless transformed the messengers into potent symbols of political disorder. Some movement leaders felt it necessary to dissociate themselves from these media-magnified creations. (Aware of this unwanted legacy, the freeze movement of the eighties anticipated this marginalization and went to considerable lengths to lodge itself in the political and cultural mainstream.)

As schism weakened the antinuclear movement's political focus, its more moderate wing improved its fortunes at *Time*. One story gave a sympathetic account of a SANE-sponsored ad in the *Times* showing a concerned Benjamin Spock gazing down at a little girl, a potential victim of the dangers of unlimited tests that would harm "countless children worldwide." The story in the news weekly lauded SANE as the "most respectable of a number of organizations trying to change public opinion about testing" but added that "it was not always so." At one time it provided a safe haven for "crackpots and leftists of all stripes." A housecleaning of fellow travelers in 1960 had made it more even-handed since then, for it found equal fault with Soviet and American testing programs. (The CNVA had applied a similarly even-handed policy.) Contrasting SANE with the Student Peace Union, the account told how the organization had purged itself of its "radical membership," paying the price of dividing it from the SPU, whose leadership was reported as being "impatient" with SANE and deriding it for its increasing irrelevance. SANE did not escape a mild chiding—prompted by its unrealistic calls for placing the Berlin issue in the hands of the United Nations and its criticism of the fallout shelter program—but it clearly had achieved a position within the news weekly's editorial mainstream (*Time*, April 27, 1962, pp. 22–23).

Coverage of this phase of the movement by the *Times* peaked at the end of April when the largest group to date marched through midtown Manhattan to protest Kennedy's decision to resume testing. Several themes threaded through the story: the warmth of the day, the peacefulness of the demonstrators, synopses of speeches by organizational leaders, and related activities in other cities (*NYT*, April 22, 1962, p. 1). Little distinguished the sympathetic story itself, except for an accompanying analysis that did little to dispel the impression of a movement spinning its wheels. Headlined "Pacifism Finds New Adherents in Shadow of Nuclear Warfare; Charges of Communism, Doubts about Efficacy and Shifts in Membership Beset Groups, Large and Small," the unusually thorough full-page analysis credited the growth of the movement to the startup of nuclear testing and especially the last six months of "vociferous" activity. Whereas the previously mentioned paradoxical analysis of the student peace pickets found widespread student apathy despite the movement's prominent coverage, here the writer found an equally paradoxical absence of efficacy despite movement growth: "There is doubt even among some members of the organizations as to their ability to influence public thinking and officials in Washington." Two factors dragged the movement down, "its beatnik image, which the organizations are trying to eradicate, [and] the damaging specter of past and current charges of Communist penetration."

As a whole, coverage in the *New York Times* does not portray a movement riddled with irrational, oddball elements; these seem to have appeared primarily at those times when movement goals clashed (temporarily) with administration policy. In such reports these elements seem to have been singled out for projecting the wrong kind of image, since the coverage did not draw sharp political distinctions among individuals in the coalition. The communist theme raised by Senator Dodd was old news, unsupported even by FBI investigations and the House Un-American Activities Committee.

By contrast, the plucky WSP had threatened a boycott of milk products to last at least four weeks after an atmospheric test. This was said to "worry" dairy producers. Aside from mentioning this single instance of direct pressure, the article characterized other movement groups as disorganized (some did not know the extent of their membership) and as mainly concerned with image. James Peck, a member of the War Resisters League and CNVA, shared with "most" leaders of the movement a concern with its public and media image. "He notes that there is a tendency of the public at large to dismiss the demonstrators as beatniks. He ascribes this to the appearance during rallies of a small minority, probably beatniks, who are dressed in outlandish clothes" (*NYT,* April 22, 1962, p. 2). At the apparent peak of its influence, with its leadership praised and even seemingly consulted by Kennedy, the movement continued to disintegrate, caught in the grip of a media-defined set of priorities that substituted polite deference for political effectiveness.

In summary, the *New York Times* provided high visibility to movement activities, especially the rise of the WSP and an increase in student activism whose true significance seems to have been questioned by student leaders themselves. The increased coverage tracked an openness to oppositional politics by the administration, which shared the policy objectives of the movement but which also was pleased to take advantage of the propaganda opportunity afforded by resumption of Soviet testing. The attention lavished on these groups stood in contrast to the underlying theme of futility that accompanied the coverage. The State Department rebuffed the students, and the WSP received friendly but patronizing treatment. A further explanation for this treatment comes by contrasting this coverage with an emerging story type that called attention to physical appearance.

In this coverage, particularly after resumption of U.S. testing, stories made increasing references to beatniks, who had been singled out by police and reporters for their appearance and apparent bad behavior. There were no specific policy differences to distinguish beatniks from the others, who were at pains to distance themselves from these "irresponsible elements." Because press accounts did not offer details, presumably it was adherence to middle-class norms of behavior and appearance that separated the sheep from the goats. A seemingly unimportant political distinction, it nevertheless worked to cleave the movement.

### *Media Coverage:* Time *Magazine*

While the *New York Times* assessed movement politics by reference to an implied protocol of political etiquette, stories in *Time* indulged in a robust frontal attack. The Soviets' announcement of renewed testing was featured in a cover story illustrated by a portrait of a bellicose Khrushchev foregrounded against a roiling mushroom cloud: "Power—brute power—is the basic weapon of Communism. When the Cold War going gets really tough the Communists shove aside all their books of theory, all their piously professed concern for mankind." A compilation of reactions from senators, representatives, negotiators, and nuclear scientists included comments by Linus Pauling, who remarked that the United States need not resume testing since it already had enough weapons to wipe the Soviet Union off the face of the earth. His opinion was not deprecated, just overwhelmed by the flood of others running the other way. A boxed feature asserted that additional tests were necessary—despite the overkill capacity of existing stocks—because the nation needed more precise and cleaner weapons. The search continued for a clean bomb, and the neutron bomb would need extensive testing (*Time,* September 8, 1961, pp. 20–21).

On the latter issue, only two months earlier the science editor had established that most scientists thought such a weapon to be impossible since it would require a temperature of one million degrees centigrade in order to start a fusion reaction: "Until something comes near this goal, there is little point in demanding explosive N-bomb tests. The best N-bomb that could be built today would no more explode than if it were made of putty" (*Time,* July 7, 1961, p. 43). Thus, much as it had done in its case for a clean bomb, *Time* continued to segregate the skeptical, cautious discourse in its science section from its political agenda that made unsupported claims based on that discourse.

Further justification for deterrence came in a philosophical debate on the case for waging nuclear war for Berlin: "Can western civilization use the horrible weapons of thermonuclear war to save itself, or would such a war destroy the very things the West stands for?" Harvard historian H. Stuart Hughes argued that such a war would be too costly to contemplate. Hans Morgenthau, leading exponent of the realist theory of international relations, agreed, saying, "There is a breaking point for a civilization as there is a breaking point for an individual man," which he found surpassed by the estimates that nuclear war would kill 100 million Americans and destroy 90 percent of industry.

Philosopher Sidney Hook argued the case for total war, pitting the callow Soviet "mere survival" position against Aristotle's argument for the worth of a life worth living. Morgenthau responded that Aristotle was thinking not of the incineration of millions in a few seconds but of the heroic action of individuals such as Socrates. Hook replied that total war was not inconceivable in antiquity—both Carthage and Judea fought it—and concluded that the choice between death and subjugation was a false one: "The only faith that I have in the Russians is the faith that they want to survive. I believe that if they know *they* cannot survive a nuclear attack against the West, there will be none. . . . If we surrender, Communism with all of its evils will take over the world. But if we are prepared to fight, and if the enemy is foolish enough to attack us, then, if we are prepared, the losses will not be as great as some anticipate" (*Time,* October 13, 1961, p. 29).

*The Fallout Shelter Bubble* — By the early sixties the Soviets were thought to have achieved sufficient weapons to withstand the full fury of a nuclear attack and massively harm the United States in retaliation (Freedman 1989, 132). A civil defense program, it was argued, would increase survivability and thereby reclaim a strategic and political advantage. The defense of Europe by nuclear threat—extended deterrence—depended on this perception and stimulated a gruesome theoretical musing on the size of the casualties the United States might tolerate to defend Europe against a Soviet invasion. Herman Kahn suggested one-third of the American population as an acceptable threshold (Freedman 1989, 133). It was in this context that an odd debate developed on the value of fallout shelters for preserving American lives in the event of a nuclear war.

On July 25, 1961, Kennedy responded to the deepening Berlin crisis by asking Congress for an appropriation of $93 million to fund a fallout shelter program. Supporters of the program—including Willard Libby and Henry Luce—had been claiming since 1958 that such a program would ensure the survival of 90 percent or more of the U.S. population (Karp 1992, 172). *Time*'s coverage of the issue—an extension of its support for a war-fighting strategy—equated fallout shelters with smallpox vaccinations, a part of the normal fabric of life. A combined fallout and blast shelter system would reduce deaths from 160 million to 25 million, allowing a core of survivors to climb out to reassemble society and "prosper once more." Moreover, their survival would serve as a deterrent that might prevent the launching of an attack in the first place.

Sounding very much like real estate developers, entrepreneurs boosted the mundane comforts of shelters. Lone Star Steel, a Dallas firm, offered a $2,550 model that included a window and a garden scene painted on its wall, "complete with a shade that can be pulled down at night." A model equipped with an elevator, pool table, and a keg of wine served the needs of wealthier customers. For those who could not afford the low-end model or find a bank willing to assume the risk of financing one, the government would offer twenty-year home improvement loans. A list of practical suggestions for stocking the shelter included a polyvinyl wrapper for anyone who died in the shelter. It was equipped with chemicals to keep "odors" down and doubled as a sleeping bag until tapped for its primary use. In case intruders who did not share Aristotle's call to heroic sacrifice insisted on entry, pistols were at the ready and became part of the list of must-haves for shelter supplies.

Thus far, however, the government was said to have set a "sorry" example for the nation, for only the postmaster general had installed a shelter in his home.[4] The piece closed with the cheerful views Edward Teller had enunciated four years earlier: on emerging from their fallout shelters, Americans would find 95 percent of their land to be green. By then civil society would be restored and those industries that had taken precautions would be moving back into business. In the end it was the willingness of the American people to prepare for such a war that might spell the difference between victory and defeat (*Time,* October 20, 1961, pp. 21–25).

Despite these patriotic urgings, the fallout shelter bubble had burst by the following February. The Soviets had exploded massive bombs, creating some doubt about the efficacy of the shelters and the optimistic estimates regarding the amount of time people would need to spend underground while the radioactivity dissipated. Scientists estimated it might take up to seven months before the environment would be habitable. The most devastating criticism came from those who questioned the moral foundation of a program that encouraged a selfish "ground-hog psychology," but these objections did not touch the crux of the issue: shelters would save lives (*Time*, February 2, 1962, p. 15).

Willingness to offer one's self as hostage to nuclear war supported a variety of story lines that varied from Nelson Rockefeller's call to the responsibilities of power (the question is not whether we like nuclear weapons but whether we love freedom) to a cover piece on the urgent need for resuming the U.S. testing program. The latest round of tests "might" have provided the Soviets with improved nuclear weapons, the absence of certitude being due to the inherent mysteries surrounding nuclear energy and the "inscrutable designs of an iron-fisted dictatorship." No supporting evidence accompanied the suggestion of these advances, although some military and scientific leaders expressed fears that the Soviets might have developed an antimissile missile: "The free world had no doubt that one of Khrushchev's chief aims was purely and simply to terrorize and intimidate the world." If the objective for exploding such enormous bombs (in excess of fifty megatons) was to stampede the free world into a state of "defenseless fear," it had missed its mark, as evidenced by the remarks of average citizens: "When a rattlesnake is loose in the house you get down your gun and go after it" (*Time*, November 10, 1961, pp. 21–25).

A month later these speculations became hard realities when the lead article in *Time*'s nation section reported the findings of a National Security Council (NSC) intelligence estimate: the Soviets showed real advances in antimissile missiles, and they had produced cleaner weapons with greater yield/weight ratios (*Time*, December 15, 1961, p. 21). The Pentagon concurred with the NSC estimate. The Soviets had made "spectacular" improvements in yield/weight ratios and explosion efficiencies. Moreover, the reduced weights of these warheads enabled them to be transported on existing missiles capable of reaching American soil. A caption under a picture of a Soviet rocket concluded, "The facts leave little choice" (*Time*, March 2, 1962, p. 18).

## Resumption of U.S. Testing and the Cuban Missile Crisis, May–November 1962

The United States resumed its testing program on April 25, 1962, after a media campaign that highlighted Soviet advances in nuclear technology and Kennedy's reluctance to resume atmospheric explosions. The tests that followed were consistent with Kennedy's reluctance; the total yield of the DOMINIC series of forty tests amounted to about twenty megatons, one-tenth that of the Soviet series (Seaborg 1981, 150–51). In September 1962 the United States and Great Britain offered a way out of the inspection dilemma by proposing a treaty that would permit underground testing. Before the negotiators could advance on the proposal, however, the Cuban missile crisis engulfed the world's attention. The public face of the crisis spanned less than two weeks and developed with no advance notice, leaving the movement with little time to prepare an effective protest.

### *Tardy and Unfocused Reaction*

*Time*'s cover story on the resumption of American testing highlighted the "arranged reaction" to the tests. It characterized the American peace movement as "dispirited" and quoted a demonstrator who said, "It's awfully hard to keep up a sustained campaign." Explaining the mild reaction were the "lessons of experience," recounted in a short history of the nuclear age ostensibly showing that if the advice of those who doubted the wisdom of atomic testing had been heeded, "Khrushchev would now be the world's master" (*Time,* May 4, 1962, pp. 18–22).

Those in the antinuclear movement, like most Americans, were taken by surprise by the missile crisis. The crisis did elicit a reaction, but it seemed tardy and unfocused. The WSP acted first, staging a small rally at the United Nations. A photo accompanied a short story that gave a matter-of-fact account of the women and babies in the group's ranks (*NYT,* October 24, 1962, p. 24). The following day SANE published a small boxed ad, a memo to the Soviet Peace Committee in Moscow, asking it to "urge [its] government" to consider a plan for suspending arms shipments to Cuba and for dismantling the missile bases there in return for closing U.S. missile bases in Turkey (which in large measure was the deal that ultimately settled the crisis) (*NYT,* October 25, 1962, p. 34).

By far the largest demonstrations, and the most prominent coverage, occurred after the crisis had mainly passed. By now it was clear that the movement's moment had passed as well. Coverage in the *New York Times* alternated between the odd and the merely ineffectual. A Saturday demonstration at the White House combined protests by the SPU, a counter-demonstration by the Young Americans for Freedom, and a small group of Nazis. They were joined, according to a front-page account, by a prominently featured Reverend Sidney Lansing of Franklin, New Jersey, "resplendent in red and gold robes with a silver skull cap surmounted by an eight-pointed star." He bore a sign declaring the president a traitor, as a result of which the police hustled him off until he produced a placard with a less offensive sentiment. The SPU was the most measured of the groups, yet its efforts seemed uncoordinated. On hearing of a proposed deal to swap the Soviet bases in Cuba for American bases in Turkey, an SPU protester said, "Sure, I could go for that." When told later that Kennedy had not yet accepted the deal, a "bearded protester" said, "I guess this puts us back where we started. . . . But I better not try to give you an answer until I hear from the leadership." Immediately following the story a very short item said that about a dozen students at the University of Texas had called for a peaceful solution but had disbanded after attracting "practically no attention" (*NYT,* October 18, 1962, p. 1).

The largest rally was staged in New York the following day, a rally of 8,000 pacifists at the United Nations. The story mainly followed the police as they stopped a group of anti-Castro demonstrators from meeting and disrupting the peace demonstrators. There was little to protest, for the crisis was nearly over, and the story reported that an aura of goodwill predominated (*NYT,* October 19, 1962, p. 20).

The Cuban missile crisis passed with little resistance from the peace movement, which had warned of such an eventuality but whose disorganized ranks no longer had the necessary political focus to launch an effective protest: "There was no use minimizing the fact, that we came near being blown up, and that our total impotence to avert the crisis had its effect on all of us" (in DeBenedetti 1980, 169).

## Détente, December 1962–May 1963

The end of the crisis brought a conciliatory letter from Khrushchev offering a point-by-point negotiation of all outstanding questions on a test ban agreement (Seaborg 1981, 178). Kennedy responded favorably, largely because of his belief—shared by the Soviets—that a treaty would deter the Chinese from developing their own nuclear weapons. In June 1963 Kennedy spoke at graduation ceremonies at American University in Washington, D.C. His speech made good use of the spiral metaphor as he spoke of the superpowers' being caught in a "vicious and dangerous cycle in which suspicion on one side breeds suspicion on the other, and new weapons beget counter-weapons." As Freedman dryly points out, in a period of détente there is less need to establish credibility in nuclear threats than to emphasize that nuclear war would be the ultimate disaster (Freedman 1989, 244).

Regarding it as the "best speech of any president since Roosevelt," Khrushchev suspended jamming Voice of America broadcasts so as to promote it. Given instructions to "bring home the bacon," on July 15, 1963, after only eleven days of negotiations, Averell Harriman initialed a treaty that banned atmospheric tests. That October the Senate ratified the treaty Kennedy regarded as a "shaft of light in the darkness" (Giglio 1991, 217–18).

Despite the important diplomatic breakthrough, no doubt brought on by the enormous relief after the crisis had broken, the negotiated treaty remained only a partial success. The intractable problem continued to be inspection. Kennedy knew that for the treaty to be acceptable to the Senate, it had to include provisions for on-site inspections. The Soviets objected to these on grounds that such inspections would likely take place in Central Asia, an area of both considerable seismic activity and significant strategic importance. Suspicious seismic disturbances would require inspections that would cover approximately five hundred square kilometers. Since the United States insisted on a minimum of six such inspections per year, the Soviets feared their defenses would be compromised (Seaborg 1981, 191). The American position on what the Soviets considered excessive inspections scotched hopes for a complete ban.[5] "[Khrushchev] would no more allow inspectors to travel about than Orientals would allow other men into their harems" (Beschloss 1991, 618).[6]

### *The U.S. Is Powerful after All*

Except for one article in the *Sunday Magazine* section of the *New York Times* (May 19, 1963, p. 111), there was little coverage of the antinuclear movement in either source following the missile crisis. I will, however, analyze *Time*'s coverage of the advance on the test ban treaty because of an interesting reversal in the weekly's view of American military strength, a linchpin of its case against cessation of American weapons development. The reversal helps to explain a key finding that scholars have repeatedly noted in their study of public opinion on arms spending.

Coverage of U.S.-Soviet relations perceptibly softened in tone following the missile crisis. Prior to the crisis cover art had portrayed Khrushchev in a number of angry and threatening guises. After the crisis he appeared in a chastened, thoughtful countenance, and a lead article detailing a Soviet offer to accept on-site inspections described him as "mellowing." A later account of Kennedy's conciliatory speech at American University included references to the spirit of Moscow as a "love feast" and Khrushchev as a back-slapping, friendly bear (*Time,* July 26, 1963, p. 23).

With this turnabout on the desirability of arms control, the administration (and the news weekly) now required a significant reassessment of Soviet military strength. A hint of how this would be accomplished came with an analysis of the military outcome of the crisis. According to *Time,* emplacement of Polaris missiles on submarines compensated for the removal of land-based Jupiter missiles from Turkey (the face-saving swap for the removal of the missiles in Cuba), Italy, and Great Britain. The Polaris had greater range and firepower than the Jupiter, and the Soviets had not yet devised an effective defense against it (*Time,* February 1, 1963, p. 21).

The deemphasis on deterrence in arms discourse became plain in a piece that explained why the United States had stayed at Geneva. Whereas prior negotiating sessions had once been regarded as "long and futile," now the magazine urged patience, for the central concern was Kennedy's worry of the spread of weapons to other powers: "I am haunted by the feeling that by 1970, unless we are successful, there may be ten nuclear powers instead of four, and by 1975, fifteen or twenty. I regard that as the greatest possible danger and hazard" (*Time,* March 29, 1963, p. 17).

Just prior to Senate consideration of the test ban treaty, a cover story assessing the strength of the American military declared the United States to be the mightiest nation in human history—"few realized its staggering dimensions." (Recall that a year earlier *Time* had warned of advances in Soviet arms technology that threatened American superiority.) Testifying before the Senate Foreign Relations Committee, Secretary of Defense Robert McNamara said the United States had in excess of sixty thousand megatons of nuclear materiel. (The article reported that one twenty-four megaton bomb dropped from a B-52 is capable of opening a crater a mile wide and hundreds of feet deep, starting fires 40 miles from its center, and sowing enough radioactive debris to kill people 350 miles away.)

The American arsenal held other advantages as well: the Soviets had fewer than half the bombers, a fraction of the ICBMs, and no weapon comparable to the Polaris. The only area in which the Soviets seemed to have an advantage was their explosive yield—their bombs were bigger. On this score McNamara believed the United States parried the Soviet advantage by its capacity to launch a greater number of smaller weapons on a variety of delivery vehicles. Thus the larger Soviet weapons provided only a thin illusion of deterrence value since they were much harder to defend. "Our missile force is deployed so as to assure that under any conceivable Soviet first strike, a substantial portion of it would remain in firing condition. Most of the land-based portion of the force has been hardened as well as dispersed." Even if a sizable portion of the siloed Minutemen were destroyed, the Soviets had no effective defense against the submarine-based Polaris. As far as the putative lead the Soviets had in developing an anti-missile missile system—an argument justifying resumption of testing a year earlier—Kennedy now said, "The problem of developing a defense against a missile is beyond us and beyond the Soviets technically, and I think many who work on it feel that it can never successfully be accomplished."[7]

Another professed reason for resumed testing was a significant technological lead the Soviets might have achieved in a single test series. Now McNamara disputed this as well: "The consensus is that the Soviets could not in a single test series, however carefully planned, achieve a significant or permanent lead in the strategic field, much less a 'superweapon' capable of neutralizing our deterrent force" (*Time*, August 23, 1963, pp. 11–14).

By a single proclamation all the arguments deployed to advance the case for testing had now been declared null and void and reality reconstructed to build support for the treaty.[8] Neither the administration nor the news magazine seemed to have any memory of its earlier pronouncements, perhaps because the brush with the logical extreme of deterrence theory—willingness to sacrifice the larger part of civilization on principle—had caused the doctrine to pall on the nation. The Senate ratified the treaty by a vote of eighty to nineteen in September, after only three weeks of hearings.

Domestic political constraints on Kennedy's ability to negotiate hampered the peace movement's initiative for a comprehensive ban. Thought to be a minor loophole, the secrecy surrounding underground testing actually quickened the pace of nuclear arms development. This and the increasingly technical nature of the issues surrounding disarmament would pose daunting obstacles to future popular movements against nuclear arms races. Kennedy's Arms Control and Disarmament Agency stimulated the growth of a government-funded cottage industry on the technical issues of disarmament. This would erode the legitimacy of popular opinion on highly technical issues and thus negate an important movement political resource (Boyer 1984).

Following the treaty Kennedy's doctrine of flexible response enabled a slow, incremental escalation of U.S. involvement in Vietnam. As military historian Michael Sherry points out, "The Cuban crisis did not so much ease the Cold War as direct it into different channels, ones less likely to produce nuclear conflict" (Sherry 1995, 250). Weakened by internal dissent and lulled into complacency by the agreement, the antinuclear movement would be awakened in a new form—the New Left—by an escalating war in Vietnam. Students, civil rights workers, and intellectuals would change the focus of movement politics from nuclear testing to American foreign policy in the Third World (DeBenedetti 1980, 168).

## Analysis

During the Kennedy administration the antinuclear movement added two traditional constituencies to its base, despite serious internal problems in the movement coalition. Coincidentally this took place when the movement achieved its greatest sustained visibility in the *New York Times*. The CNVA, in the Eisenhower era consigned largely to the obscure inner pages, appeared on the front page twice. Although reports stressed the repressive nature of the Soviet political system over the CNVA's even-handed application of pressure on both the Soviet Union and the United States (an even-handedness that belied the charges that such organizations were communist dupes), the group's rise to media prominence corresponded with official support for a movement goal.

Kennedy's sympathy with the peace movement's goal for a test ban, especially with regard to the WSP and the student groups, served as a cover for his equally important goal of strengthening the military. This cued the media to anoint respectable protest, especially among college students and the WSP. No such sympathy existed, however, for the beatnik nonconformists, whose unspecified misdemeanors made them targets for the police. They became a handicap as the *Times* used their presence as an indication of movement instability, a view supported by movement spokespersons who, increasingly dependent on external support, accommodated themselves to media- and elite-defined expectations of respectability that nearly supplanted their political goals. This further alienated the moderates from the idealists in a process that may be fairly characterized as a self-fulfilling prophecy and a major contributing factor in the fracture of the movement coalition.

The *Times* did not view the addition of two new constituencies to the movement as increased support for arms control. Rather, the paper treated the groups as if they were ethnic subcultures, part of the national scene, to be sure, but somehow detached from the political mainstream. The coverage compartmentalized the significance of their activities within their specialized identities as students (idealistic but uninformed) or as wives and mothers (concerned and "obviously proud of what they are doing"). In both cases coverage called attention to cultural status rather than independent political force; both groups gained political significance to the extent that an administration spokesperson was on hand to lend them credibility. This was in part a result of the change underway in media assessment of movement participants, who had become increasingly susceptible to selective framing as their numbers increased and as movement leadership fragmented. With celebrities such as Linus Pauling on the sidelines, unable or unwilling to lend moral gravitas to the effort, and with a wider spectrum of people attracted to the movement, the news media had wider discretion in their portrayals. Moral authority had begun to compete with novelty and conflict, standards of newsworthiness that could easily dovetail with state prerogatives (Gitlin 1980).

As to correlation of media frames with administration policy, the unruly beatniks seemed to appear on the scene whenever international tension escalated. For example, they appeared in the Hiroshima anniversary demonstration that took place during the Berlin crisis, in stories that followed Kennedy's decision to prepare a round of atmospheric tests, and after U.S. testing began. They constituted but a fraction of the coverage, but they posed an important symbolic presence used in the analysis articles to cleave the movement. The internationalist wing of the peace movement tried to distance itself from the beatniks, even though they seemed to amount to a tiny minority that lent some color to what even the *Times* characterized as an ineffectual, "plodding lot." Here, then, is an ironic reversal of the process described by Gitlin (1980) in his analysis of the New Left. Gitlin argues that movement leaders lost control of the antiwar movement of the Vietnam era to rowdies attracted to the flamboyant leadership and violence favored by the media. In the case of the test ban, the movement's leaders lent credence to media characterizations of movement division and thus were accomplices to its marginalization. What weakened each movement was a leadership that failed to reach beyond its elite perimeter and thus shared some blame for the dominant rhetorical themes of futility that structured media coverage. It must be remembered, however, that the press called repeated attention to these elements, holding the movement to a higher (and less democratic) standard than it did the government leaders, whose views traversed an equally wide spectrum.

The Kennedy years brought some moderation to *Time*'s views on deterrence. These softened after the missile crisis, unlike the situation in the Eisenhower years, during which any move toward détente brought ridicule on those figures advocating it. By the end of the period the news magazine had even recognized SANE as a legitimate agent in the debate. The legitimacy was qualified, however, on the organization's willingness to adhere to the rule of the cold war–inspired loyalty oath.

By the period's end Norman Cousins had become an administration insider, acting as a trusted go-between after the end of the missile crisis and paving the way for rapid negotiation of the treaty in Moscow (Cousins 1972). The White House encouraged Cousins and other notables, including James Wadsworth and two of Eisenhower's former secretaries of health, education, and welfare, to form the "Citizens Committee for a Nuclear Test Ban" in early August (Terchek 1970, 84–85). The highly organized campaign for the treaty's ratification, including endorsements by over 70 percent of the nation's newspapers and McNamara's testimony, succeeded in shifting the tide of public opinion: those favoring it grew from just over half in July to 81 percent in September (Terchek 1970, 56, 118). Nevertheless, to garner the support of conservative Democrats such as Henry Jackson and to preempt an attack from the Republicans, Kennedy chose to frame the campaign for ratification in terms of national security rather than as a first step in disarmament. As a result, the ratified treaty did little to prevent an arms race that continued by way of underground tests. Nor did it stand in the way of nuclear proliferation to China. Its chief benefits were to reduce the levels of radioactivity in the atmosphere and, perhaps most important, to set an important precedent for arms control negotiations with the Soviet Union.

Kennedy's strategy for ratification was in keeping with the large body of scholarly research showing that Americans support arms control to the extent that they feel the nation's security is not endangered. As the analysis of *Time* magazine's coverage shows, however, official perceptions of security bend to the necessities of political expedience. In this case a year seemed sufficient for obliterating the "facts" of the past.

An example of such a perceptual shift was Kennedy's decision to resume testing because he anticipated a fight for ratification in the Senate, a fight that would require a symbolic display of American military power analogous to the May Day parades of tanks and missiles held by the Soviets in Red Square. The Senate testimony provided that display. Media cooperation in this ritual helps to explain the repeatedly observed finding that Americans tolerate negotiation only when they feel secure (Russett 1990). This cooperation took the form of memory lapses when, year after year, expert testimony from the Department of Defense and the armed forces raised the phantom of communist military ascendancy. Such testimony and uncritical reporting contributed to an escalation of an arms race, later legitimized as responsiveness to public opinion (see Bartels 1991; Hartley and Russett 1992). The press cannot, of course, establish independent knowledge of the true strength of the nation's defense, let alone that of a foreign power. Indeed, even defense experts' estimates vary depending on the technique used (e.g., military spending, numbers of weapons, war scenarios, military doctrine [Fischer 1983]). Nevertheless, its uncritical coverage of an issue that recurred on a regular basis is a remarkable example of one-sided deference to official views, despite their transparently self-serving nature.

The antinuclear movement by definition represented a point of view rejected by most foreign policymakers. Their rejection—abetted by the news media—reduced the scope of public debate and contributed to a climate of suspicion that rejected a comprehensive ban on testing.[9] Although the result of a less complicitous media must remain speculative, a less paranoid climate might have led to a more effective arms control treaty, one that might have reduced the fabulous expenditures that were to come.

## Notes

1. This lends credence to Russett's comment on the supremacy of domestic considerations with regard to foreign policy: "Policies of arms control and disarmament, negotiation or threat, conciliation or the use of military force are adopted in large part because they gratify friends and disarm adversaries at home, not because they necessarily seem sensible in some abstract principle of the national interest abroad. Furthermore the political horizon shaping those decisions is typically a short one, not a vision for the long haul" (Russett 1990, 7).

2. *Time* used the occasion of the meeting as an opportunity to swat at the movement. Although the CNVA protesters had been "done out" of a promised rally in Red Square, they were permitted to publicly condemn Soviet and American resumption of tests. All this the reporter characterized as a "grand diversion" (*Time,* October 13, 1961, p. 32).

3. Contrary to their appearance as "mere housewives," Swerdlow points out, many in the WSP rarely did housework because they were sufficiently affluent to afford cleaning help. Their cautious approach to the media yielded dividends, as the following passage from a *New York Times* article indicates: "For the most part they stress femininity rather than feminism. They are amateurs, women who, in less urgent times, would never have put down the mop to write a Congressman, much less demonstrate with their children in the street" (in Swerdlow 1993, 72). In contrast to this image of restraint and traditional gender-role behavior, the WSP made vivid impressions on both American and Soviet negotiating teams in Geneva. One of the WSP cornered a Soviet delegate and asked why the Soviets were so fearful of the Americans. He replied that a ring of American bases in thirty-three countries surrounded the Soviet Union. The WSP delegate asked whether closing down one base would ease Soviet fears. He quickly responded that it would. The exchange made its way to reporters, who quizzed Kennedy about the WSP proposal. Momentarily taken aback, Kennedy promised to ask Arthur Dean to follow up, but he expressed doubt that there was much in the story (Swerdlow 1993, 196–97).

4. Although the program remained official U.S. policy for years, the public relations campaign came apart at the seams less than six months later. Three unrelated factors were its undoing: First, the shelters came under attack by critics who argued that the Soviets could easily defeat their deterrent value by increasing the size of their bombs, which would have the effect of converting the shelters to ovens. Second, cler-

ics had a field day with the sophistical arguments of those who defended the ethics of using pistols to push out their hapless neighbors. Last, many of the shelter manufacturers were exposed for selling shoddy goods. In the end even Eisenhower informed the press that he would not build a shelter (Karp 1992, 169–82).

5. Newhouse reports that the failure to achieve a total ban brought sighs of relief to some in the Pentagon and the AEC who feared that a comprehensive ban would have closed up U.S. weapons labs while the Soviets would have continued making more weapons (Newhouse 1989, 194).

6. Seaborg argues that this was not the sole reason for the failure to produce a comprehensive treaty. Beyond the number of inspections, the methods and numbers of inspectors involved posed significant other challenges to a negotiated treaty.

7. It is difficult to determine which statement was true, whether the Soviets had made advances toward such a device at the time of U.S. resumption or whether neither power was near such an achievement. Seaborg claims that analysis of the Soviet tests suggested a true advance in that direction (Seaborg 1981, 152). If this is true, Kennedy's statement reported in *Time* downplayed these advances to build support for the treaty, unchallenged here, despite assertions to the contrary only a year earlier.

8. Edward Teller was an important witness against treaty ratification. He argued the Soviets already had a lead on high-yield weapons and could gain parity on smaller weapons by testing underground. His testimony was countered by Harold Brown, a former associate at Livermore. Moreover, Herbert York, Brown's predecessor at the Department of Defense, argued that most scientists favored the treaty and did not share Teller's assessments (Knopf 1991, 301–2).

9. Recall that Khrushchev was willing to accept three inspections, whereas Kennedy, recognizing the "realities" of Senate ratification, required eight; from today's perspective these seem like small differences.

# 6 Politics in a Black Box

In driving nuclear testing underground, the Limited Test Ban Treaty did little to stop the arms race, but it deprived the antinuclear movement of its most compelling and visible organizing issue (Kleidman 1993, 120). With the movement weakened by internal discord, the various organizations and groups constituting it left arms control for issues such as nuclear power, civil rights, and the war in Vietnam. It rallied briefly in campaigns prior to the antiballistic missile (ABM) and Strategic Arms Limitation Talks (SALT) treaties of 1972, but the national antinuclear movement remained moribund until the onset of the first Reagan administration. By then a trend begun nearly ten years earlier awakened and invigorated the second major antinuclear movement of the cold war.

This chapter traces the evolution of arms policy after the Limited Test Ban Treaty. This history will help to explain the significance of the radical departures on arms control that transpired during the Reagan era and how these stimulated the antinuclear movement to reunite on a common issue. As in chapter 3, I also provide a brief history of the protest movement in this period and a general overview of public opinion on arms control. These broad strokes should provide a helpful context for interpreting media coverage of the nuclear freeze movement, which is discussed in chapter 7.

## Parity and Détente

By the time of the Nixon administration, the Soviets had closed the missile gap and enjoyed what arms experts regarded as parity, at least in raw numbers (Freedman 1989). This estimate was necessarily imprecise, however, because whereas the Soviets chose to build large warheads and mount them on land-based ICBMs, the United States spread its firepower among a greater number of smaller warheads on three forms of conveyance: land- and submarine-based ICBMs and B52 bombers, the "strategic triad." On the one hand, the Soviets seemed to have the edge in concentrated firepower and throw-weight,[1] but the United States had more missiles fitted with multiple warheads (deployed during the first Nixon administration) and a credible second-strike capacity to be delivered by low-flying bombers and virtually undetectable submarines.

Though apparently ominous, the greater throw-weight of the Soviet arsenal was not strictly a measure of its destructive force but the result of a technological lag in guidance systems. Put simply, if you are not sure exactly where the missile is going to land, you want to make sure its explosive force is large enough to destroy the target even if you do not score a direct hit. American advances in miniaturization and guidance systems, as well as in explosive efficiencies, permitted smaller warheads that in theory could be more precisely targeted. There was a tacit agreement that these reciprocal strengths—known in the arcana of arms control as "offsetting asymmetries"—opened a political window of opportunity for arms control; in any event, the Soviets felt secure enough to negotiate an arms agreement, and most important, Richard Nixon had changed American views of Soviet behavior.

To promote maximum flexibility in his chosen domain of achievement, Nixon moved foreign policy-making to the White House, away from what he considered the establishment-dominated State Department and CIA, both of which he regarded with skepticism and even personal animus (Newhouse 1989, 209). Instead of relying on them, he established a new national security system headed by himself and his national security affairs adviser, Henry Kissinger. Working in tandem, Nixon and Kissinger adroitly used the Soviet-Chinese rift to maneuver the ABM treaty through the process now known as SALT I. Signed in May 1972, the treaty limited each side to two antimissile sites and thus exposed each to nuclear annihilation, a condition that would prevent one from launching an attack on the other in the logic of mutually assured destruction (MAD). SALT established a five-year interim agreement on a ceiling on long-range missile launchers, the first step toward limiting offensive arms. The treaty was premised on an assumption of rough parity by the two superpowers; neither could achieve definitive superiority without committing to a major investment in a new generation of weaponry. MAD bought relatively cheap deterrence in the form of a second-strike capacity that would reduce the temptation of a first strike. As a bonus, the theory provided a natural cap on the undisciplined growth of the strategic defense budget (Meyer 1990, 35–36).[2]

In large part, SALT succeeded because Nixon changed his view of the Soviet Union as an unswerving ideological opponent. After all, anyone bent on maintaining a foreign policy based on an assumption of communist orthodoxy would have to explain why the Soviets had positioned forty-five divisions on their border with China. Nixon exploited the rift between these one-time partners and now competitors. He opened formal relations with China as a move to pressure the Soviet Union to reduce its support of North Vietnam. Soviet interests, on the other hand, lay in an improvement of trade relations with the United States, which it would pursue independent of Marxist-Leninist orthodoxy. The realpolitik attitude motivating both powers was apparent from the circumstances surrounding the signing of the ABM treaty: several Soviet merchant ships had been hit by American bombers in North Vietnamese waters the previous month, and only a few days prior to the summit Nixon had ordered the mining of Haiphong harbor. Despite what under typical cold war circumstances would have been considered a dangerous provocation, comparable to the downing of the U2, compelling self-interest led to a successful summit at which Brezhnev himself signed the treaty. The achievements of that summit, however, soon came under fire from conservatives and political opportunists who took advantage of an issue that had become increasingly appealing to the news media.

In his analysis of nuclear arms limitation issues, John Newhouse notes that by the early 1970s arms control had become an attractive issue for television news. Senator Henry Jackson's move to link exit visas for Russian Jews with détente, for example, made an inviting combination of personality and conflict for reporters. As once complex issues of arms control became associated with personality and conflict, they began to be drawn into the media spotlight. In a circular process the media began to highlight the ostensible decline of American military strength and the pitfalls of arms control agreements. The demand established, supply issued from those who sought to promote themselves by promoting controversy: "And here the symbiosis tightened. Instead of being detached observers, media people become figures in their own right, because as a practical matter, the enlargement of their role and status contributes to shaping, if not inviting, many of the stories they cover. The tendency was always there, but the heavy diet of conflict and the dominant role of television news built the tendency into a fact of daily life" (Newhouse 1989, 251). The increased publicity came at a time when Nixon's defense of détente had been overtaken by the necessity of defending himself against charges of obstructing justice in the Watergate scandal.

The collapse of the Nixon administration brought an end to its chessboard maneuvering in a tripolar world. With its chief supporters weakened, détente lay open for an attack from the right, for whom the fall of Saigon symbolized a weakening of American military might. Gerald Ford sought a second arms agreement with the USSR, but an energized right wing in his own party forced him to ask for greater concessions from the Soviets, who were then behaving in a decidedly undétente-like manner in Angola. As the Republican primaries approached, Ford continued rightward, pressured by the dominant conservative wing within his party. Among Ford's concessions was his unprecedented invitation to an outside group of experts—Team B—to challenge the established process of determining the strength of the nation's military defenses. Their success led to the reincarnation of the Committee on the Present Danger (CPD), a group originally formed in 1950 to build popular support for a military buildup in Europe to block Soviet aggression. The Soviet drive could be contained, the original CPD had argued, only by a credible military force and an aroused public opinion whose presumed natural tendency was to slide to isolationism. On December 15, 1950, following the CPD's public announcement of the aggressive designs of the Soviet Union, Harry Truman used similar language to declare the need to raise U.S. military forces to 3.5 million so as "to meet the present danger." The rallying cry thus formalized George Kennan's containment thesis (Sanders 1983, 55).

During the cold war, the CIA was charged with developing an annual estimate of Soviet military strength. Its National Intelligence Estimate guided the size and shape of the defense budget, U.S. negotiating posture, and even the concept of deterrence itself (*NYT,* December 26, 1976, p. 14). Increasing conservative dissatisfaction with détente and distrust of the interpretation that found essential parity in U.S. and Soviet force levels pressured Ford to permit CIA director George Bush to invite a group of outside experts to establish a panel whose role was to develop a worst-case scenario.

Two catalysts led to the Team B "experiment": a doubling of the CIA estimate of Soviet military spending (10 to 15 percent of GNP rather than 6 to 8 percent)[3] and the Pentagon's discovery of a Soviet civil defense effort (*Washington Post,* January 2, 1977, p. 4). In selecting members for the team, Bush looked for hard-line critics of defense policy. Led by Harvard historian (and future CPD member) Richard Pipes, Team B announced a much higher estimate of Soviet force levels; indeed, the group could not avoid this conclusion, for its members had been selected to find just such a disparity.[4] Team B did not stop with a numerical analysis; it concluded that the Soviets were bent on achieving strategic supremacy and thus a capacity to win a nuclear war (Scheer 1982, 60).

The political forces that had provided the military rationale for NSC-68 reconstituted around the issue of U.S. strategic vulnerability.[5] Using the same name and even meeting at the same Manhattan club as its predecessors had, the CPD began sounding an alarm about the state of U.S. strategic forces and what it considered a wrong-headed pattern of thinking regarding the Soviet threat:

> The principal threat to our nation, to world peace, and to the cause of human freedom is the Soviet drive based upon an unparalleled military buildup. The Soviet Union has not altered its long-held goal of a world dominated from a single center—Moscow. It continues, with notable persistence, to take advantage of every opportunity to expand its political and military influence throughout the world: in Europe; in the Middle East and Africa; in Asia; even in Latin America; in all the seas. (In Tyroler 1984, 3)

The CPD set out to persuade the public that a weakened state of U.S. defenses threatened to let Europe drift into the Soviet sphere of influence and that negotiation with the enemy amounted to bargaining with the devil: "The notion of a stable world order in which nations based on differing political principles cooperate rather than contend is alien to Soviet psychology and doctrine" (Tyroler 1984, 11). The rhetorically potent ideological argument was back, and its logical implications for arms policy inevitably followed.

### *Jimmy Carter and the Collapse of Détente*

Détente collapsed during Jimmy Carter's term of office because of conservative opposition, a conflicted view of détente, and external events. Carter stirred up wave upon wave of conservative opposition, first with a campaign pledge to reduce the defense budget by $7 billion and then at a preinauguration briefing at which he announced his desire to reduce the strategic arsenal to two hundred missiles. Shortly after an unsuccessful meeting with the CPD, the Team B report was leaked to the press in what was to be the opening round in a war of wills between Carter and his neoconservative critics (Herken 1985).

Carter's formulation of détente included elements of cooperation and competition, a not unrealistic view but one that destabilized foreign policy because it failed to indicate precisely when one should cooperate or compete (Garthoff 1985, 564–65). Carter duplicated this equivocal formulation in his cabinet by appointing two advisers whose posture toward Soviet policy differed fundamentally, Cyrus Vance as secretary of state and Zbigniew Brzezinski as assistant for national security affairs.

Vance accepted the position on the condition that "only the president and his secretary of state were to have responsibility for defining the administration's foreign policy publicly" (Vance 1983, 35). He preferred a quiet, cooperative diplomatic path to be carried on within the strict confines of the State Department. The more combative Brzezinski regarded the United States as being engaged in an "overarching geopolitical struggle" with the Soviets (Garthoff 1985, 565). He thus regarded Vance as overly optimistic and temperamentally unsuited for standing up to Carter on important issues. Vance was fine when dealing with "decent parties" but at his worst when dealing with the "thugs of the world" (Brzezinski 1983, 37, 43–44). Carter intended the opposing views to create a range of policy options from which he could select an appropriate response. What he did not anticipate was that these two very different perspectives would not be represented by two equally matched foes.[6] Brzezinski easily dominated the more diffident Vance, who submitted his resignation shortly after discovering that Brzezinski had convinced Carter to attempt a rescue of the embassy staff held hostage in Teheran.

Influenced by Brzezinski's views and his desire to look tough after the Soviet Union had invaded Afghanistan, Carter increased defense spending, approving development of the "Missile Experimental" (MX)—the largest ICBM to date—as an ill-fated concession to right-wing critics of SALT II (Herken 1985, 289). The Senate never ratified SALT II, for political support crumbled over the course of Carter's term in office. An emboldened opposition pointed to Soviet interventions in the horn of Africa and Afghanistan as evidence of Soviet expansionary designs and to the revolution in Iran as evidence of American impotence traceable to a naive faith in détente and the military it had weakened.

Notwithstanding his move to the right to outflank conservative critics in his reelection campaign, Carter had spent his political capital, leaving SALT II unratified, even as Ronald Reagan attacked it as symbolic of U.S. capitulation to the Soviet drive for power. As a member of the CPD, Reagan insisted that a strategic "window of vulnerability" had developed, a product of Carter's ineptness.[7] Carter's move to appear as conservative as his challenger merely weakened his appeal for those seeking a foreign policy alternative (Meyer 1990).

## The New Cold War

The first Reagan administration attempted to recast the American view of the USSR; no longer merely a self-interested power, it was once again an implacable ideological foe. Yet there was a certain extravagance in the characterization, in part due to Ronald Reagan's ambivalence on nuclear weapons and his tendency to rely on popular culture, especially movies, for his metaphors. Reagan's characterization of the USSR as the "evil empire" traded on public familiarity with a villainous power of a similar name in *Star Wars.* The same movie would later become associated with a fanciful Reagan proposal to defeat nuclear war entirely. Reagan's extreme views were an outgrowth of his idealism. In the first stages of his presidency this manifested itself in the metaphor of a shining city on a hill doing battle with the evil empire. Accordingly, he drew on the political analysis and advice of the CPD.[8]

The public was sometimes skeptical of and other times outright frightened by the Reagan military alarm. Indeed, analysis of public opinion data reveals that defense spending contributed only marginally to Reagan's victory.[9] Despite this, Reagan committed to a military buildup (begun by Carter) that between 1980 and 1985 increased the military budget by over 50 percent, from $197 billion to $296 billion, adding $330 billion in real growth. Empirical justification for the buildup rested on a revised CIA estimate of Soviet military spending that doubled the earlier estimate. By 1983, however, the CIA had returned its estimate to the earlier figure: "Since 1983, based on evidence of lower weapons production than had been predicted, both the CIA and later the Defense Intelligence Agency have sharply reduced their estimate of Soviet defense spending back through 1975, setting annual growth, after inflation, at about 2 percent instead of the 3–4 percent growth previously estimated. The cumulative effect of this revision was to drop the estimate of total Soviet defense spending in 1981 and later years by more than 10 percent" (Stubbing 1986, 10).

Richard Stubbing, for twenty years a senior Defense Department budget analyst and then a professor of public policy at Duke University, summarizes an extensive analysis of force comparisons and concludes that in general, "when data about military spending, weapons production, manpower, and overall capabilities for the two superpowers are considered, it is difficult to perceive a radical shift in the military balance over the course of the 1970s" (Stubbing 1986, 14). Indeed, the "window of vulnerability" began to disappear from administration rhetoric by the spring of 1983 as Reagan pressed Congress for additional funds for the MX. The story of the MX provides a guide through the thicket of bureaucratic infighting among those responsible for arms control during the first term of the Reagan presidency.

### *The Travails of Missile Experimental*

Eventually named the "Peacekeeper," the MX was to be the latest word in the American ICBM arsenal. Precise and deadly, the MX would fly 6,000 miles to within 600 feet of its target and carry up to ten warheads with a combined destructive force 170 times more powerful than that of the bomb that destroyed Hiroshima. It represented the latest evolution in arms technology that answered the threat posed by a generation of Soviet missiles designated as SS-18 and SS-19. The SS-18 and SS-19 were also MIRVed[10] and represented what the Soviets favored—huge land-based weapons that could carry heavy payloads. What alarmed some analysts was that the Soviets were getting better in guidance systems as well, making the heavy payloads seem even more menacing. Some argued that these missiles could now destroy the siloed Minutemen—the principal weapon in the U.S. arsenal—and thus weaken their deterrence value. But perceptions of a technological advantage can yield political leverage as well. For example, the overwhelming advantage the United States held in ICBMs had sobered the Soviets into climbing down in the Cuban missile crisis. First voiced by Europeans and then by American conservative critics, a view of increasing Soviet power translated into fears of increased influence over European affairs, especially Germany (Freedman 1989, 367).

Reagan's election quickened the trends started by Carter and produced a sea change in the rhetoric used to characterize nuclear weapons. The senior figures—Reagan, Bush, Alexander Haig, and Caspar Weinberger—"created the impression of leaders for whom nuclear weapons held little awe" (Newhouse 1989, 337). Haig, for example, denied them any special quality. As he put it, they do not exist "in a world of their own." They are more powerful, "but fundamentally, they remain an expression of strength of the nation possessing them" (Haig 1984, 220). So extreme was the administration's position that the views of the Joint Chiefs of Staff seemed moderate by comparison: "The chiefs, aware that America's strategic forces still held advantages over the Soviet Union's, wanted to sustain existing limits and prevent what was being called 'breakout,' i.e., a massive increase in Soviet forces. They didn't share the administration's strong preference for scrubbing SALT and reestablishing American superiority in strategic weapons. They preferred the relative certainties of parity to the uncertainties of a major new cycle of competition" (*Newsweek,* October 1, 1984, p. 27).

Superficially Reagan's views on nuclear arms resembled those of the CPD, but some analysts argue that they resulted from his incomplete understanding of the technical and diplomatic significance of these weapons. During NSC meetings, for example, Reagan's attention flagged when discussions among rival factions within his cabinet turned on disagreements over the relative importance of warheads and launchers, the subject of a long-running debate between State and Defense Department officials and thus important to the direction of an arms control strategy. After the issue had been (imperfectly) resolved, Reagan said to some White House visitors that he never fully understood "what this throw-weight business [was] all about" (in Talbott 1985, 237), and in an interview with *Time,* he said he did not know that the Soviets had concentrated their nuclear forces in land-based ICBMs (Talbott 1985, 263).

Freed from the restraints imposed by an understanding of technological issues or diplomatic nuance, Reagan's views tended to extremes. On the one hand, he held an ideal vision that contemplated the total abolition of nuclear weapons—in Reykjavík Reagan and Mikhail Gorbachev nearly agreed to eliminate all nuclear weapons; on the other, he dreamed of a perfect defense against them.[11] If the weapons were to continue to exist, however, the United States would hold the clear advantage. Indeed, in early budget discussions Weinberger proposed a plan for "deterring or prosecuting a global war with the Soviet Union" (in Newhouse 1986, 337). Reagan also doubted the Soviet economy's capacity to sustain a quickened arms race, believing that the USSR would eventually face increased pressure to begin negotiations on reducing nuclear weapons (Cannon 1991, 297).

Lack of leadership and a strong interdepartmental policy-making structure led to competition for influence at the cabinet level (Haig 1984, 223; Talbott 1985, 9). In the first year of his presidency, Reagan concentrated his efforts on a tax and budget package, leaving his cabinet members and their assistants to wrangle over arms control. Here the State Department and the Joint Chiefs of Staff favored adhering to SALT. Opposed were Secretary of State Weinberger, presidential adviser Edwin Meese (to whom the NSC looked for cues), CIA head William Casey, and arms control adviser Lieutenant General Edward Rowny.

A vacuum of expertise and interest at the highest levels created political opportunities for hard-liners such as Richard Perle, whose ideological self-assurance made up for his comparatively lower-echelon arms control position in the Defense Department (Talbott 1985, 17). The Soviets were puzzled by all this, especially the extremity of White House rhetoric and U.S. intransigence on arms control.[12] Administration hard-liners characterized Soviet peace feelers as moves to consolidate the gains made in SALT II (Haig 1984, 228), an advantage to be parried by deployment of new systems, such as the MX.

The fate of the MX, its role in arms control policy, and especially its interaction with a renascent peace movement define and demarcate the periods of policy-making in the Reagan administration. Because the movement's chief goal was to stop any further advances in weapons technology, any further deployments or funding programs would be perceived as fatally wounding it. In making this claim I differ with analysts such as David Cortright (1993) who argue the movement continued to exert influence through the second Reagan administration. The success of the arms buildup and Reagan's landslide reelection suggest the movement's major influence was limited to issues of public awareness during the first Reagan administration.

## Reconstitution of the Peace Movement

A number of developments led to the reconstitution of the antinuclear movement: a turn to the right in national politics that had stimulated resurgent cold war militarism, an existing organizational and communications network of peace and environmental groups (Kleidman 1993, 135–36), a single unifying issue, and some important establishment allies.

The movement found a favorable political environment in the alarm caused first by the nuclear reactor failure at Three Mile Island and then by the unusually harsh rhetoric coming out of the White House. Furthering prospects for movement success was the growth of many antinuclear groups that were unaligned with either of the warring wings in the test ban era. This made the movement less susceptible to the ideological disunity that had plagued it during those days (Kleidman 1993, 137).

The movement also received an important boost from an influential ally, the more moderate analysts in the arms control community whom Reaganites had excluded from executive appointments (Meyer 1990, 40). Since the test ban, nuclear issues had become not only invisible but also increasingly complex and remote. Kennedy's Arms Control and Disarmament Agency had weakened the influence of popular opinion on nuclear issues (Boyer 1984). The more moderate arms controllers thus made for a potentially sympathetic and politically influential ally. Exclusion of these moderating voices also helped to stimulate dissent among officials outside Reagan's inner circle, who responded in part to the ideological purity of the Reagan appointments and in part to threats business interests saw in the administration's policy of deficit spending to pay for the nuclear buildup (Ferguson and Rogers 1986, 146–54).

Modeling itself on an umbrella coalition of the sixties and seventies—the Mobilization Committee to End the War in Vietnam—the Mobilization for Survival (MfS) sought to reestablish the threat of nuclear holocaust in the public consciousness. Responding to an article in the *Progressive* in which antiwar activist Sidney Peck called for organized resistance to American nuclear policy, in 1977 organizers of the coalition brought together a wide range of organizational forces—40 national organizations and 280 local groups poised to address four general goals: to abolish nuclear weapons, eliminate nuclear power, stop the arms race, and meet human needs. Although consciously patterned on the antiwar movement of the sixties, the MfS lacked the single large issue that would stir its disparate ranks into concerted action (Meyer 1990, 147–48). Tellingly, even though the movement defined the issue on which it sought action, the essence of that issue—the nuclear freeze—represented a shift from the politics of passion and moral authority (e.g., "no radiation without representation) to the dispassion and prestige of expertise, technical virtuosity, and the authority of numbers.

The chief strategist of the freeze was Randall Forsberg, a nuclear defense expert who had studied arms control in a graduate program at MIT. Forsberg believed that it was possible to force a nuclear weapons debate on Congress and the president if grass-roots peace groups and, especially, the American middle class could be mobilized to join the movement. Mindful of the complexities of arms control, Forsberg believed that any attempt to eliminate all nuclear weapons and, eventually, all arms of any sort would have to begin by removing the principal dynamic of the arms race, the incremental ratcheting effect known as "technology creep." By doing so, what appeared to be a simple holding action could put a stop to the arms race itself. Deceptively simple, the proposal represented a radical departure from the arms control programs of the past: "While previous arms control agreements had set numerical limits on weaponry and allowed technological modernization, the freeze would end both numerical increases and technological improvements in nuclear forces. It was not an attempt to manage the arms race but to end it" (Meyer 1990, 160).

In December 1979 Forsberg persuaded the MfS to unite around her draft proposal, an analysis of American and Soviet weapons systems and an argument for a bilateral, technically verifiable freeze that would leave the powers with net parity of strength. Fluent in the technical issues of arms control and respectful of the complexities confronted by arms control experts, Forsberg believed that organizing a movement around an issue that addressed technical concerns would force experts to consider radically different methods of arms control (Meyer 1990, 167). This proved fatal on two counts. First, the issue was not capable of sustaining enduring moral passion because its heart was technological, analytical, leaving it vulnerable to a cause that, though perhaps more idealized, held greater inspirational power; ironically, this cause came from Reagan, who envisioned a defense system that would eliminate nuclear war altogether. Second, this turn of events left the arms controllers to reclaim the technical grounds from which they had been pushed in the first place. Comfortably back on their turf, they judged the freeze as simplistic and unverifiable.

The movement's chief political strategy echoed the commonsense quality of its proposal. It strove to win over a large moderate base by sticking to a single issue, hammering on the idea of multilateralism, and using populist rhetoric designed to return nuclear issues to popular understanding and democratic control. Politicians who ignored the wide appeal of the measure would be backed into the dubious position of devaluing public opinion (Meyer 1990, 161). Such linkages, however, would depend on the cooperation of the news media.

### *Media Strategy*

Many freeze movement leaders were veterans of the antiwar movement of the sixties and recalled the mass media's tendencies to target the flamboyant and weird at the expense of political substance (Gitlin 1980), a tendency also noticeable during the test ban movement. Leadership distrusted the national press and formulated an end-run strategy that mirrored its overall political strategy of empowering ordinary citizens to question the assumptions of the arms race in their own neighborhoods. Freeze activist Pam Solo drew this contrast between the open, democratic approach of the movement and the secretive nature of arms control elites: "While the Freeze's commitment to democratic procedure represented the organizing and cultural preferences of those initiating the movement, it was also an instinctive response to militarism. The secrecy, the cult of expertise, and the bureaucratization of military-mindedness cut people off from decisions that affect lives so profoundly. This realization solidified the Freeze's commitment to democracy as both a goal and a way of conducting its business" (Solo 1988, 62). The freeze movement avoided the top-heavy organizational models characteristic of the Washington lobbyists and established not a headquarters but a national *clearinghouse* in St. Louis so as to reinforce the movement's structure, namely, a loose grass-roots coalition (Cortright 1993, 15). Randall Kehler—a veteran of the Vietnam War movement—was appointed national coordinator. Placing the clearinghouse in St. Louis allowed the movement to promote a rock-solid middle-American image while it avoided the coastal cities that housed the national press (Kleidman 1993, 148).

In its earliest stages the grass-roots strategy effectively tapped an existing network of traditional and antinuclear organizations, churches, and professional groups such as the Physicians for Social Responsibility (PSR), Federation of American Scientists, and Union of Concerned Scientists. These groups brought the movement an increased flow of funds and considerable media attention. The national media focused much of their attention on the head of the PSR, Helen Caldicott, who provided an important rhetorical catalyst for the freeze. The publicity garnered by Caldicott's strategy of legitimating fear of nuclear war dramatically increased the PSR's reach. Between 1979 and 1982 its membership grew from a few hundred to twenty thousand. Some analysts argue, however, that Caldicott's medical visions of nuclear horror numbed her audiences instead of activating them into effective political action. Hogan, for example, argues that media fascination with Caldicott and her "radical, irrational, alien, and condescending" rhetoric weakened the movement's appeal, for she paid little more than lip service to the actual proposal, which she regarded as a mere step in swift bilateral disarmament or even unilateral U.S. disarmament (Hogan 1994, 63–64, 71).

In its early public phase, the freeze coalition's media strategy worked to perfection. Images of ordinary citizens speaking against the arms race in local political venues such as town meetings filled television newscasts. These recalled the sympathetic images of morally impassioned Quakers that had appeared in the *New York Times* during the test ban movement. Groups also used the local mass media for education and outreach. In North Carolina, for example, SANE sponsored sixty-second ads that aired on dozens of radio stations. The ads had been recorded by Dean Smith, then the basketball coach of the University of North Carolina Tar Heels, who agreed to be a spokesperson for the movement (Cortright 1993, 61–64). Freeze activist David Cortright assesses the movement's overall media effort as unsophisticated and inadequate, however, especially as it contrasted with the Reagan administration's savvy and highly organized media counterattack. Nevertheless, the early media successes of the freeze caught the ready attention of national politicians.

## *National Politics and Beyond*

By the early spring of 1982, the movement had achieved some political success. The passage of local freeze referenda in Vermont and Massachusetts surprised national politicians, some of whom who saw an opportunity to ride the wave of a grass-roots movement (Solo 1988, 72). On March 10, 1982, Senators Ted Kennedy and Mark Hatfield and Representatives Ed Markey, Sylvio Conte, and Jonathan Bingham brought the freeze movement to the floor of Congress, where supporters proposed a variety of freeze resolutions. By this time many Democrats were finding the freeze a useful screen for their endorsement of increased spending on nonnuclear high-tech arms, such as laser-guided bombs, sophisticated tanks, and battlefield missiles of the sort used in the 1991 Gulf War—a way of mollifying dovish constituents while remaining strong on defense. According to Ferguson and Rogers, "Allying with the 'freeze' became [for Congress members] little more than a way of disaffiliating with a military buildup of the size Reagan projected" (Ferguson and Rogers 1986, 151). Democratic support for the freeze transmuted into a way of slowing down the Reagan push for increased nuclear arms.

Meanwhile Forsberg's strategy for engaging mainstream support was successful as well. A massive rally in June 1982 that brought 750,000 people to New York City to demonstrate on the eve of a UN session marked the crest of the movement's public success. The *New York Times* characterized the event as "the largest political demonstration in the history of the United States" (*NYT Sunday Magazine,* July 11, 1982, p. 14). As the movement grew, however, its media strategy was undermined by a number of unrelated factors, among them an inability to manage its message because of the thin resources devoted to the national media (Kleidman 1993). As the analysis in the following chapter demonstrates, this may have well been beyond the control of even the shrewdest media specialist.

The Reagan administration opposed the freeze to the last using three main arguments. At first it claimed the movement was supported by funding from the KGB, the Soviet intelligence organization, an argument that harked back to the days of red-baiting. Later, Reagan spokespersons claimed a freeze would lock in a Soviet lead in strategic weapons, thus appealing to the window of vulnerability. Finally, Reagan outflanked the antinuclear movement's moral appeal by promoting a space-based missile defense—the Strategic Defense Initiative (SDI)—popularized as "Star Wars."[13] Most American experts doubted the technical basis of the SDI proposal, but the Soviets regarded it as destabilizing because although they also doubted it could be completely leakproof, it might provide an effective shield against a ragged retaliatory attack, leaving the United States with a highly effective first-strike capacity that increased its political leverage (Garthoff 1985, 1027). Despite its fanciful prospect, SDI provided Reagan with an idealist's image that made people forget he had just promoted one of the largest peacetime defense increases in U.S. history.

A year after the New York City rally, the House voted for a freeze resolution described in *Time* (May 16, 1983, p. 13) as so vague and confusing that "both pro- and anti-Freeze legislators claimed victory." A legislative aide to Markey contested this view, saying that the press saw any amendment to the proposal, no matter how meaningless, as a setback. Although the *New York Times* characterized the resolution as "substantially modified," leaders of the movement claimed to disagree with this assessment and said they were elated by its passage (Waller 1987, 287).

The skeptics would be proven right, since congressional support for the freeze declined soon after passage of the resolution. (The Senate resolution never emerged from its Republican-dominated Foreign Relations Committee.) The House resolution had passed by a vote of 278 to 149, but practical support for implementing it dissolved with no agreement on precisely which weapons were to be affected: "It became clear to all concerned that very few Representatives were actually enthusiastic or thoroughgoing freeze supporters and that most were simply responding to constituent pressure that (at the moment) demanded a general anti-Reagan military vote" (Leavitt 1983, 5).

That fall a Soviet fighter shot down Korean Airlines flight 007, an incident that recalled the darkest moments of the cold war and seemed to undo the twenty years of arms control diplomacy it had stimulated. Randy Kehler declared KAL 007 a disaster for the movement, which by the end of 1983 had retreated to a "freeze fundamentalism," offering only weak opposition to the MX and Trident missiles and the deployment of European missiles (Meyer 1990, 218). Congressional approval of the MX had already divided and weakened the movement. Referring to Les Aspin and others who had voted for the freeze, Kehler remarked, "You think you have expert support, but the experts are just using you as a wedge to hit Reagan, but they don't support your position. And to the extent that we told people that two-thirds of the House of Representatives was with us on the freeze, we misled them and we misled ourselves" (in Meyer 1990, 235). By the close of 1984, the public face of the movement had dropped from the mainstream media radar. Ronald Reagan's landslide reelection had thoroughly demoralized its supporters.

*Public Support*

The late seventies and early eighties marked a period of wide swings in opinion regarding the desirability of arms buildups and arms control. Following a course explained by some political scientists as expressing the simultaneous desires for strength and peace (Russett 1990; Graham 1989; Kohut 1989), public support for an arms buildup increased during the Carter presidency and then declined during Reagan's term (see figure 4).

What is puzzling about public opinion during this period is that at a time when a large percentage of people favored increased military spending, an equal and at times much higher percentage favored a multilateral nuclear freeze. A search of the public opinion database at the Roper Center at the University of Connecticut revealed five polls using the official text of the resolution ("would you favor or oppose an agreement between the United States for an immediate, verifiable freeze on the testing, production, and deployment of nuclear weapons?"). Those surveys showed steady and

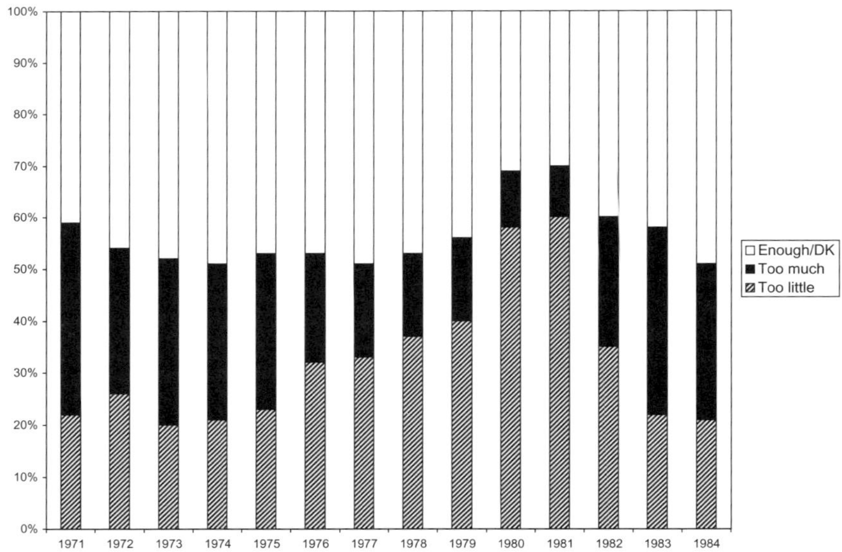


Figure 4. Public opinion on defense and military expenditures, 1971–84. *Source:* Hartley and Russett 1992.

increasing support for the measure, ranging from 67 to 79 percent between 1981 and 1988.[14]

Political scientists argue that the simultaneous desire for both peace and security explains the apparent paradox at the core of public opinion research on American attitudes toward defense issues. Russett (1990), for example, says that these define the "acceptable range" of alternatives in foreign policy-making. If the two exist in equal parts, however, as the poll data suggest they did, and there is no empirical means of gauging defensive strength, the average citizen has no alternative but to turn to the media for the information needed in organizing priorities. For the greater part of the population, this information may be limited to the most salient issue (see Zaller 1992). Salience establishes only a general awareness. How the news media frame the issue influences how members of the public think about it. Analysis of media coverage of the antinuclear movement during the first Reagan administration should provide some indication of the balance of views that prevailed.

## Notes

1. Throw-weight refers to a missile's usable weight, that is, the weight of its warheads and guidance system.

2. Two years after the ABM treaty, Nixon signed James Schlesinger's National Security Decision Memo 242, which repudiated MAD in favor of flexible response, the doctrine of graduated escalation established by Robert McNamara. Nuclear weapons were once again fair game in a conflict (Meyer 1990, 35).

3. This may have been plausibly interpreted as a sign of the Soviets' inefficiency—twice the cost to produce the same number of weapons—rather than an indication of their intent to achieve war-fighting capacity (Stubbing 1986, 10; Scheer 1983, 57–59).

4. "The conditions were that the outsiders be mutually agreeable to the advisory board and to Mr. Bush and that they hold more pessimistic views of Soviet plans than those entertained by the advocates of the rough parity thesis" (*NYT*, December 26, 1976, p. 14). Among the Team B analysts were Paul Nitze and William Van Cleave, who prior to their temporary assignment at the CIA had spent several months planning the formation of the CPD with Eugene Rostow (Scheer 1983, 57). Van Cleave's views on Soviet force levels were so alarmist that Caspar Weinberger made sure to exclude him from the administration (see Garthoff 1994, 34).

5. Concerned by the potential spread of nuclear weapons to the Soviet Union, Truman asked his secretaries of state and defense to formulate an appropriate response. The National Security Council issued its report—NSC-68—in April 1950. It presented the Soviet Union as a dangerous aggressor and recommended increased

U.S. military preparedness, advising the administration to "increase our atomic armaments as rapidly as other considerations make appropriate" (in Freedman 1989, 71).

6. Brzezinski insisted that although there were some differences of opinion on the issues of Soviet-Cuban influence in the horn of Africa, the timing of a Brzezinski trip to China and the announcement concerning normalization of relations, and the wisdom of the Iran rescue mission, "on most issues, at most times [he and Vance] were in basic agreement." The problem was a press that "seized" on every disagreement as illustrating the gulf between the two and, perhaps, as characteristic of a disorganized presidency. This framing became so insistent that the press invented disagreements even when there were none. Nevertheless, Brzezinski's memoirs contain a stream of unflattering references to Vance: "For his part, Cy was extraordinarily deferential to the President; he had a way of very pleasantly blinking his eyelashes to indicate agreement and deference, and I was struck by how often that habit manifested itself in Cy's dealings with the President" (Brzezinski 1983, 38–40, 42).

7. The window had actually been "discovered" by Carter's Pentagon expert William Perry, who believed the Soviets had developed a breakthrough in guidance systems that could guide a new generation of powerful missiles to a crippling strike on U.S. land-based ICBMs (Cannon 1991, 163).

8. Sixty of the 182 members of the CPD would serve in the administration (Tyroler 1984, ix–xi).

9. Miller and Shanks (1982) reported party identification and dissatisfaction with Carter's performance as far and away the most important predictors of a vote for Reagan. Defense played a marginal role. Aldrich, Sullivan, and Borgada (1989), however, found that issue position on foreign affairs played a small but significant role in predicting vote.

10. MIRVs (multiple independently targeted reentry vehicles) are missiles carrying multiple warheads (usually six to ten) that can be targeted at the moment of release.

11. Another example of this outlook was Reagan's decision to scrap SALT for START (Strategic Arms Reduction Treaty). Haig argues that unlike other administrations, this one aimed for systematic reductions of weapons in all categories rather than limitations in selected ones (Haig 1984, 222).

12. Concerned by the rhetoric, in 1981 the KGB advised its station personnel in western capitals that the United States was preparing to attack the Soviet Union (Newhouse 1989, 336).

13. For a rhetorical analysis of Reagan's proposal and its effectiveness at morally outflanking the freeze, see Bjork 1989.

14. See, however, Hogan and Smith's (1991) analysis of public opinion data on the freeze. They argue that support for the measure was shallow since it depended on the answers to a variety of questions, including whether the freeze would leave the United States in a weakened state (a version of the window of vulnerability argument) and whether the Soviets would cheat on it.

# 7 Freezing Out the Opposition: The Reagan Presidency

This chapter resumes the study of patterns of news coverage, looking now at how they corresponded with the Reagan administration's views on arms policy and its response to a vigorous antinuclear movement. In previous chapters, on the test ban, I selected the *New York Times* and *Time* magazine as examples of the media because of their prestige and influence on public officials and other media sources. In this chapter I continue to follow coverage in the *New York Times* but substitute television news for *Time*.

I make this substitution for several reasons. First, 1963 was the first year in which Americans who got their news from television outnumbered those who relied on newspapers. That year 55 percent said they got most of their news from television; 53 percent relied on newspapers. By the early eighties nearly two-thirds watched television newscasts, whereas only 44 percent read a newspaper (Mayer 1993, 603). The evening news broadcasts had become a nightly ritual and a principal source for information about the outside world. Second, unlike the Eisenhower and Kennedy years, for which records and archives are spotty, detailed records of newscasts during the Reagan years and the actual taped footage are available from Vanderbilt University. Finally, television coverage allows us to see whether its specific nature—its visual aspect and a proclivity for dramatic story telling—significantly changes the quality of coverage. For the analysis of television news, I selected the *CBS Evening News* because it was the most highly rated newscast during this period.

Once again, I look most carefully at those stories in which long-standing patterns change, signaling a reorientation in perspective on the movement. For the *New York Times* I looked at the most prominent stories, national news items that appeared in the first section of the paper. During twenty-seven months of coverage, the paper published fifty-seven stories on the freeze movement and related items, including the debate in the House and Ronald Reagan's speeches and comments on the merit of the issue. During roughly the same period, CBS broadcast forty-one stories, the first in March 1982 and the last in February 1984. I have set early 1984 as the outer limit of the news analysis because of Congress's decision to fund the MX in November 1983 and the drop-off in media coverage soon thereafter.[1]

Generally speaking, the development of arms policy during the first Reagan administration can be divided into three periods: a period of dissent regarding the shape of new arms control policy that led to a flawed START proposal, a period of negotiations with the Soviets that eventually stalled on those flaws, and a short period of fast-moving events during which the House passed a toothless freeze resolution that provided cover for approval of the MX shortly thereafter. I will explore each of these in greater detail in this chapter, but figure 5 provides a bird's-eye view of the general patterns of freeze-related coverage through these three periods.[2]

The graph shows the familiar pattern of heightened visibility at or near major policy changes. Note the correlation with the absence of a unified

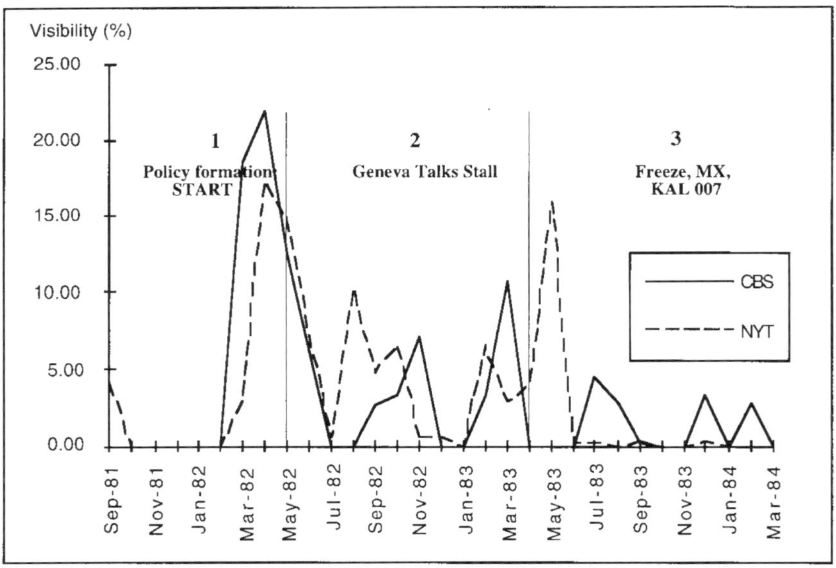


Figure 5. Presidential policy and movement visibility in the *New York Times* and the *CBS Evening News:* Reagan administration.

arms control policy and high movement visibility in early spring 1982. Note also the drop in coverage after the announcement of the START proposal, despite the New York City demonstration in June 1982. Once again, visibility increased as the Geneva talks began to stall. After the House vote on the freeze and the KAL incident, however, movement visibility drops off again. On the surface the patterns of coverage suggest media sensitivity to administration initiatives and dissent.

A comparison of the two sources shows much similarity, with a few expected and unexpected differences. The *New York Times* led television coverage, in the first instance by seven months, and continued to do so until the House debate in May 1983. Note also that the *Times* paid more sustained attention than CBS. The comparison also shows that although the *Times* was first on the scene, it was also the first to leave after officials had disposed of the issue. Television provided the movement with more follow-up coverage after the House debate (although it is possible that the *Times* provided local coverage in its metropolitan and regional pages, which I did not analyze).

One possible reason for television's greater sustained interest was its policy of assigning a single reporter who followed the freeze movement more or less regularly. By contrast, the *Times* assigned a variety of beat reporters who covered the movement as it intersected with their prescribed beats of the White House, Congress, or the specialized areas of arms control and national politics. Such reporters were more likely to note official reaction to the movement rather than to cover it as a news story in its own right. This may explain why, when government officials perceived that the movement had stimulated debate and an arms control proposal—goals defined by editorial staff rather than movement leadership—they were less likely to feel its political pressure. It is this structural difference that I hypothesize accounts for the differences in perspective for the two news sources.

I will look at media treatment of four groups in the controversy: (1) the movement itself, including its leadership; (2) potential movement supporters (the public); (3) government officials, including members of Congress and individuals in the Reagan administration; and (4) sympathetic allies, such as the moderate arms controllers and the Catholic bishops.

## Reagan Arms Control Policy: Confusion and Dissent, January 1981–April 1982

Although eventually returning to familiar patterns, at first the Reagan administration gauged the merits of arms control proposals by their distance from those of the past, especially SALT II. Reagan distanced himself from the issue, allowing it to fall prey to the interests of the departments chiefly affected by the proposals. Accordingly the State Department was sensitive to the diplomatic interests of similar organizations overseas, especially the North Atlantic Treaty Organization (NATO). Defense saw its mission more narrowly as providing the most effective defense for the United States. The necessity for reconciling the negotiating posture with a plan of action—the single integrated operational plan (SIOP) that specified Soviet targets in case of nuclear war—made the Joint Chiefs of Staff the most pragmatic in an administration eager to strengthen U.S. military power.

Whereas Jimmy Carter seems to have been pushed into a military buildup, Ronald Reagan relished it. Within two weeks of taking office, Reagan requested an immediate $32.6 billion increase in defense spending, this following a $26.4 billion increase by Carter the previous year over a total budget of $200.3 billion. The issue was not the desirability of a more confrontational policy but rather the details of its implementation (Garthoff 1994, 14–15), and this is where departmental interests enhanced philosophical differences.

As Reagan took office, a debate broke out between those favoring a hawkish though pragmatic path and those bent on a more ideologically confrontational posture against the Soviet Union. These differences manifested themselves in a number of issues, but I will focus on arms control and specifically on a debate that centered on what would constitute the units of negotiation, launchers or throw-weight.

Secretary of State Alexander Haig represented the pragmatists, who had to deal with the NATO alliance's wariness of new Soviet missiles pointed in their direction and of American intentions to deploy Pershing II and Tomahawk cruise missiles as a counterweight. Thus they favored discussions about launchers because they knew launchers were negotiable. Unlike his ideological adversaries, Haig saw the tough new policy as a means for engaging with the Soviet Union and bringing it into line (Garthoff 1994, 17).

Secretary of Defense Caspar Weinberger and especially influential civilian officials such as Richard Perle and Fred Iklé took a confrontational hard line. Unwilling merely to contain communism, they were eager to roll it back (Garthoff 1994, 32). This group insisted on reducing the Soviet advantage in throw-weight. This was a hard-line position because throw-weight was the basis of the offsetting asymmetry for the Soviets. Insistence on throw-weight as the unit of account underlay the confrontationalists' strategy of forestalling any agreements until the United States could build up and modernize its own forces. To understand the significance of these developments, it is necessary to take a short detour into the political significance of nuclear weapons in Europe.

After World War II the Soviet Union amassed a large standing army in eastern Europe. Because the United States could not respond with troop emplacements of its own, it threatened to launch ICBMs from its soil should the Soviets ever decide to attack West Germany or any other NATO ally. U.S. ICBMs provided formidable deterrence value until the Soviets began deploying their own. This had the effect of "decoupling" the deterrent: if the Soviets invaded, could Europe count on the United States to launch its missiles and risk its own population? It was to the Soviet advantage to plant this doubt in western European leaders' minds and thus leverage an accommodation with the NATO countries that would isolate them from American influence.

Decoupling became an issue in the seventies after the Soviets deployed a new intermediate-range missile in the Urals, designated by the United States as the SS-20. The SS-20 substantially outperformed its predecessor, the SS-4, in range, accuracy, and firepower, yet it narrowly circumvented the restrictions placed by the first SALT agreement. The United States thus had two roads of response: restrictions on the SS-20 in SALT II or deployment of an answering technological response, a missile capable of flying unmolested into the Soviet Union. The Tomahawk—a cruise missile that flew at altitudes low enough to avoid radar detection—and a longer-range Pershing II took the latter road of response. Renewed arms talks were a step down the former. Thus was born what came to be known as the "dual-track" strategy, a balanced application of threat of deployment and negotiation to reach the perception of security (Talbott 1985, 26–37).

For the Europeans the relaxation of superpower tensions was crucial to maintaining the strength of the NATO alliance as well as disarming domestic opposition. The delicately balanced dual-track strategy seemed like the answer, but the rhetoric of the incoming Reaganites alarmed the alliance. Blaming détente generally and SALT specifically for Western vulnerability, Caspar Weinberger's response to Europe characterized the administration's attitude: "If the movement from Cold War to détente is progress, then let me say we cannot afford much more progress" (in Talbott 1985, 46).

George Shultz (Haig's replacement) provides further indirect evidence that a significant portion of the administration resisted accommodation. He reported in his memoirs that the Soviet ambassador had (futilely) proposed new talks at all levels in December 1982: "There was lots of powerful opposition around town to any effort to bridge the chasm separating Moscow and Washington. It came from Bill Clark and the NSC staff, from Cap Weinberger and others at the Defense Department, and from Bill Casey and his soulmates at the CIA" (Shultz 1993, 159).

Until the new weapons systems were safely funded, Weinberger and Perle continued to insist on reduction of the Soviet advantage in throw-weight in heated discussions with the State Department. When pressed to change their position for the sake of a consensus National Security Council (NSC) position, Perle managed to smuggle in a condition that could be traced back to an obstructionist intent.

### *The Media: Touching a Sensitive Nerve*

The freeze movement made its greatest gains during the first year and a half of the divided Reagan presidency. The period preceding the formulation of the START proposal provided the freeze movement its best opportunity for gaining new recruits and influencing public opinion. In fact, both the print and electronic media did provide the movement high visibility and favorable coverage. The content of the coverage, however, demonstrates how strategic errors led the movement to squander its best opportunities.

In early coverage the news media did not distinguish between general public sentiment and the freeze movement itself, suggesting that the movement gave voice to public sentiment rather than organizing it in the first place. The *New York Times,* for example, began its coverage in early September 1981 with a front-page story on Bishop Leroy Matthiesen's attempt to close down a Texas nuclear bomb factory and granted legitimacy to the movement by noting that it had crossed traditional pacifist (i.e., extremist) boundaries: "Some members of the movement are pacifists but many are not" (*NYT,* September 8, 1981, p. 1).

CBS began its coverage seven months later when it reported on a series of Vermont town meetings, the result of local AFSC staff efforts to put the freeze on the meeting agenda (Solo 1988, 55). Like the *Times,* television news legitimated the movement by pointing to its grass-roots support. In this first story earnest citizens went on record as being opposed to the arms race and persuaded the town council to pass a freeze resolution. Bruce Morton (who became the principal CBS reporter assigned to the movement) said this was but one example of a wider movement that included five state legislatures and twelve city councils, including "middle of the road" Fort Wayne, Indiana. Contrasting this movement to that of the sixties (a contrast that would become a dominant theme in the coverage),

Morton said that Vermont was "no hotbed of radicalism" (*CBS Evening News,* March 3, 1982).

A few weeks later a Bill Moyers commentary noted the growth of opposition to nuclear weapons in the United States and Europe. The news anchor, Dan Rather, preceded Moyers's commentary with a story refuting a charge by unnamed U.S. officials that the movement was partly financed by the Soviet Union, thus blocking a Reagan administration effort to use a classic jeopardy argument, an old-fashioned disloyalty smear on the movement. Moyers argued that support was too wide for such a charge to be taken seriously. He said that recently published essays by Jonathan Schell (*Fate of the Earth*) "open the public mind to dimly perceived truths" and concluded, "Citizens seem to be determined to close the gap between policies of the government and desires of the heart that the species survive" (*CBS Evening News,* March 22, 1982). Typical of news coverage in general at this stage, the Moyers commentary invested the movement with the moral authority of popular sovereignty, endowing "the people" with the authority to require government responsiveness on an issue traditionally left to its discretion.

Indeed, movement strategy for enlarging the scope of political debate and democratizing the issue had succeeded, even with the editorial board of the *New York Times:* "The problem is not nuclear but political. The freeze movement members are not lobbyists pressing for a specific piece of legislation. They are people, ordinary citizens, pressing for something much less intricate. They want to put nuclear restraint back on the track, to give diplomacy, and peace, a chance. The wonder is that the Reagan Administration seems so determined to take the other side" (*NYT,* March 16, 1982, p. 22).

By the end of March the *Times* considered the movement and the sentiment it tapped significant enough to warrant several front-page analyses by its political reporter, Hedrick Smith. One such analysis followed a news conference on March 31, 1982, where Reagan off-handedly remarked that the Soviets had achieved a "definite" margin of offensive superiority in land-based missiles that would allow them to wipe out American missiles in a preemptive strike—the window of vulnerability. This claim had been rejected by Carter's hard-liners, Secretary of Defense Harold Brown and security adviser Brzezinski, and was never believed by Weinberger.[3] A follow-up story surveyed a number of official reactions, including one from a State Department spokesperson who downplayed the remarks and an analysis containing Weinberger's statements to Congress that U.S. defense policy was intended to prevent the Soviets from ever achieving such superiority (*NYT,* April 1, 1982, p. 1). Though contested and qualified, even by administration officials, the claim nevertheless made its way into public discourse as an established fact.

In a later analysis Smith attributed the freeze movement's success to the absence of an administration consensus on arms control, which had eroded congressional support for the MX and other weapons systems that would have added $1.6 trillion to the defense budget over the next five years. The public opposed this, Smith asserted, citing a poll in which 70 percent favored increases smaller than those proposed by Reagan. (This was in fact close to the same number of people who favored the freeze.) "Now, with its ambitious military buildup, assertive talk of confrontation with Moscow and public comments about limited nuclear war, the Reagan Administration seems to have touched a sensitive public nerve and fed the climate of controversy" (*NYT,* April 9, 1982, p. 1).

Significantly, Smith referred to polls that indicated a seeming anomaly: notwithstanding public acceptance of Reagan's claim, Americans wanted to move ahead with arms control anyway. This reading of ambiguous public opinion data bolstered the freeze movement's cause, an interpretation that would change after Reagan's START proposal.

Television news approached the story in a characteristically dramatic way, responding uncritically to an administration leak intended to strengthen the case for increases in the military budget. In an April 1 broadcast, CBS Capitol Hill correspondent Phil Jones began his report with this announcement: "CBS has learned that [Senator] Howard Baker has agreed to hold an unusual super secret briefing on the Soviet threat." At pains to refrain from revealing the details, Jones revealed that Baker was in possession of a confirmed statement from a Soviet general that "Russia is now on a war footing."[4] Already having gotten the briefing, Senator David Boren (D-Okla.) said that the Soviets had continually tried to achieve superiority in every area and asked, "What are we to do about it?" The assessment portrayed the situation as being much worse than Americans thought it to be. Nevertheless, Jones provided no specific information that would lend support to the alarming "findings" (*CBS Evening News,* April 1, 1982).

No movement spokesperson was on hand to comment on the balance of nuclear power, in part because of the movement's horizontal, locally based structure and the decision to locate its clearinghouse in St. Louis. Putting it beyond convenient reach of national media centers restricted the movement's control of its message, a fact made increasingly apparent later that spring when Ground Zero ascended to public attention.

*Ground Zero and the Arms Controllers* — Led by Roger Molander, a former NSC staffer and arms control adviser, Ground Zero was a campaign designed to point out the dangers of nuclear war. Molander sympathized with the freeze movement's general purpose of raising public awareness of nuclear issues, but he opposed the proposal itself, saying it was simplistic and unverifiable. His opposition to the freeze proposal represented the arms control community's general reluctance to ally with the movement, a severe blow to overall movement strategy since the merit of the proposal rested heavily on its technical credibility. Meyer notes that the movement's natural allies among the liberal arms controllers—the Council for a Livable World (CLW), the Federation of American Scientists, the Arms Control Association, and even SANE—preferred to endorse traditional arms control measures, that is, incremental and calibrated decreases in force levels. These bread-and-butter issues had allied the arms controllers functionally to the political establishment since the Kennedy era. Meyer notes CLW member Jerome Grossman's reaction, which was typical among this group: "We had to be dragged kicking and screaming to support the freeze" (in Meyer 1990, 164).

Because Ground Zero marked the movement's first round of public activities since the Vermont town meetings, the media covered it extensively but conflated it with the freeze and obscured its central political message in the wash of sideshow activities. Much of a *New York Times* front-page article on Ground Zero, for example, cataloged the whimsical events that made up the week's events. These included a "run-for-your-life" race in which participants established that people cannot outrun a nuclear blast wave and a "swim for peace" in which a seal was used to demonstrate that animals are no better equipped to survive a nuclear war.

The scrupulous "nonpartisan" quality of Molander's position had made it attractive even to administration officials. Eugene Rostow (head of the ACDA) and Ronald Reagan favored this educational campaign. The presence of such highly placed allies in this nonpartisan venue would not contribute to the movement's democratizing strategy, however. The article noted that while many freeze advocates favored direct political action, others "acknowledged the possibility that entering the political process as a lobbying group might fragment the movement, which has been growing rapidly" (*NYT*, April 18, 1982, p. 1).

Here and in following instances media contrasted the movement's laudable efforts to educate the public on the dangers of nuclear warfare with the dangers to its coherence and unity that the movement faced when it entered the political process to translate sentiment into policy. Molander's campaign to restore traditional arms control undermined the freeze by differentiating its message, offering a middle-ground position that would block its chief goal of changing fundamental thinking on the arms race. Here was one thread of what would (perhaps inadvertently) become the most effective rhetorical strategy against the movement: futility. It would be reinforced visually by an infantilization of the movement's image in television reporting.

CBS noted the weekend kickoff of Ground Zero week with scenes of children and balloons, a visual theme that would come to dominate Bruce Morton's reporting of movement activities. There was little substance in the report: a soundbite from Roger Molander proclaiming that people needed to be educated on the dangers of nuclear war followed by footage from several cities showing crowds of varying sizes at rallies, with toy bombs in evidence. The theme of nationwide support for a serious political issue ran counter to the festive images of balloons and children that dominated coverage (*CBS Evening News,* April 18, 1982). With disciplined communication absent, the distractions of colorful images diffused the movement's message, moving it from the freeze movement's call to stop the arms race and military buildup to Ground Zero's more general concern with the risks of nuclear war.

Again conflating Ground Zero with the freeze, the next day a CBS report on a Ground Zero demonstration began with this observation by the anchor: "A chess game across from the White House drew more onlookers today than a Ground Zero demonstration protesting the horrors of nuclear war, but there were speeches, songs, and rallies across the country sparking the week-long campaign designed to build opposition to the nuclear arms buildup." A lengthy three-minute report followed on the larger freeze movement from the standpoint of movement events in California. Interspersed with references to sixties demonstrations and dancing protesters, the report quoted industrialist Harold Willens, a freeze supporter, as well as Ronald Reagan's daughter, Patty. Highlighting California's significance as a mirror of the nation, the report revealed that polls showed two-to-one support for the freeze. A pollster said: "It's a strong, unusual spontaneous grass-roots movement. They better run fast to get ahead of it." The reporter heightened the importance of the November vote on the resolution, saying it would be closely watched by the president (*CBS Evening News,* April 19, 1982). Television news had thus established the first criterion of political success for the movement, the first in a series of moving targets.

With the emotional appeal now intertwined with an uncontroversial abhorrence of nuclear war, the movement's technical authority came into question by the arms controllers. A *New York Times* analysis of the movement's significance traced its origins to the Carter and Reagan military buildups and the absence of an arms control initiative. The analysis presented cases for and against the freeze, but the case against was bolstered by "many arms control specialists" who argued it would serve as a disincentive for the Soviets, who stood to gain "many of the limits on American forces they have been seeking." Moreover, they asserted, negotiating an agreement that would increase stability, rather than "merely decrease the number of nuclear weapons, requires expertise, more than a passing acquaintance with military issues and considerable patience. When, for example, does modernization become a new weapons system? How does one go about verifying production of cruise missiles? The freeze, specialists assert, is misleading in its purported simplicity" (*NYT,* April 24, 1982, p. 8).

The experts also worried that the issue was becoming too partisan, a political weapon wielded against the administration, and that as such, it represented "all things to all people." One reason for its amorphousness was the movement's loss of control over issue definition to opponents and even to congressional supporters, with the *New York Times* having contributed to this confusion by its failure to distinguish between the two freeze resolutions before Congress. The Kennedy-Hatfield resolution, the experts said, was difficult to distinguish from the Jackson-Warner proposal: both called for negotiations, not an immediate moratorium.

In fact, the two differed in a very important way. The Kennedy-Hatfield proposal—a nonbinding resolution—called on the president to "decide when and how to achieve a mutual verifiable freeze on the testing, production, and further deployment of nuclear warheads, missiles, and other delivery systems" (in Meyer 1990, 225). Jackson and Warner proposed a freeze *after* the Americans and Soviets had achieved a sizable reduction in their stores of nuclear weapons. This was in fact a ploy (assumed by Washington pundits to have been designed by Richard Perle) to co-opt the language of the movement even as the proposed resolution supported Reagan's goal of avoiding arms control (Garthoff 1985, 1023; Meyer 1990, 226).

In the end, the analysis continued, the fate of the freeze itself was not all that significant. Rather, it said, "the force of the freeze is . . . likely to be affected by the extent to which the position put forth by the Reagan Administration is viewed as a 'serious' negotiating posture by arms control specialists here and overseas" (*NYT,* April 24, 1982, p. 8). In short, the *Times* equated movement success with a good faith offer of an arms control proposal in general, not adoption of the movement's particular proposal. Of greater significance was the *Times*'s reliance on arms controllers for their appraisal of the freeze. This assessment, however, drew on the traditional policies of finely calibrated arms negotiations, not the radical departures represented by the Reagan military buildup or Forsberg's call to end the arms race altogether.

To summarize, in this first phase both media sources failed to distinguish the movement from a national reaction to Reagan's arms policy and no doubt to its scary rhetoric. The news legitimated the movement on the basis of mainstream participation in it. For example, the Vermont town meetings served as a favorite symbol, a wistful look at preindustrial, rural American democracy in its most idealized form, described by Gans (1979, 44) as one of the enduring values of American journalism. But this early coverage also included distracting themes that called attention to festivity rather than to nuanced renderings of the facts. The festivals of Ground Zero illustrated by images of children and balloons seemed overmatched by the paradoxically "super-secret" meetings in congressional chambers. Meanwhile, concern over the window of vulnerability, the administration's disputed case against the freeze, shifted the rhetorical balance in favor of technical expertise.

## START, May 1982–March 1983

As the warring sides in the Reagan administration came to loggerheads on a variety of proposals, an energized peace movement increased pressure on European leaders, while the U.S. freeze movement helped to turn public opinion against Reagan's arms control policy. With the pressure on, in February 1982 William Clark, the head of the NSC, asked assistant secretary Richard R. Burt to draft a memorandum outlining the "terms of reference" defining an arms control position, the proposal later named START (Strategic Arms Reduction Treaty). These terms would also serve as the foundations of the administration's public relations strategy in speeches, press briefings, and congressional testimony. The criteria and their implications were as follows:

1. Equality: the military balance had shifted in favor of the Soviets
2. Stability: to be recovered once the American military had been beefed up

3. Reduction: a repudiation of SALT
4. Comprehensibility: the new agreement would have to be simple to gain public support
5. Deference to allies: compatibility with the INF talks

The campaign's aim was to present a proposal that looked good to Congress and the public, "however bad it looked to the Kremlin" (Talbott 1985, 247–48). In fact, START was little more than a public relations ploy to outflank increasing popular support for the freeze movement (Garthoff 1985, 1023).

As the May 1, 1982, deadline for a consensus proposal approached, both sides lobbied the Joint Chiefs of Staff for their support. The chiefs finally decided to go with the State Department on the pragmatic advantage it held for designing an achievable SIOP. The Weinberger-Perle proposal envisioned both powers with smaller but more numerous weapons sites. The chiefs saw this as incorporating the worst of both worlds; they recognized the dubiousness of the throw-weight advantage, the difficulty of persuading the Soviets to give up their sole advantage, and the problems of designing a SIOP for multiple targets.

The START proposal—very much one-sided—asked each side to reduce its warheads and launchers by two-thirds (Newhouse 1989, 345). This would have effectively cut into Soviet strategic muscle while leaving the United States with an advantage in bombers and submarines, as well as sparing the MX and other new systems waiting in the wings.

Reagan used the compromise paper to craft a speech for delivery at Eureka College on May 9, 1982. Innocent of its implications for the Soviets, Reagan would have to alter the START position a little more than a year later to gain congressional support for the MX (Cannon 1991, 305). A month earlier Haig had rejected the freeze proposal as perpetuating "an unstable and unequal military balance," saying, "It would reward a decade of unilateral Soviet buildup and penalize the United States for a decade of unilateral restraint" (in Newhouse 1989, 346). For its part, the Soviet Union responded with an equally one-sided counterproposal: "Washington and Moscow were returning to an earlier period when what passed for arms control was played to the galleries, with propaganda advantage the priority goal" (Newhouse 1989, 351). This circular war of propaganda fed Reagan's suspicions that the Soviets were not interested in negotiation, a conclusion favored by the confrontationalists, who benefited by the continued stalemate (Cannon 1991, 308).

### *Media Coverage: Separating the Movement from the Public*

Seriously flawed, START nevertheless altered the news media's perceptions of administration policy and the movement. After the Eureka speech the media began to distinguish between the movement and the general public, despite continued high levels of support shown in opinion polls. As the issue was loosened from the moral gravity of popular sovereignty, it moved onto the arcane grounds of nuclear technology and strategy. Here ordinary citizens and even presumably sophisticated journalists could not discern the hidden political implications of ostensibly technically grounded (and therefore incontestable) arguments. Detached by the media from the sources of its political strength, the movement became susceptible to a futility attack.

The *New York Times* headlined its story on START "Reagan Asks U.S.-Soviet Cut of 1 in 3 Nuclear Warheads as Step to an 'Equal Ceiling.'" The report acknowledged that the Eureka proposal would be more costly for the Soviet Union because of its greater dependence on land-based missiles, but the thrust of an accompanying analysis characterized Reagan's remarks as generally firm but conciliatory and the proposal as "sharply reducing each side's strategic arsenals" (*NYT,* May 10, 1982, p. 1). In fact, START would have required the Soviet Union to cut about half of its ICBM warheads and two-thirds of its SS-18s and SS-19s, while it permitted an increase in U.S. ICBM warheads and left off the table U.S. plans for deploying two hundred MX missiles and modernizing other strategic forces. Raymond Garthoff, a Soviet scholar and member of the diplomatic team that negotiated SALT I, summarized the net effect of the Eureka proposal for the Soviets: "Overall, while the proposal would have alleviated the vulnerability of American land-based intercontinental missiles, it would have greatly increased the vulnerability of Soviet land-based missiles. As a Soviet general remarked to me in 1983, 'You [the United States] want to solve your vulnerability problem by making our forces vulnerable.' And he was right" (Garthoff 1985, 1025–26).

A "disappointed" Senator Edward Kennedy accused Reagan of hiding his intent to build a new generation of weapons. But because neither the reporter nor someone from the arms control community offered supporting evidence (which presumably would have exposed the one-sidedness of the proposal), Kennedy's rebuttal, though correct, appeared as conventionally partisan.

The next day a more sobering analysis by Leslie Gelb asserted the Eureka proposal would be hard to negotiate. The problem was that the Soviets would be asked to trade their current advantage in land-based missiles for an American concession in the future (not building the MX and Trident II). Gelb's analysis traced the outlines of the difficulty for the Soviets, who would have been expected to eliminate twice as many missiles to make up for the danger they posed to American missiles. A second phase would deal with the issue of equalizing throw-weight, a concession intended to "mollify" Weinberger. Other problems centered on the nature of cruise missiles (how to verify which were nuclear), ways of counting them (how many warheads they carried or what the CIA believed they could carry), and the overall issue of inspection. Exaggerating costs to the American side, Robert McFarlane concluded, "Everything is on the table and Moscow's leaders have to make some tough choices and so do we" (*NYT,* May 11, 1982, p. 1). These two analyses produced the impression that although the START proposal seemed tough, it was a proposal nonetheless and welcome for that reason. Gelb's analysis came closest to discerning the nonnegotiable nature of START but stopped short of that conclusion.

In fact, hardly anyone on the *New York Times* editorial staff could make sense of the varieties of weapons and their offsetting qualities so as to discern the hidden intent of START. An editorial following the speech praised Reagan for restraining the arms race even as it chided Senator Edmund Muskie for "missing the mark" in his accusations that the proposal was a secret agenda for sidetracking disarmament (*NYT,* May 11, 1982, p. 18).[5] Anthony Lewis similarly praised Reagan's change in rhetoric and his "realism" in forgoing arms control until a military buildup was in place (*NYT,* May 13, 1982, p. 27). Flora Lewis commended Reagan for his change of heart and credited the debate in the House and the nation for producing it, though she recommended the debate avoid the "details," leaving these to the negotiators (*NYT,* May 13, 1982, p. 27). Tom Wicker saw the proposal as the "death knell" for the MX, assuming it was to be used as a bargaining chip to induce the Soviets to dismantle their land-based missiles (*NYT,* May 14, 1982, p. 31). William Safire was the only one on staff who detected the win-win position of the White House—the proposal reduced the immediate political pressure and increased the chances of a Soviet rejection that would allow the United States to strengthen its position before returning to the negotiating table (*NYT,* May 14, 1982, p. 31).

Unlike the *New York Times*'s labored and opaque analysis, television coverage of the speech came to a comparatively sharp focus. On Sunday, May 9, 1982, CBS reported Reagan's Eureka proposal to give up on SALT and begin START. "Officials" acknowledged the Soviet Union was being asked to give up more of its present strength than was the United States, but, the report maintained, there was something in it for both sides, "and if it seems tough, remember that it is a negotiating position." The Democrats responded through Edmund Muskie, who pointed out that Reagan had proposed a reduction of a class of weapons on which the Soviets were most dependent, that the United States was being asked to give up less from its balanced triad, and that the proposal was a secret agenda for sidetracking disarmament while the United States got on with rearmament in a "hopeless" quest for superiority (*CBS Evening News*, May 9, 1982).

This first clear statement of the proposal's hidden implications (albeit delivered by a partisan critic) contrasted with the Leslie Gelb analysis, in which START's political intent was discernible only to individuals sufficiently knowledgeable and motivated to understand the varieties of warheads and delivery vehicles on each side, the different counting systems used to make the estimates, and the significance of the land-based missile system to the Soviet Union. The superficial thrust of Gelb's analysis was that negotiations would be "difficult"; the deeper message was that only experts could make sense of it. In the CBS report the message needed to be simple because the structure of television news limited the time in which to make it. In this case, simplicity provided a clearer statement of the truth.

One possible reason for this clarity, identified by Neuman, Just, and Crigler (1992, 53–55), is the propensity for television news to use techniques of framing, identifying problems and solutions and making moral evaluations so as to make stories easier to understand within the constraints imposed by time. Newspaper reporting, by contrast, is more likely to focus on factual presentation, which examples such as these have shown to be less likely to clarify extremely complex issues. This is confirmed by Neuman, Just, and Crigler's research, which shows that television news has a clear advantage over print media for conveying information on technical issues such as SDI. As they point out, "Abstract, distant, or more difficult issues seem to be more daunting in print than on television" (ibid., 86–87, 89). Notwithstanding its advantage on these technical issues, television is no more immune than other media to constraints on journalistic practice.

I interviewed Bruce Morton, the principal CBS reporter assigned to the freeze, and asked him about his coverage of the movement. The passage of fifteen years had understandably fogged his recollection of many of details, but he spontaneously volunteered that START changed the terms of the debate: "After all, Reagan was proposing a reduction. Surely that was more significant than a freeze."[6] Morton also said that sustained attention to such issues as the window of vulnerability is less likely in such contexts because of the absence of "news pegs," convenient newsworthy opportunities for fixing sustained attention on an issue. These occur regularly in the course of an electoral campaign, Morton said, but did not do so during the movement.

Despite the difference in reporting styles, the administration's START proposal marked a change in both media sources' coverage of the movement. The first sign of this was their reinterpretation of public support for it.

*Public Opinion* — START altered the *New York Times*'s coverage of the movement. A front-page analysis of increasing citizen activism (in reaction to Reagan cutbacks in social programs) included this passing comment on the significance of the freeze: "Political analysts generally agree that President Reagan's recent decision to negotiate on arms reductions with the Soviet Union without preconditions resulted in large part from the political strength exhibited by the antinuclear movement" (*NYT*, May 16, 1982, 1). The movement had, in other words, passed the test set out a month earlier by the arms controllers. Insistence on its own proposal would now represent an impediment to responsible arms control.

Two weeks later the paper reported the results of a poll that showed overwhelming but now qualified support for the freeze. Headlined "72% in Poll Back Nuclear Halt If Soviet Union Doesn't Gain," the front-page story reported that the success of the freeze hinged on whose version of Soviet strength the public believed. Responding to this claim, a White House official declared the issue as "very much up for grabs" (*NYT*, May 30, 1982, p. 1). Yet comparative Soviet strength was not a material issue for the freeze campaign or for public opinion reported only a month earlier, when Hedrick Smith had interpreted public opinion as favoring arms control *despite* an ostensible arms lead by the Soviets. Now the *Times* interpreted public opinion as favoring the freeze *only* if the Soviets did not gain by it, an oblique reference to the window of vulnerability and an indication that its flawed assumptions had been imported into public discourse.

Ten days before reporting the same poll, CBS broadcast an unusual analysis of the Reagan administration's case against the freeze. Unusual for its use of the news anchor—Dan Rather—the analysis was supported by ostensibly disinterested expertise offered by Herman Kahn, a senior fellow at the Hudson Institute, a conservative think tank.[7] Rather began by explaining the theory of the window of vulnerability. An animated sequence showed Soviet missiles arcing from their launch pads into U.S. Titan and Minuteman missiles silos, a "nuclear age Pearl Harbor." Rather: "Many experts believe the Soviets have built up enough advantages to pull off such a crippling first strike." Kahn: "They have significant kinds of advantages, not enough to make me lose sleep at night, but if one is President, it would be totally irresponsible to depend on Soviet caution and prudence." Rather continued that the answer to the threat was to counter with a massive military buildup: MX, B1, Trident II, cruise, and Pershing II missiles.

Rather asked Kahn whether the United States really needed to build the weapons or whether the threat to build them could be used to bolster its bargaining position. Kahn responded: "I think that's a weak argument. Russians won't let you trade programs for dismantling." "That means," Rather continued, "that we have to put muscle behind our words, the total estimated price tag—more than seventy-five billion dollars. Can we afford them?" Kahn: "If we feel that our lives are being threatened sufficiently, we can rearrange our expenses." Rather: "If we freeze now, there is no way to catch up, no way to ease the nightmare of a Russian first strike. If we keep nuclear weapons at the present level, there is no incentive for either side to negotiate reductions" (*CBS Evening News,* May 20, 1982). The best case against the freeze, once again accepting as fact the window of vulnerability, and unopposed by other experts, was made by the most credible news sources, a television commentator and an expert (see Page, Shapiro, and Dempsey 1990).

Less than two weeks later, CBS ran a story on the poll reported in the *New York Times.* Just a few months earlier, CBS commentators had reported a groundswell of support, but now Bruce Morton revealed that a poll showed "very wide but very shallow" support for the freeze. Though 72 percent were in favor, the numbers changed as soon as qualifications were added. For example, if the freeze gave the Soviets greater strength, support for the freeze dropped to 30 percent. Similarly, support dropped to 17 percent if either the United States or the Soviet Union could cheat on it. On the question of whether a buildup or freeze was more dangerous, 49 percent regarded a buildup as more dangerous. Morton concluded, "The public doesn't seem to know much about the issue." Only 30 percent knew Reagan's position, and 59 percent believed it was too complicated for ordinary citizens to understand (*CBS Evening News,* May 29, 1982).

This confusing analysis of public opinion embodies a number of contradictions and indicates that the administration's plan to obfuscate its true arms control strategy was working. The first point—that support dropped if the Soviets had an advantage—was relevant only given information that the media had failed to establish through credible sources. Moreover, only

Kennedy and Muskie had clarified the significance of START as cutting into the muscle of Soviet strategic forces and thus its role as a smokescreen for obstructing arms control. Their assertions, however, could have been construed as partisan, for they represented conventional political opposition rather than disinterested expertise. After all, a month earlier the briefing detailing the USSR's war footing had affirmed Soviet gains, and the Rather-Kahn report provided seemingly disinterested support for the window of vulnerability; thus the movement now jeopardized U.S. security.

Support for the freeze remained shallow in large part because of an absence of information and highly partisan cases argued under the guise of "expert analysis." Thus it was not at all unreasonable for citizens to feel the issue was too complex to understand; in fact, the public did lack information sufficient to form an informed opinion, whether for or against the measure. Indeed, even the highly informed editorial staff at the *New York Times* could scarcely understand the implications of an arms control proposal characterized by the secretary of defense as "a nonnegotiable package . . . a two-faced proposal which was clearly going to fall of its own weight and did" (in Garthoff 1985, 1025). Only a handful of administration figures and the arms control community understood its implications. Despite all this, the public supported negotiations over an arms buildup. With expert support absent for what was largely a technical issue, the popular movement became increasingly vulnerable politically. Evidence for this comes from news coverage of the New York City freeze demonstration, the largest political gathering in U.S. history.

*The New York Demonstration* — On the surface *New York Times* coverage of the New York City demonstration seems impressive (nearly four times the usual coverage of a major story), but only a small fraction of it (about 15 percent) focused on the central political message voiced by the rally's speakers. The remainder, including the front-page story, dwelled on descriptions of the participants, both the bizarre and the ordinary—with repeated references to the sixties—and the logistics of crowd movement, thus disembodying the demonstration from its political purpose (Gitlin 1980).

A short boxed story summarizing the results of the poll reported two weeks earlier accompanied the spread of pictures and articles. It said that although the public favored the freeze, its support depended on the Soviets' not gaining by it: "The survey found the public greatly concerned about giving the Soviet Union a military advantage and easily swayed in favor of or against a freeze depending on the conditions surrounding it" (*NYT*,

June 13, 1982, p. 43). The burden had shifted to public judgment, which remained ill-equipped factually to judge which side was ahead.

One might argue that New York reporting would rightfully focus on logistics as at issue was a local event with implications for snarled traffic in a highly congested area. To see whether papers outside New York emphasized this issue less, I also looked at coverage in the *Washington Post*. The *Post* account did spend less space on logistics but repeated many of the themes found in the *Times*. The lead fairly represents these: "Led by a bearded flutist, in a buoyant atmosphere of balloons, banners and anti-nuclear chants, an estimated 550,000 protesters gathered here today in the nation's largest disarmament rally and one of the biggest demonstrations in U.S. history." The account did not address the proposal itself but noted the rally had brought together groups with "widely different proposals for slowing down the arms race." What united them was not the freeze proposal but a general fear of a nuclear holocaust.[8] Much of the account sorted out the participants—ordinary people as well as veterans of the sixties (but less bitter). Indeed, the absence of bitterness moved the writers to liken the demonstration to a "crafts fair or even a carnival midway." There were passing references to the political implications of the nation's "largest disarmament rally"; sympathetic members of congress characterized it as "overwhelming" and bearing "real clout." The last word, however, went to Weinberger, who assessed the demonstration's political significance: "I don't think that anybody rushes back and says, 'We have to change policy' . . . or something because there's been a rally" (*Washington Post*, June 13, 983, p. 1).

CBS covered the New York City demonstration in much the same way: "The largest anti-nuclear protest in U.S. history included famous rock stars, politicians, and hundreds of thousands of lesser lights." Bruce Morton's report began on a familiar note: "Children led them, puppets followed." The crowd was mostly American, in their twenties and thirties, and mostly white, and it included many "veterans" of the sixties antiwar movement. The piece used a familiar formula, released balloons (symbols of the weapons "they want to get rid of") and a sunny, placid mood. Two soundbites followed, one from a victim of Hiroshima ("no more Hiroshimas") and one from Helen Caldicott: "There are no capitalist babies, no communist babies: a baby is a baby is a baby."

Morton characterized the rally as a big success but raised the political bar by asking where the movement would go from there. Morton noted that Reagan did not support the freeze: "So the question is, will the freeze, which has grown quickly, be able to move from rallies to the tough politics necessary to change his mind?" (*CBS Evening News*, June 12, 1982). By detaching the movement from national sentiment, such reports rendered it an interest group with a political agenda no more worthy than any other.

After the anchor's mention of an Ann Landers column on the horrors of nuclear war (of which several thousand copies arrived in the White House), the next brief story described how ten of eleven members of the Soviet Union's only peace movement had been arrested for violating a 1930 law banning the organizing of clubs. The contrasting story on the arrested protesters highlighted the absence of a democratic brake on the Soviet government and thus supported Reagan's argument that the freeze would only encourage the Soviets to hold out for the gains the American protesters would deliver them.

The variety of themes of futility underlined a major change in the way the news media regarded the movement, which they viewed initially as a spontaneous impulse from the American public as a whole and later as an interest group led by veterans of the sixties. Denied the opportunity to defend the merits of its proposal and thus to reinforce the basis of its support, the movement lay open to the vagaries of political opportunism.

*Congress* — In early August the House rejected the Kennedy-Hatfield freeze resolution by a two-vote margin. Again, the *New York Times* indicated that the line of division cut through the issue of strategic arms advantages; support for the freeze would depend on whose version one believed. In an accompanying news analysis, both sides laid claim to victory. Freeze supporters said that Reagan had to spend valuable political capital defending his position and that the movement—now bent on direct political action—had developed a "hit list" of the 204 representatives who had voted against the measure and were vulnerable to strong opponents. A State Department official assessed the significance of the vote's risk-free nature: "All of these guys are up for re-election in November, and they could have considered a vote for a nuclear freeze a safe political bet" (*NYT*, August 7, 1982, p. 2).[9]

Indeed, two months later an article on the significance of the issue for Senate and House races revealed that few votes would be determined by the incumbent's position on the freeze (*NYT*, October 19, 1982, p. 18). Because the movement had failed to redefine the issue of public support for the freeze—permitting opponents to draw attention to the technical issue of military balance—public opinion remained vulnerable to competing interpretations (the article repeated the May poll results). Straining for nonpartisanship, the movement had made another strategic error by failing to endorse Democratic candidates. This move, coupled to Republican support of movement offshoots such as Ground Zero, had so thoroughly clouded the issue that nether movement leaders nor citizens could discern supporters from opponents.

Following the New York demonstration, media coverage dropped off, despite the movement's success in state-sponsored freeze referenda. These had won majority support in all but one state and in numerous cities. Nevertheless, although a front-page *Times* analysis by Adam Clymer on the "lessons" of the election assessed these victories as revealing "widespread concern on the arms control issue that stands a reasonable chance of becoming an important part of the 1984 Presidential campaign," he added that, with "only a couple of exceptions . . . neither this nor any other issue of foreign or military policy mattered in electing candidates in 1982" (*NYT,* November 4, 1982, p. 1).

CBS spent little time on the House debate on the freeze resolution. Instead, that summer and fall the issue wove through its coverage of the Democratic presidential race and various state referenda. At the Democratic midterm convention, a panel supported the "idea" of a freeze but fuzzed the language so that any number of policies (e.g., ratification of SALT II or merely talking about arms reduction) could be favored. (Les Aspin, a key figure in the MX debate, helped to blur the resolution's meaning [see Drew 1983, 49].)

The ambiguity helped to promote the party's tough-mindedness as it strove to shed a "peacenik image." As Democratic presidential aspirant Senator Gary Hart declared, "We're Americans; we care as much about defense as anyone else" (*CBS Evening News,* June 26, 1982). Because the movement had not aligned itself with the Democrats, it had little political leverage on their platform. Democrats and Republicans tried to have it both ways, simultaneously advocating both peace and defense. By not providing any sustained examination of the Reagan arms control package or illuminating the issues driving arms control in general, television news contributed to making the freeze an apple-pie-and-mom issue, easy to support but difficult to argue meaningfully within the complicated parameters set in motion by the technical nature of Forsberg's proposal.

Television news traced the freeze referenda through statewide fall elections. In mid-September it reported on the Wisconsin primary, which included the first such referendum on the nuclear freeze. Once again, children played a prominent role in the coverage. Over an image of several boys swinging languidly from a tree, a reporter asked, "To freeze or not to freeze," to which a boy of about ten responded: "Nobody wins if you drop a bomb on one side. They're just going to come back and drop one on your side." The increasing prominence of children in these reports as movement spokespersons suggested a linkage with naïveté and symbolic politics (Edelman 1988). Its principal ideas overtaken and claimed by others, the movement had devolved into a child's innocence, its principal motivation becoming fear.

Although television had earlier established the elections as an important test of the freeze, coverage of its successes was modest—twenty seconds in the middle of a newscast in which the anchor mentioned that the freeze movement had made a successful transition from the streets to the polls: it had scored a "near clean sweep" in eight of nine states, with only Arizona turning it down (*CBS Evening News,* November 3, 1982). Reinforcing Morton's assessment after New York City, the brief mention indicated that television news no longer considered the movement a noteworthy political force, despite its having achieved the criterion of success set out for it earlier.

In summary, the freeze movement achieved its greatest prominence just as the Reagan administration offered its START proposal. Despite this proposal's one-sidedness and goal of derailing the freeze movement, the *New York Times* found much to like about it. START signaled that the movement had done its job of stimulating an arms control proposal. Less than four months had elapsed from media characterizations of the movement as earnest, serious, and high-minded to depictions of it as irrelevant and even intrusive.

Television coverage of the freeze changed character as well, exaggerating the shift in the *Times,* which spent some time considering some of the nuances, if not the intent, of the Reagan arms control proposal. CBS provided some critical exposure of START by airing Muskie's remarks on the program as a way of sidetracking disarmament, but the report noted the partisan quality of his analysis owing to his status as "Democratic spokesman." Much more important was the one-sided, cartoonish depiction of the Soviet threat delivered by a long-time proponent of a war-fighting nuclear strategy but not identified as such and thus enjoying the prestige of nonpartisan expertise. Significantly, the news anchor himself presented the administration's case for the window of vulnerability as established fact rather than contested theory. Soon afterward the news interpreted the results of the CBS-*New York Times* poll through the assumptive framework of the window of vulnerability. Coverage of the New York demonstration extended the frame established early on, concentrating on the festivities surrounding the events and not the central message of the movement. Meanwhile images of the participants as "mainstream and white" converted the apparent asset of large numbers into the liability of skewed demographics. The repeated references to the sixties ran counter to the assessment of the demonstrators as mainstream, however. As evidence of the effects of these themes, a poll taken in early June 1982 revealed that 50 percent of the public believed that "protesters from the past" made up the movement, while 38 percent believed it to be a grass-roots movement. By December 1982 the numbers had shifted to 55 and 32 percent, respectively (Hogan and Smith 1991, 569).

## The MX and Star Wars, April–September 1983

Reagan's START speech at Eureka college provided a holding position until the administration could build congressional support for an arms buildup. As evidence of its success, that August the House amended and thereby rendered meaningless a resolution to freeze the deployment and manufacture of nuclear weapons (the amendment called for substantial reductions in nuclear arms before a freeze). The Republican-controlled Senate never considered it. Meanwhile, at the Geneva talks the problems with the Eureka proposals soon surfaced, making it clear that they were unnegotiable. Edward Rowny, the principal U.S. negotiator at Geneva, spent much of the year lecturing and staging walkouts as part of his attempt to "turn the tables on the Soviets," payback for what he considered their past excesses (Talbott 1985, 285). By year's end talks had stalled, leaving the administration in a poor public relations position with Congress, which grew increasingly skeptical of the MX.

The missile had come under mounting criticism for its expense and a curious sequence of basing schemes required to protect it from a Soviet strike. To understand the significance of these, recall that it constituted a response to a perceived first-strike threat to the Minuteman—the window of vulnerability. A variety of basing arrangements had been proposed to make the MX immune to attack, including moving it around in trucks, railroad cars, and planes; concealing it in a maze of tunnels; and even hanging it from a dirigible. Each was rejected, either for its expense or unacceptability to those who would have to live next door to the missiles. The latest scheme—Dense-Pack—would arrange the proposed 100 MXs within a comparatively small area. The initial incoming Soviet missiles would create shock waves that would destroy any following missiles in an orgy of "fratricide," leaving half the MXs to retaliate and thus eliminating the window of vulnerability. Skeptics called the scheme "dunce-pack."

In the face of this controversy and the growing peace movements in the

United States and abroad, the House rejected MX funding in December 1982, despite Reagan's insistence on the missile's value as a bargaining chip and its necessity should START fail. In January 1983 Reagan asked national security adviser Robert McFarlane to develop a strategy to build support for the MX. McFarlane appointed Brent Scowcroft, national security adviser under Gerald Ford, to head the President's Commission on Strategic Forces. The commission's task was not to assess the strategic value of the MX but to fashion a proposal that would garner congressional support. Accordingly McFarlane appointed a number of former NSC staff members and SALT negotiators, including Henry Kissinger. These individuals gained credibility not only though their outsider status but also by being associated with SALT, which Reagan had regarded as one of the major causes for the window of vulnerability (Drew 1983, 46). The effort set in motion a chain of events that would lead to the Strategic Defense Initiative, Reagan's ideal solution to what he regarded as the fundamental immorality of deterrence theory (Cannon 1991, 323).

On April 11, 1983, the commission issued a report that gave lukewarm approval to the MX. To finesse the basing problems, the commission recommended replacing fifty Minuteman missiles with the MX, basing it in the vacated silos—those presumably vulnerable to Soviet attack. This effectively undermined the main argument for building up U.S. strategic weapons in the first place. Despite the absence of theoretical support, the Scowcroft commission report provided the cover congressional supporters needed to approve the MX. If the window of vulnerability had existed, the scheme for deploying the MX would actually have widened it at a cost of nearly $15 billion by the time Reagan left office, with more than $8 billion needed to complete the task (Cannon 1991, 170). That fall the United States began to deploy Pershing II and Tomahawk cruise missiles in England, prompting Soviet negotiators to walk out of the stalled Geneva talks. The dual-track strategy for arms control had become a dual-track military buildup.

The political campaign to finance the MX accompanied a parallel effort to develop an alternative to nuclear deterrence itself. Unlike many in the administration, McFarlane preferred the incrementalist philosophy of traditional arms control. Part of the game plan for successful negotiation included bargaining away a plausible-sounding technological advance that frightened an opponent. McFarlane knew the Soviets feared space-based nuclear weapons systems, so he began to explore their technological feasibility with scientists such as Edward Teller and their strategic military value with the Joint Chiefs of Staff. Teller proposed some fanciful ideas, including X-ray lasers that would destroy Soviet missiles as they emerged from their silos, and the chiefs worked up a briefing paper for Reagan that outlined a general plan for a defense against strategic weapons. According to Lou Cannon, the plan delighted Reagan, who had been captivated by the idea of a biblical Armageddon in its modern guise as nuclear holocaust and who was personally determined to leave in his legacy of distinctive accomplishments the elimination of the concept of mutually assured destruction.

The briefing paper issued by the Joint Chiefs of Staff did not represent a technical blueprint for the design of such a system—far from it. Its only significance was that the chiefs had for the first time endorsed a strategy that represented (for Reagan) a middle ground between the two morally abhorrent positions of a preemptive U.S. strike on the Soviet Union or the American absorption of a Soviet strike. Not sufficiently discouraged by aides who knew that such a system remained at best a hope rather than a realistically achievable technological breakthrough, Reagan could not wait to announce it. On March 23, 1983, at the end of a planned speech on the defense budget, he surprised the nation (and most of his staff and conservative backers) with his proposal for a massive program of scientific research to develop the technology that would release the earth from nuclear terror: "I call upon the scientific community in our country, those who gave us nuclear weapons, to turn their great talents now to the cause of mankind and world peace, to give us the means of rendering these nuclear weapons impotent and obsolete" (in Cannon 1991, 332).

Reagan's hope for such a solution flew in the face of scientific plausibility, but it supported a $17 billion program that has yet to develop even a rudimentary missile defense. Nevertheless, its formidable moral appeal would further dull the luster of the freeze movement's proposal.

Sherry argues that SDI also restored American faith in the redemptive value of technology and realigned conservative and liberal opinion on the value of nuclear arms. By offering to share SDI with the Soviets, Reagan at a stroke converted conservative distaste from the Soviet Union to nuclear weapons themselves as he simultaneously embraced the liberal utopian vision of the elimination of the nuclear threat (Sherry 1995, 407–8). One indication of Reagan's success at diverting attention from the freeze is that by April 1983, attendance at antinuclear demonstrations had declined and the number of magazine articles written about nuclear weapons had dropped significantly. Weart calculates that by 1986, magazine articles on missile defense exceeded those written on nuclear winter, nuclear testing, and other fearful aspects of the subject. As important as SDI was for diverting public attention, however, the government continued to build nuclear weapons at an undiminished pace: "The European movement similarly withered when it became clear that its drive to block new missiles was a failure" (Weart 1988, 386).

### *Media Coverage: The Loss of Moral Authority*

During this period the movement's loss of control over its political message proved fatal as its moral authority collapsed. Had its leadership been more politically astute, the movement might have been better able to take advantage of the situation presented in late winter of 1983 when the Geneva talks stalled and public support for the arms buildup began to decrease. To a considerable degree, the movement could have taken credit for this decline.

In early February 1983 the *New York Times* reported a poll on defense spending that showed a growing number of Americans no longer believed the United States to lag behind Soviet Union military prowess. Only 11 percent said that more money should be spent on new weapons; a quarter said spending levels were about right, while half believed that the United States spent too much. Despite Congress's failure to approve the MX, the public believed the military standing of the United States had improved vis-à-vis the Soviet Union: a year earlier 44 percent believed that the United States trailed the Soviet Union; now less than a third believed this. The *Times* attributed this change not to the efforts of the freeze movement, however, but to the state of the economy, dragged down by federal deficits and high unemployment. A number of officials and citizens quoted in the poll story opposed "throwing money" at military problems the way money was thrown at social problems in the sixties and seventies (*NYT,* February 6, 1983, p. 1).

Both the administration and the freeze needed a public relations boost. In fact, the day following the poll results, a story in the *Times* described the leaders of the freeze movement plotting a "more political approach." The story's placement on an interior page indicates the movement's waning influence, with "many political analysts" judging that the movement had peaked, despite its success in the November referenda.

The *Times* here characterized discussion among freeze organizers as internal division and weakness and provided indirect corroboration of the unilateralism charged by the freeze's opponents. That this characterization took place after the movement's success at the polls seems paradoxical. As I have shown, the administration itself was and continued to be deeply divided on its approach to arms control negotiation. The *Times* portrayed the obstructionist proposal of START—itself the result of the deep division—as conciliatory, whereas it dismissed the freeze as a simplistic slogan. (The *Times* opposed the referenda in an editorial, calling the idea a "simplistic, sloganeering response to a complex issue" [*NYT,* October 24, 1982, sec. 4, p. 20].)

Television coverage, meanwhile, continued to focus on the futility of movement action. Bruce Morton began a report on a movement conference with a visual of a folksinger strumming a guitar and the comment that "on the surface the movement had lots to sing about," yet as Forsberg admitted, there had been no slackening in the production of nuclear weapons. Morton repeated his earlier diagnosis that the movement continued to be middle class and white, the result of its failing to reach out to Hispanics or blacks.

In fact, the movement for the test ban had been equally white and middle class (as had previous peace movements). What had changed was perhaps an unintended consequence of the New Left movement of the sixties and the reporter's implicit assumption that the freeze was an echo of it. Because social justice had been a major plank in the New Left's program, that movement had set a standard for widened political participation among a broader social spectrum of Americans. The freeze had been called to task for its failure to satisfy a normative standard that, although perhaps symbolically important, was politically irrelevant. In other words, the news had hoist the freeze on the New Left's petard.

A second problem, according to Morton, was that the freeze movement had little labor support (Lane Kirkland, president of the AFL-CIO, had been a member of the CPD, a fact not mentioned in the report). Morton also devalued the November referenda. Once seen as an important criterion of success, they were now characterized as "beauty contests" with little effect on congressional elections (*CBS Evening News,* February 7, 1983).

Such was the weakened position of the movement that the *New York Times* noted House passage of the freeze resolution in May 1983 not as a movement success but as a symbol: both supporters and opponents claimed victory, and the amended version of the resolution had captured the essence of the Reagan position—reductions of weapons first before imposition of a ceiling. Republican House leader Robert Michel termed the adoption of the amendment "a victory unthinkable only weeks ago." Tip O'Neill also claimed victory, saying the freeze nevertheless remained a first priority. The freeze faced an uncertain future, however: Republicans dominated the Senate, and "'if it ever gets to the President's desk, it's going to be vetoed,' said Representative William Carney, Republican of Suffolk, L.I." (*NYT,* May 5, 1983, p. 1).

An accompanying analysis (in the paper's B section), while crediting the freeze movement with expanding the scope of debate, said the resolution remained symbolic: "The freeze movement, born of quiet concerns about the arms race, took form in church, school and other local groups. Even now, with the phrase 'nuclear freeze' part of the political lexicon, the movement remains an inchoate mass. While arms experts sort out the nuances of the resolution, politicians are viewing the last few months' debate as an expression of public anxiety about the arms race" (*NYT,* May 5, 1983, sec. B, p. 6).

Les Aspin, who voted for the resolution and two months later managed House approval of the MX, said the resolution "was never going to pass and be signed by the President, and in that sense many people thought it was not a serious piece of legislation. Yes, this was a symbolic vote, and, yes, it is a vote on the President's arms-negotiating stance. But you could make a pretty good case that the White House is not immune to those sort of things. If it weren't for the people and freeze movements, the White House wouldn't be negotiating now" (ibid.). Aspin had served on the Scowcroft commission, managing Democratic support for the MX. He had arranged the legislative agenda such that a freeze vote would come shortly before a vote on the MX, smoothing its passage as he predicted that Congress would be reluctant to vote three times to pass "pacifist issues" (Drew 1983). With its political power diminished by the media's shifting criteria of success and congressional logrolling, the movement's most important source of authority would come under attack next.

*Moral Politics and Self-Interest* — In early May 1983 the Catholic bishops as a body issued a pastoral letter that denounced the use of nuclear weapons and endorsed the freeze.[10] The political significance of the letter rested on two points: its language closely paralleled the text of the freeze resolution before Congress, and the bishops would disseminate it in every parish as a teaching resource. Although the letter did not have the authority of church doctrine, it nevertheless had the potential for influencing opinion among roughly a quarter of the nation's population.

Contemplating potential erosion of support for a military buildup, administration officials lobbied the bishops to moderate the letter, in one case, for example, asking them to change one sentence from "halting" the development of weapons to "curbing" them. Declaring themselves pastors, not politicians, the bishops voted overwhelmingly in favor of the more strongly worded version. The *New York Times* provided prominent and friendly coverage, placing the story of the bishops' letter on the front page twice in one week and quoting large portions of the declaration. One such story was accompanied with this comment: "The bishops take a forceful and historic position in their letter, breaking some new ground in church thinking and assuming a leadership role in the effort for disarmament. Many of the 50 million Catholics in the United States consider the bishops' action to be the boldest and most decisive step on social issues in the history of the American hierarchy. It caused the White House great concern and efforts were made to modify drafts" (*NYT,* May 4, 1983, p. 1).

A follow-up article charted the reactions of Catholics to the bishops' letter. Far from drawing on a random sample of Catholics from across the country, however, a *Times* reporter had gone to a parish in Preston, Connecticut, home to Electric Boat's facility for manufacturing nuclear submarines, where he joined a dozen parishioners who had gathered after mass to discuss the letter. Some worked in the boatyard and were understandably divided on the issue. An engineer raised the issue of Soviet atheism: "I don't think they care what God's words are. They've got to listen to something that's meaningful to them—our deterrent force." Another said the stigma of working for the movement had been removed. On the larger question of whether it was a mortal sin to work on the Trident missile, the local bishop observed that the pastoral letter said only that it was a matter of conscience (*NYT,* May 9, 1983, p. 1).

By converting a symbolic moral burden into a practical one and applying it to those least capable of bearing it as a practical matter, the *New York Times* made the bishop's call seem onerous indeed. This transformation in turn constituted an unfair test of the freeze. Questioning its moral force in this context was somewhat like testing the authority of a church prohibition against theft by asking a group of people whether they would steal bread to feed their hungry children. The *Times* had not applied such a test to House members who had first voted for the freeze and then the MX, nor had it judged the quality of elected officials' work based on the consistency of their actions.

The paper took a similar tack a week later in a more secular setting. Several House members who had voted for the freeze resolution were now lobbying the Defense Department to "woo" the nuclear fleet into northeastern ports, even though it would be carrying nuclear-tipped cruise missiles, the most destabilizing element in U.S. strategic forces. The motive again was self-interest, this time jobs to relieve blue-collar unemployment:

> Alan Sagner, chairman of the Port Authority, is also general chairman of the New Jersey Campaign for a Nuclear Weapons Freeze; last November, a nuclear freeze referendum in New Jersey carried the state by 66 percent. "I don't see any inconsistency as chairman of the Port Authority in doing everything we possibly can to get the fleet home-ported here and our efforts for a nuclear freeze. If there's a nuclear exchange, they're not going to go for three or four battleships in New York or Boston. Anything that we can do to reverse the trend, to start building the port back up, is very important from an economic point of view and from a symbolic point of view. It feeds on itself." (*NYT,* May 14, 1983, p. 1)

Television news had questioned the moral integrity of the Catholic bishops from the start of their campaign. In a story aired on April 8, 1982—at the height of movement influence—Bruce Morton led a story on Catholic activism with the question, "Are priests becoming too political?" He contrasted cold war support offered by Cardinal Fulton Sheen a generation earlier ("nuclear war may be justified") with several contemporary bishops who considered it morally wrong and recommended against working in nuclear factories and withholding tax payments. Reflecting on this change, Morton asked rhetorically, "Is the church being radicalized?" A reporter for a Catholic newspaper mentioned that the church had taken on a broad range of social issues—including civil rights—and opposed right-wing rule in El Salvador. Morton detected confusion among Catholics perplexed by the seeming ideological inconsistency of church's rigidity on celibacy and the role of women in the church. He concluded that fifty million Catholics united would be a powerful force but questioned how many would follow (*CBS Evening News,* April 8, 1982). Like the *New York Times,* television news held nonpoliticians to a higher standard, questioning the integrity of a message that seemed inconsistent with liberal ideology and overlooking the bishops' role as moral teachers and the consistency of their message with their stand on abortion. Their stand on women's rights may have seemed inconsistent with liberal ideology but not with church doctrine.

The media's emerging view that the movement had lost its moral authority could be detected on the eve of its apparent political triumph in Congress. By this point television regarded the movement as merely an interest group, and not a particularly successful one at that. In March 1983 CBS reported the successful vote in a House committee in support of the freeze, in spite of administration lobbying efforts. The report began with a visual of a group of cheering freeze supporters standing on the Capitol steps. It then followed a lobbying freeze delegation into the office of an undecided representative from Connecticut. Repeating a theme from earlier coverage, a young girl urged a Republican congresswoman to vote for the resolution.

The theme of naïveté and futility carried through the report as Morton noted that since Reagan opposed the measure, its passage in the House would be meaningless, and anyway, the campaign so far had been symbolic: "This is really just a game. The freeze is a symbol. The genuine issue will come in votes on individual weapons. And the opposition there is not a rally. It is the defense lobbyists who last year gave six and a half million dollars to congressional candidates, a tactic the freeze movement did not employ."

To illustrate his point, Morton revealed that defense contractors had provided $1.1 million to members of the House Armed Services Committee and Defense Appropriations Subcommittee. Gordon Adams, a specialist and author on congressional defense politics, said the movement was out of its league in what he called the "iron triangle"—arms manufacturers, key members of Congress, and Defense Department offices—all of which were unified in their desire to support weapons systems the freeze would stop. The report then cut to the freeze rally with guitar-strumming singers on the Capitol steps. Morton conceded that the movement against the Vietnam War showed civilian amateurs could make a difference but then qualified that concession: "Of course, it also showed that it can take a long time as well" (*CBS Evening News,* March 8, 1983).

At first the news media had regarded the referenda as being important for demonstrating the power of the movement, implicitly vesting its authority in public opinion, which seemed indistinguishable from the movement itself. As the administration and then Congress resisted, however, standards of political efficacy shifted from the authority of majority opinion to the purchase of congressional access. Throughout Morton's world-weary reports, the dismissal of the movement's cause on its inability to compete in the "big leagues" and the implicit equating of the freeze movement with other interest groups diminished its strength by denying it access to the source of its greatest power: popular sovereignty over an issue that held the gravest consequences for the life of every citizen. What the *New York Times* had characterized a year earlier as an earnest attempt by "ordinary citizens" to put nuclear restraint on track had transmuted into an ineffectual attempt at interest-group politics.

*KAL 007 and the MX* — The movement suffered a loss of public support for arms control after a Soviet fighter shot down a Korean Boeing 747 airliner on September 1, 1983. By mid-September a Gallup poll revealed that half the public thought Reagan was "not tough enough" with the Soviets, an increase of 16 percent from the figures yielded by a poll conducted only a month earlier. The negative reaction to the Soviet Union—heavily promoted by Reagan (Sherry 1995) and the media (Entman 1991)—lowered Americans' estimation of the nation to a point not seen since the fifties (Gallup 1984, 219, 224, 227).

The Reagan administration made the most of this change in public sentiment as it successfully lobbied for a House vote to end a fifteen-year moratorium on the production of chemical weapons and approval of its military budget, the largest to date. A move by Democrats to delete $2 billion in production funds for the MX (research funds were not a target of the attempts at reduction) was also defeated.

That December CBS covered a conference at freeze headquarters. Bruce Morton reported the plans for a new campaign and opened with the by now predictable lead that the delegates had some things to "shout about"—the Vermont town meetings and state referenda, the big rally in New York, and the House vote for the freeze. On the negative side, however, the House had approved the MX, and freeze constituents continued to be overwhelmingly white and white collar. In a brief soundbite Randy Kehler said he wanted to broaden the campaign and to focus on political action committee (PAC) money. But, Morton reminded the audience, the 1984 Congress would be the same one that voted in the MX. Moreover, the freeze people would be outspent: in 1984 four profreeze PACs gave candidates $140,000, while a single defense contractor gave $200,000.[11] To compensate, the freeze would use people, a million volunteers for the coming election campaign. So far they had been amateurs, said Morton; could now they be effective pros? The report ended with an image of a mother and child, the visual cue that once again emphasized innocence and fecklessness (*CBS Evening News,* December 3, 1983).

In its last phase of movement coverage, television news returned to a familiar metaphor, the contest that this time pitted the movement against Congress. Accordingly, stories described the underfinanced and underorganized movement fighting against the rich and powerful defense industry PACs. Although this schema could have plausibly provided the raw material needed for a sympathetic account of a morally charged issue facing down cynical self-interest, the stories merely called attention to the movement's artlessness and lack of means. The moral resources for the movement had already been preempted by the implicit questioning of the Catholic bishops' right to recommend the freeze to their following on the grounds that their stand was inconsistent with liberal Democratic ideology. The movement was thus left to its meager political and financial resources. These were caricatured by stories that spent an inordinate amount of time on images of children. Although sympathetic, they nevertheless called attention to the ingenuousness and powerlessness of the movement rather than to the substance of its proposal and the proposal's implications for arms control.

The following year Ronald Reagan's reelection applied the coup de grâce to the movement. Forsberg had targeted Reagan's campaign as a test of the movement's political leverage. His landslide victory so disappointed and discouraged movement volunteers that they lost the drive to carry on (Hogan 1994, 185).[12]

## Analysis

The media window of opportunity for the movement opened to its widest point during the first several months of the campaign, during the height of bureaucratic infighting within the Reagan administration. Both media outlets admitted movement messages without qualification on technical, political, or moral grounds. The absence of an administration arms control position provided the movement an opportunity it never fully grasped—a chance either to articulate the substance of its proposal or to force greater attention to the fictive claim of the "window of vulnerability," the administration's principal justification for a massive military buildup.

The movement also failed to capitalize on the Scowcroft commission's report, whose basing recommendations for the MX contradicted the administration's case for the window of vulnerability. By that time, however, Reagan had revealed his plan for a missile shield that undercut the remaining moral grounds of the movement (see Bjork 1989).

The coverage of the *New York Times* and CBS news showed some interesting similarities and unusual differences. Television and newspaper alike noted that "citizen concern," not centralized leadership, drove the movement. With the movement lacking prominent leadership, the *Times* reduced the freeze to a mushy preference for peace that permitted both Democrats and Republicans to support it without any political risk. The absence of such leadership also allowed the *Times* to transform the freeze into a nonspecific, generalized desire for arms control (including even the flawed START proposal) and use the arms control community as a sounding board for judging its value (*NYT,* April 24, 1982, p. 8).

Far from having a nonpartisan position, the arms controllers viewed the freeze as leverage on an administration that had severed their institutional links to the executive branch. Their protestations that the freeze was too partisan seemed to express veiled fear of its being effective enough to threaten their self-interest. Some support for this interpretation comes from Albert Carnesale, then dean of the Kennedy School of Government at Harvard and a former SALT I negotiator:

> The arms controllers who have been working on all of this complicated stuff were afraid that they might ultimately lose support for arms control rather than gain it. Now, there isn't a lot of support for arms control—it's never had a huge constituency—and the freeze movement was at first viewed as a godsend. But then there grew this fear that it might pass right by, and suddenly [there was] this big political movement for this unachievable nirvana. And when it's not achieved nobody will want to bother with this boring complicated stuff. Their motives were understandable; they were trying to build political support to get something done, and the more complicated you make things the more people fall off the edges. . . . [But] the arms controllers felt that the freeze people were overselling the proposal, that if you put all those words together you can't get here to there—or it's going to take a long, long time, and its still not going to be comprehensive. (In Leavitt 1983, 7)

Carnesale and a group called the Harvard Nuclear Study Group later published a report titled *Living with Nuclear Weapons,* in which they characterized the freeze and the Reagan military buildup as "atomic escapism," recommending as the most reasonable alternative the familiar incrementalism of traditional arms control and what amounted to technology creep. The report recommended that the United States work harder in certain areas of arms control but simultaneously develop Stealth technology and air-launched cruise missiles and replace the Minuteman with a smaller, single-warhead "midgetman." The group could not come to agreement on the desirability of the MX, however (see *Time,* May 30, 1983, p. 16). Its claim to the "middle ground" was in no way less political, but because the *New York Times* had defined it as expert, it seemed to transcend politics.

The *Times* and CBS similarly portrayed movement-related activities with apolitical themes of festivals and whimsy. Both sources focused on the color of the events, not their underlying political themes or the significance of the numbers at the New York City demonstration. Because images so dominated television coverage, the portraits of the freeze supporters restricted the movement's influence. As I have shown, the reports focused predominantly on children and what children do. This had some potential for raising the moral stakes by defining the children as potential victims of a dangerous arms race (much as the test ban had successfully achieved in its campaign), but neither the movement nor the media made a compelling connection. With the movement unable to build pathos for the issue, the children became merely novel actors in what was otherwise conventional interest-group politics. In one example Bruce Morton and his camera crew recorded a girl's protestations to a nonplussed Republican House member undecided on the merits of the freeze resolution. Although the "child bites adult" story may have been appealing for its novelty, it was a measure of television's absence of interest in the substance of the issue Morton finally defined as "only a symbol." On this issue both CBS and *Times* coverage also agreed, but for different reasons.

Whereas the *New York Times* relied on the arms controllers for judging the merits and greater meaning of the issue, television coverage focused more on the legislative process, where (perhaps inadvertently) it limned the influence of the defense industry. Whereas the *Times* delegitimated the movement on the grounds of expertise, television news judged it deficient on its ability to raise sufficiently large amounts of PAC money. The reporting lacked moral bite, however. To be fair, the reporter gave no indication of countenancing the system; in fact, the reports made plain the connection between PAC money and the election of representatives favorably disposed to voting for the weapons systems developed by their benefactors, leaving it to viewers to judge whether this was ethically sound and an appropriate use of their elected representatives. In any case, the movement failed to take advantage of the moral high ground offered by the report.

While the *New York Times* used the expertise of its columnists (Hedrick Smith and Leslie Gelb) and the arms controllers to gauge the movement's influence, the credibility of the administration's position on Soviet arms strength, and the merits of START, thus rendering an ambiguous judgment, CBS used partisan experts. In one instance Herman Kahn and the anchor bolstered the administration's case against the movement, both presenting the argument as fact rather than as a contested theory. No such case was presented for the freeze, nor was Randall Forsberg consulted to offer a counterargument.

Balancing the narrowly partisan case for the administration was the revelatory analysis of the influence of the "iron triangle" offered by a partisan expert from the left. The failure to identify him as such provided the report with greater credibility than it might otherwise have had. In this respect the seemingly blind reliance on expert judgment without regard to underlying political theory or preference was fair to the extent that it was truly random. By contrast, the *New York Times* used public opinion to support its framings. Because public opinion was sufficiently ambiguous on the issue of movement support, especially with reference to the window of vulnerability, the statistics served both sides of the argument. CBS made a single reference to public opinion in one story, with no further references to these statistics in any of its subsequent reporting.

The different structures of the organizations influenced the quality of their reporting. In the case of the *New York Times,* its seasoned reporters and columnists were superbly positioned in executive departments and bureaucracies to get firsthand information and interpretation from the highest sources in government. Their reporting bore the strengths and weaknesses of this advantage, as seen in their essentially defensive reporting on the movement as an instinctive reaction to a process gone awry rather than as a substantive issue in its own right.

By contrast, Bruce Morton followed the movement as it interacted with "ordinary citizens." His focus, however, was on the people and not with the issue, whose substance he failed to explore fully except in the context of the single poll that reported shallow public support. He thus treated the movement as a fun activity, a way for the sixties generation to relive an earlier dream, this time with their children. The most visually appealing icon—children—came to symbolize the humanity of the issue. The reporter could not help but see the issue as a symbol because television news had failed to examine it with any sustained interest. In some ways this had become nearly impossible, for the evolution of nuclear arms and the technical complexities of arms control had outstripped people's abilities to understand them. The process and the technology had become sequestered within a black box whose contents were ascertainable only to a small group of experts. But this was only one of the changes evident in the state of public knowledge and influence on this issue, a topic I explore further in the conclusion.

## Notes

1. Movement activists such as Robert Kleidman (1993) and David Cortright (1993) date the movement's trajectory through the 1984 presidential election and on to 1987. Walter Mondale and other Democratic candidates made the freeze an issue for a time, but Mondale jettisoned it after getting the nomination (Cortright 1993). Following the election, foundation support began to dry up, forcing cutbacks and consolidation. The formal movement organization merged with SANE in 1986 and adopted the organization's familiar internationalist position on military, economic, and ecological issues (Kleidman 1993, 166). My analysis follows a more restricted path through the movement's public life in the national news media. Since I am interested in the resources the mass media provide to movements, and in the mass media's response to official policy and rhetoric, my attention is

fixed on this coverage. Indeed, as I will demonstrate, media attention does not necessarily overlap with the movement's true lifespan.

2. For press coverage, I calculated visibility by multiplying the reciprocal of the page number by the number of words and summing the story values for that month. For television coverage, I used the number of minutes of coverage in a given month. The final figure for both sources is a percentage of total coverage.

3. Weinberger made sure to exclude alarmists such as William Van Cleave, head of Reagan's transition team, who proposed an expensive program to shore up United States defenses to close the window (Garthoff 1994, 34).

4. In fact, it was the Soviets who thought the United States was on a war footing, taking seriously Reagan's remarks that it was possible to win a nuclear war (see Talbott 1985). In November 1983 the KGB interpreted a high-level military exercise by the United States and NATO as possible preparation for a nuclear strike on the USSR. Reagan had contributed to their unease by remarking that he considered it "a scenario for a sequence of events that could lead to the end of civilization as we know it" (in Garthoff 1994, 138).

5. A follow-up on May 16 praised Reagan for his "conversion," especially his decision to forgo "linkage," that is, conditioning negotiations on Soviet restraint in Afghanistan and Poland. The editorial presumed the Soviets would "crow" about the effect of the freeze movement, but it remarked that "few knowledgeable Americans actually favor a freeze or think it can work." It concluded, "Mr. Reagan's new approach is neither extreme nor only defensive. It deserves a solid reply" (*NYT,* May 16, 1982, sec. 4, p. 22).

6. The telephone interview took place on August 20, 1997.

7. In the fifties and sixties Kahn had argued for a nuclear war-winning strategy (see *Time,* January 3, 1961, p. 16).

8. Meyer notes that the planning coalition included 80 national and 150 local groups. Conflict among such diverse groups was inevitable and took the familiar shape of the ideological differences between the far left and more moderate environmental groups (Meyer 1990, 184–86).

9. On the political benefits of avoiding a definitive stand on an issue, see Page 1978, 178–79.

10. The bishops nevertheless continued to affirm their support of the just-war doctrine and supported Reagan's call for deep cuts in both nations' nuclear arsenals (Hogan 1994, 188).

11. Kleidman (1993, 161) reports that state and local freeze and peace PACs had actually raised more than $5 million. Nevertheless, this represented only a fraction of the amount raised by defense contractors and conservative organizations.

12. See Cortright 1993 for an account of diminished movement activity beyond this period.

# 8 Coordinates of the Oppositional Space

A survey of the media's behavior over the course of these two movements demonstrates its dampening effects on oppositional politics. I will begin with my empirical findings and then broaden the view to see what relevance these have for the wider underlying issues of participatory democracy.

The central finding of this study is that news coverage of the antinuclear movements is highly correlated with the administration's policy of the moment. In some ways this is because dissident movements are sensitive to administration policy and because in an increasingly media-influenced political environment, presidents are sensitive to movements that win media sympathy. The antinuclear movements reacted to changes in policy, and the various presidents anticipated these reactions, in some cases crafting public relations gestures that blunted the force of their influence. Such was the case with Kennedy and Reagan. Thus, looking at patterns of overall media visibility is by itself insufficient to draw any conclusions, other than to note the obvious phenomenon of event-driven coverage around administration-driven policy changes. Applying a template sensitive to news frames, however, begins to tease out patterns that reveal the direction of influence. Here the findings clearly point to an immense advantage held by government.

Peace movements are fragile creatures, capable of holding themselves together against the onslaught of government attack and the vagaries of media scrutiny only under the most extraordinary circumstances. A marriage of convenience between reformers and radicals on a single issue—in the early stages of the cold war, the cessation of nuclear testing; during its last stages, the cessation of weapons development—partly explains the delicacy of their coalition. A political culture that suspects collective power, reflected in the standards of news media coverage, also explains why they find it difficult to thrive. They are, however, capable of growth and resilience, provided they find a favorable political medium.

The test ban movement withstood an internal conflict precipitated by the decision to sacrifice a fellow organizer to the wolves and even managed to add two important constituencies to its ranks because of the strategically minded favor imparted by a White House seeking to realign its military forces. The *New York Times* bestowed its favor as well on the two new groups—students and women—taking its cues from the approving executive branch. But this relative strength lasted only until external crises lowered media attention to the "deviants" in the movement's midst. In the early stages of the freeze movement, media enthusiasm for citizen involvement pressured the White House into a variety of responses, including attempts to link it with communist plots and then more elaborate and effective ruses that included a sham arms control proposal and a utopian scheme for rendering nuclear missiles harmless. Aided by the news media, these efforts successfully redirected pressure from the White House to the movement itself. When, then, do movements enjoy the advantage?

Walter Lippmann's (1922) sour assessment of public opinion and of the limitations on the press that contribute to the public's ignorance has inspired several generations of political and media scholars. This study partly supports his contention that "there is a very direct relation between the certainty of the news and the system of record." By this Lippmann meant that the news will be reliable and useful to the extent that it records the outputs of a well-oiled, functioning government bureaucracy. In other words, we can depend on the news for reporting the temperature provided the thermometer is calibrated and working properly. The more ambiguous the situation and the less certain the outcome, however, the less dependable the news.

This parallels one of this study's findings: the antinuclear movements made their greatest strides in situations of political uncertainty. In those times, when the administrations were divided and provided less certain cues, the movements gained credibility, not necessarily because their messages were more credible, but because the official message was devalued. Recall, for example, how a divided Eisenhower administration opened the front pages of the *New York Times* to the modest demonstrations of the peace walkers and the Quakers and also how a seriously divided Reagan administration raised the credibility of the freeze, but only until START ostensibly closed the administration's ranks. This supports Bennett's (1990) findings that public opinion is a less reliable indicator of media attention than is dissent among elites, a principle formalized by Gadi Wolfsfeld (1997, 29) as the devaluation of the official message by the loss of elite control over the political environment.

To what extent, then, can we rely on the conventional news media to bring us news of nonmainstream politics? The short answer is that it depends on the special interactions of the groups and institutions involved; each has specific, limited influence on the character of the messages that emerge into public light. For government, this influence comes from the policy of the moment and the scope of internal debate. But news organizations exert control as well.

For news organizations, editorial policy and organizational constraints particular to the specific medium affect coverage patterns. The "cold war consensus" on communism allowed influential publishers such as Henry Luce to attribute sinister motivation or wide-eyed credulity to the leadership and supporters of the test ban movement. By the eighties the consensus had eroded to such an extent that it failed as a conventional standard of political judgment. It had been replaced by deference to technical expertise, accompanied by a shift in the standards of political judgment. My contention is that these changes are not unrelated, an argument I will pick up later in this chapter. More subtly, the differing organization of work in television and newspapers led each medium to differing focal points on movement politics and thus to distinctive kinds of messages.

Movements also have some limited impact. Media treatment changes with respect to their overall strategy and the pattern of ad hoc decisions they make in reaction to a chain of interacting elements—government opposition and its influence on media coverage and then the internal dissent that follows these changes. Even a disciplined movement may falter if it does not react nimbly to changing events, if it fails to take a full measure of its political environment. The freeze, for example, self-consciously fashioned itself an image thought unassailable to leaders who had studied the lessons of earlier campaigns. To deny the government and the media the opportunity to divide its ranks, leadership equated the movement with the vaguest, most general political constituency, the "public."

Indeed, the media and politicians saw in the freeze a delicious opportunity to identify with an idea that held little or no political risk. Public opinion polls provided the most prestigious certification, namely, quantitative evidence. In the end, however, the movement fell victim to administration prerogatives (a not unexpected turn of events) but also faced unfavorable competition from a new political actor—the arms control community—and a sea change in the political culture, neither of which had entered into its strategic calculations.

These are the broad outlines of my findings. I now turn to a more detailed account of each.

## Administration Policy

Coverage patterns of the *New York Times* during the cold war varied with changes in the administration's arms control policy. During the Eisenhower years the movement appeared on the front page of the *Times* more or less on schedule with major policy initiatives, as it did in the weeks before the announcement that the administration would agree to separate production issues from arms control, the previous refusal to do so having been the major impediment to a test ban. At such times ordinary citizens would suddenly appear in front-page articles that emphasized their sacrifice, dedication, and moral purpose. From this distance it is impossible to determine whether policy affected coverage or coverage acted as a final catalyst for policy change. The stories did precede policy change by a period of several weeks, but this causal order seems implausible. Editors may have sounded policymakers, anticipated the policy change, and then felt confident in placing the peace movement on the front page. Columnists such as James Reston moved freely in Washington circles and may well have detected enough straws in the wind to alert the editorial board and the reportorial staff to imminent policy shifts.[1]

During the Kennedy administration, which accepted the desirability of the test ban movement's goals, coverage was prominent, favorable, and abundant (twice the visibility of the Eisenhower era), to the point that Kennedy's sanction of the movement created a rush of media interest in it. The movement had in effect become a reliable indicator of government policy, another functioning thermometer, but one with a more colorful dial. Recall that in one story a *Times* reporter went so far as to provide CNVA plans for a church meeting that evening, complete with time and address. This is all the more impressive when one considers that an ideological split had occurred within the movement just prior to the 1960 election and grew more serious in the years leading to the Cuban missile crisis. In fact, this split would come to diminish the effectiveness of the movement as its leadership tacitly legitimated the singling out of what the media considered deviants in its midst. As the movement weakened because of internal discord, it became increasingly dependent on the news media and, concomitantly, sensitive to its inclinations to the eccentric and to discord, a lesson apparently not passed on to the New Left (see Gitlin 1980).

Similar patterns of coverage appeared in Reagan's first term. As in the earlier movement, visibility peaked at or near major policy changes. Thematic framing shifted after START, as the news media (and even major polling organizations) accepted its assumptions regarding the window of vulnerability. Television coverage paralleled that of the *New York Times* but focused somewhat more on the legislative branch.

## Editorial Policy

Space provided to oppositional politics is affected not only by administration policy but also by the editorial preference of the publication itself. For example, *Time* magazine provided little exposure to the test ban movement until just prior to the Cuban missile crisis. Before then, the weekly only reluctantly recognized the movement's existence and used condescending terms when it did. Similarly, the military editor at the *New York Times* defended his decision to conceal Project Argus with the argument that potential public outcry might have prevented tests that were in the public's better interest.

These are examples of what Daniel Hallin (1992) has called the period of "high modernism" in American journalism, a consensus around political values and institutions that all but dropped the pretense of objectivity. For *Time*'s editors, the consensus even transcended the policies of Eisenhower and Kennedy when those presidents tried to achieve the first arms control agreement with the Soviet Union. It is against this extreme example that the space afforded to the movement by the *New York Times* seems generous indeed.

The gap between the two media treatments suggests that Hallin's analysis of the cold war consensus papers over an interesting complexity. Far from presenting a single confrontational face to political dissent, the press showed an accommodationist, sometimes sympathetic side. For example, the *Times*'s morally inflected view of the test ban movement betrayed the paper's sympathy to it. Front-page coverage of the tiny demonstration by the Quakers in Times Square underscored the power of their moral message despite their numbers, a situation symbolized by the high odds they faced as they stood in the Manhattan canyon, victims of an indifferent state. Newsworthiness in the case of the Quakers and peace walkers emerged from the larger moral meaning of their message (Ettema and Glasser 1998).

During the Reagan years the movement got good exposure in the *Times* and in television news, but news frames metamorphosed with administration policy initiatives and editorial policy. Prior to START, coverage highlighted the earnestness and scrupulous motivation of the average citizen, who became the legitimating image for the paper's agenda to return Reagan to the negotiating table. After Reagan announced START, the *Times* thanked the movement for its "quiet concern" and asked it to stop insisting on what the paper considered a "simplistic slogan," subsequently highlighting the symbolic nature of movement victories in state referenda and the passage of the House freeze resolution. Indeed, to illustrate the hollowness of these achievements, the *Times* searched for examples in which self-interest triumphed over principle. They found two such examples: Catholic parishioners in a Connecticut town that was home to their defense-industry employer and local politicians who had first advocated the freeze and then lobbied their legislators and the U.S. Navy to station a portion of the nuclear-equipped fleet in their harbors to stimulate their depressed economies.

## Difference between Media Types

The structure of the medium organization and its product create variable openings for oppositional politics. I have shown how the ideologically committed *Time* magazine provided space for open debate on the hazards of radiation, sparing even scientists such as Pauling from political smears, the result of the magazine's organizational structure, which segregated science from politics and thus disallowed the latter from making claims on the former. Ironically, the liberal *New York Times* weakened the case against the movement by conflating coverage of politics with science (unlike its uncritical acceptance of Teller's equally politically inflected views), the logical result of reserving its most prominent pages for what it considered "hard" news and its unself-conscious deference to official views.

Similar medium-specific (and counterintuitive) differences appeared during the freeze movement. Television is said to be a simplifying medium because of the constraints imposed by time and the organization of its news work. These constraints encourage the development of a fixed number of motifs and themes that help a collaborative team to develop a report that coherently integrates the disparate elements into an interesting story that can be told quickly, a process that favors the process of framing (Neuman, Just, and Crigler 1992).

In the latter stages of the freeze movement, the correspondent discussed here, Bruce Morton, selected the familiar narrative device of the horse race to assess the comparative strengths of the movement and government.

Needing to tell his story succinctly, Morton reduced the competition between the movement and defense industry interests to a single dimension, money. In doing so he provided critical insight on the interest system that drove the defense appropriations process and its effect on congressional elections. The selection of the narrative frame (the contest) uncovered a potent issue for the movement that its leadership failed to exploit in the most effective way (moral indignation).

By his more or less permanent assignment to the movement, Bruce Morton got to know movement organizers and their strategies and developed a kit of sympathetic motifs and themes. His attempts to dramatize the plight of those most vulnerable led to a symbolic association of the movement with children and the interests of children. The political weight of puppets and face painting being insubstantial, the movement's significance floated away like the helium balloons so often caught on videotape.

But horse-race journalism also led to an unexpected destination, the venality of PAC politics. Like the scientists who furnished the active reader with a countervailing interpretation in the fifties, behind-the-scenes journalism provided the active viewer with an instructive guide to the influence of money on arms appropriations. Television news offered this not as an example of corruption to be cleaned up but as realistic politics in which the movement was merely a disadvantaged player. By normalizing money influence, television news equated legislative politics to influence peddling in which citizens in search of the public good competed unfavorably with better-fixed interests.

While CBS assigned a principal correspondent to the freeze, the *New York Times* rotated a larger number of reporters who viewed the story from whatever bureaucratic perspective they routinely occupied (see Fishman 1982). Writing about a dozen stories, Judith Miller was the principal movement reporter, but a dozen other *Times* reporters also tracked the freeze from the perspectives of their beats in Congress, the White House, and metropolitan New York, as did analysts in editorial posts. For reasons of either pragmatic necessity (maintaining good relations with their sources) or their understandable inability to understand the core of the Reagan arms control proposal specifically or the arcana of arms control in general, the staff at the *Times* shifted its editorial weight in the direction of the administration after START.

In one respect all the media studied here are similar. All legitimated their notice of the peace movement by reference to the mainstream participants in it, those not dedicated to pacifism as a political doctrine or, for that matter, to serious politics of any stripe. It is the temporary political practitioner, the person drawn in from a nonpolitical context (e.g., Dagmar Wilson), who gets the media's notice. Moreover, the news looks favorably on these amateurs on the condition that they satisfy a stereotypical pattern of appearance and behavior: middle-class origins, conventional dress, moral probity, and innocence of the political implications of their action. This observation supports the work of other scholars who find in American political culture a suspicion of collective, communal power (Barber 1984) and its analog, a preference for pastoralism and individualism (Gans 1979; McClosky and Zaller 1984).

## Political Culture

The period bracketed by the two movements brought major changes in the nature of movement participants and strategies that reflected important changes in the political culture itself. The leadership of the test ban movement included an eminent group of publicly committed scientists and intellectuals—Einstein, Schweitzer, Russell, Pauling, Cousins, Muste, Reisman, and Spock—whose status certified media interest, eventually winning over even the hostile editorial board of *Time* magazine. Although some in this group left the media space tarred with the brush of "leftist" and "fellow traveler" associations, their prestige won them a forum for their remarks and petition-gathering appeals and supplied the weight of expertise for challenging administration allies such as Teller. Meanwhile, clergy and philosophers weighed in with the moral case against testing, which was uncontested by the media. Ordinary citizens could thus draw on a public discourse against nuclear testing that included credible, understandable scientific expertise and persuasive moral argument. By casting themselves as victims of fallout radiation and official callousness ("no radiation without representation"), movement participants summoned resonant principles of American political culture and drew media sympathy.

By contrast, the peace movement of the eighties made a deliberate decision to avoid linkages with political celebrities. This was to be a movement of "the people." (At the New York City demonstration, movement leadership prevented politicians from speaking to the crowd.) In a way this strategy obeyed necessity, for many intellectuals had by then left the public sphere for the shelters of academe and think tanks (Jacoby 1987). Forsberg's strategy depended on the political force of public opinion aided by the credibility of arms control expertise. But this too had also been secreted within the same precincts. Although the arms controllers offered sympathy, their self-interest functionally depended on continuing the incrementalist policies of the past, as is suggested by their qualified approval of START, a signal that the administration was moving, however unwillingly, in their direction (see Russell 1983, 16). This is not to say arms control experts consciously took their positions to preserve their status and perquisites. But the movement may have posed enough of a threat to their authority as experts—many with dovish sensibilities (such as Molander)—that they may have reacted defensively to protect their status and turf.

With public intellectuals largely absent and arms controllers standoffish, investigation of the empirical case for the freeze was left to the news media, a task for which they were singularly unequipped. Television news failed to submit the Reagan administration's claims regarding Soviet military gains to sustained critical exposure. CBS dealt with the issue in detail only once, a one-sided presentation in the guise of nonpartisan expert opinion from Herman Kahn, a proponent of the nuclear war-fighting strategy championed by the CPD who in the early sixties was satirized in *Dr. Strangelove* for his doomsday machine idea. This was not a case of tacit conspiracy but a critical failure of public knowledge to fathom an increasingly abstruse technical world. As Theodore Porter has insightfully written, numbers and the derivatives of quantification serve most effectively as tools for worlds they have largely constructed (Porter 1995, 84). By the eighties arms control, which had become such a world, lay beyond the ken of ordinary citizens and their public agents.

Exacerbating the situation was a kind of institutional amnesia that afflicted the news media. By the eighties it should have been evident to reporters covering defense appropriations that the matter of threatening Soviet force levels seemed to come to an alarming boil just as the administration was building its case for a new weapons system (e.g., the neutron bomb or the MX) or just prior to presidential election campaigns (which thus appealed to the "missile gap" or the "window of vulnerability"). Deference to official views wiped clean institutional memory, despite the obvious indications of self-serving timing. In his assessment of the political viability of the freeze movement, Bruce Morton provided some hard facts regarding the movement's inferior position in its ability to raise PAC money, but this steely realism seemed reserved solely for the movement, since television reportage presented uncritically the findings of supersecret hearings that had alerted senators and representatives to the Soviet Union's "war footing."

By the eighties ideology and moral argument had lost their value as a political resource relative to technical expertise. During the test ban movement opposition leaders and their followers strained against being labeled communists and fellow travelers. The staff at *Time* magazine made casual use of these terms, as if they denominated physical traits. Even the liberal *New York Times* felt free to label Linus Pauling a "leftist." By the time of the freeze, however, these terms had all but disappeared from the media lexicon. Neither the *New York Times,* CBS News, nor *Time* magazine (see Entman and Rojecki 1993) gave Reagan's charges more than passing notice. The credibility of the movement would ultimately depend not on its patriotism but on its familiarity with the technical arcana of arms control, hardly ever mentioned in the fifties and sixties, when charges of double standards (no democracy in the USSR) and aiding and abetting the enemy cause served as a sufficient jeopardy counterattack. Although Reagan attempted the strategy, it simply did not stick. The sole television example paired coverage of the New York demonstration with one short report describing the arrest of the tiny Soviet peace "movement."

## Quantification, Expertise, and Objectivity

The hidden assumptions and dynamics of objectivity and quantification did more to disfranchise the freeze than did any other factor. Between the two antinuclear movements the public sphere for citizen discussion of arms control issues shrank to accommodate expert opinion, notwithstanding its misuse by politicians, bureaucrats, and self-styled media experts. In 1982, for example, Defense Secretary Caspar Weinberger relied on a dollar estimate comparison of U.S. and Soviet force levels for rallying public opinion and congressional support for a record-high Reagan defense budget. Nonetheless, the dollar expenditure method, a technique that compared force levels by estimating what it would cost the United States to reproduce Soviet force structure and weapons programs, was only one of several methods of assessments that the CIA and other intelligence agencies used to evaluate the Soviet arsenal. Used alone the method was deficient, for it only crudely approximated war-fighting capability and lacked a theory that translated the investment in weapons into battle outcomes. Further, the CIA acknowledged a 10–15 percent margin of error and assigned varying levels of confidence in its assessment of the multiple layers of strategic forces: personnel, new weapons acquisitions, maintenance, and so on. In short, to produce a rigorous assessment, the dollar expenditure estimate needed to be complemented with others arrived at, for example, by calculating total weapons and their firepower, analyzing deterrence theory and battle simulation, and examining Soviet military doctrine (Fischer 1983). The news media neglected to provide such a balanced assessment, thereby depriving citizens of a public discourse that included the critical concepts and questions necessary to challenge Weinberger's claims.

This omission was perhaps the most obvious way in which quantification restricted the range of public participation in issues of defense spending and arms control. Another way lay hidden amid the interlaced assumptions of public opinion, democratic theory, and objectivity, the core of which encompassed a paradox: objectivity, lately associated with rationalism and quantification (and especially statistics), appears to maximally democratize the social world, for it checks the subjective judgment that rationalizes selfish motive and the excesses of elite power. If "ineffable judgment is a highly undemocratic form of expertise," statistics offer, in theory, the most public form of knowledge (Porter 1995, 80). The modern sample survey thus appears to offer the broadest range of popular democratic participation; all that is required of a citizen is some belief or attitude that waits to be released by the fairest forms of selection and expression: random selection, anonymous interviews using standardized questions and responses, and registration of these as numbers in a database. Far from speaking for themselves, however, numbers often require expert analysis for full comprehension of their meaning. Toussaint Loua, a French statistician, realized early that statistics do not offer the transparency democratic optimists hoped they would deliver. In 1874 he wrote: "To ascend to causes, to be able to distinguish them amidst the multitude of diverse elements that act on society, to avoid oversights, requires great sagacity, sustained attention, a profound analytical spirit, and great rigor in deductions—all things that cannot be acquired, even by the most brilliant, except with long experience" (in Porter 1995, 81).

Thus while public opinion offers the promise of maximally empowering individual opinion, it simultaneously devalues the individual as a unique, interested, located being—the ultimate source of moral appeal in a culture that champions individualism as a political value. Expertise and the dispassion of numbers—designed to drive out "corruption, prejudice, and the arbitrary power of elites" (Porter 1995, 85–86)—authorizes expertise but does not necessarily renounce politics. For example, if survey research truly represents an absolute form of objectivity, a "view from nowhere" (Megill 1994, 2; Nagel 1986) that solemnly detaches partisanship from knowledge, then what do we make of the existence of Democratic and Republic pollsters or of conservative and liberal think tanks?

Illustrating the plasticity of statistics, during the freeze movement expert interpretation of public opinion changed to suit political agendas, first to support arms control—despite uneven force levels—and then to undermine the freeze concept on the grounds that the Soviets would gain by their advantage in force levels. As Susan Herbst (1993) has observed, the larger trend toward rationalization noted by Max Weber and Michel Foucault has elevated quantification to a level that makes it an important resource for gaining political power. Sufficient ambiguity in the high levels of support in public opinion for arms control and an arms buildup permitted *New York Times* reporters to draw contrary conclusions from the same body of poll data. This marked a major change in political reporting from the time of the earlier antinuclear movement.

Reporters in the eighties referred to public opinion to bolster their coverage of the issues of defense. Numbers provided high authority, a major change from the earlier era in which celebrity and moral authority provided credibility. The danger in this trend is that although personality and celebrity may sometimes offer a false trustworthiness, individual views are susceptible to challenge, whereas numbers lend an air of unassailability, despite their inherent ambiguities in the absence of a supporting theoretical context or careful attention to the effects of framing, measurement, and sampling error. Quantification reduces ambiguity by restricting what is considered important and the scope of what may be properly said about it, but "it is no less shallow for that, since it has never understood the world we are losing" (Porter 1994, 210; 1995, 84).

Even at the height of the cold war, the media presented far from a monolithic view of the sensitive issues raised by the peace movement. As doctrinaire as *Time* magazine was in its political pages, it offered the active, reasoning reader solid scientific evidence that authoritatively denied the expert support for the hard-line, almost cartoonish ideology offered in the political pages. Ironically, however, as détente was ushered in by the technical experts in the ACDA and private think tanks, the approach to arms control became less accessible to ordinary citizens. Thus the technical discourse that issued from institutionally detached quarters in the cold war had by the eighties established a power base of its own, depriving citizens and the movement of independent authority. Now, as the news media became less monolithic in their deference to government figures, they deferred to technocracy and promoted its self-interest.

As the power of individual committed expression gave way to expertise and quantification, the movement depended increasingly on exponential increases in the size of political demonstrations, which predictably entailed a concomitant devaluation of protest as a political resource (see Lipsky 1968). Purposefully shorn of celebrity, the increasing numbers in demonstrations became a faceless mass whose political significance became as susceptible to expert interpretation as public opinion had become. In advancing the political legitimacy of the freeze via public opinion, the movement abandoned a formidable source of strength so attractive to the close-up lenses of press coverage, the committed individual who galvanizes collective power through inspiration and example.

Illustrating this phenomenon, during the fifties and sixties a demonstration of just a few hundred people could command prominent coverage in the *New York Times*. Recall, for example, the stories on the peace walkers, the Quakers, and the student pickets at the White House. No doubt novelty played some part in drawing the attention of the *Times*, but coverage occasionally presented the demonstrators as citizens with serious political statements to make. Contrast this with a story of a demonstration numbering sixteen thousand held at UN missions a few days after the June 1982 Central Park rally:

> In an assembly-line operation that began at 7:30 A.M., the police carried the unresisting demonstrators to rented city buses to be booked for disorderly conduct. Some who had been arrested in the morning were back later in the day, encouraging their friends or sitting down again for another arrest. The Police Department, which had 3,000 extra officers at the demonstration sites, said the total booked was a record for a civil disobedience campaign in the city. Patrick J. Murphy, the department's chief of operations, said, "almost everybody was very well-behaved—it was a textbook exercise." (*NYT*, June 15, 1982, p. 1)

The rehearsed qualities of the protest established its hollowness, with the report pointing to the procedural smoothness of the operation rather than the larger issues underlying it. Contrasted with the sixties, when the New Left became a victim of media interest in the flamboyant and violent (Gitlin 1980), the eighties highlighted the lassitude of the movement's anonymous constituents, thereby enervating its message and perhaps putting off the energetic participants needed to drive home its goals. Denatured by the absence of passionate engagement and moral force, the protest spent itself like a wound-down clockwork.

Another hazard of these media-savvy times is identified by Charlotte Ryan, a union activist and codirector of the Boston College Media Research and Action Project, who develops media strategies for grass-roots organizing. Ryan warns her readers that organizers may be prone to "damned if you do, damned if you don't" consequences of media scrutiny. She cites this passage from a *New York Times* story of a Nevada demonstration organized to protest U.S. resumption of nuclear weapons testing in 1987:

> Although today's protest scene at the desert proving ground was reminiscent of the 1960s, it was unlike the often disorganized, spontaneous peace demonstrations of that era and, indeed, was marketed with a promotional flair befitting Madison Avenue.
>
> In recent weeks, news organizations have received numerous announcements and telephone calls about the event. Representatives of the sponsoring groups have appeared on network television shows in recent weeks, and today's arrests, which took place at 10 A.M., Pacific standard time, were timed to gain maximum publicity.
>
> "Why do you think they scheduled the arrests at 10 o'clock?" said Don Oliver, a correspondent for NBC News. "So they could make the evening news." (*NYT*, February 6, 1987, p. 8; in Ryan 1991, 161–62)

In his analysis of the political history of the Voting Rights Act of 1965, political scientist David Garrow examined the marches, demonstrations, and violence that took place throughout the South in the early sixties, but especially in Selma, Alabama, in the winter and early spring of 1965. He argues that the most repugnant scenes of these events (e.g., a restrained demonstrator twisting away from a police dog lunging at his midsection) resulted from Martin Luther King's strategy of "nonviolent coercion," inciting local whites to commit violence on black demonstrators in the presence of the press. The following quotation from King's memoirs illustrates the intent of his media strategy: "Instead of submitting to surreptitious cruelty in thousands of dark jail cells and on countless shadowed street corners, he would force his oppressor to commit his brutality openly—in the light of day—with the rest of the world looking on" (in Garrow 1978, 225). The success of nonviolent coercion depended on the cooperation of the northern press, which trained its cameras on the savagery to produce the famous photos and film footage that aroused public opinion and federal action. The media had not merely turned the lights on the barbarisms of everyday life in the South; it shamed the nation by drawing a sharp contrast between reality and the most fundamental standards of decency, releasing the moral outrage necessary to activate political change. By the time of the freeze, movements had become aware of media practices, and the media had become aware of movement public relation strategies. Such awareness exposed an artifice that would displace the ingenuous idealism at the heart of an authentic moral appeal, thereby spoiling its chances for success.

Thus, as the second antinuclear movement moved away from (or was denied access to) sources of moral authority, it lost an important source of credibility. I am reminded of the famous Ferris wheel scene in the film

*The Third Man,* where Harry Lime uses the device to instruct his friend Holly Martins on a wider view of his nefarious trade. Holly has learned that his friend is in a black-market trade, distributing diluted penicillin to hospitals where men with gangrene and women in childbirth die for lack of a fully effective medicine. At the top of the wheel Lime looks down on the amusement park grounds and points out that if one of the tiny specks walking below were to disappear, its fate would be of little consequence to those who observed the world from this vantage point: "Look down there. Would you really feel any pity if one of those dots stopped moving forever?" Later Martins sees close up the diluted penicillin's effect on children dying of meningitis and is finally persuaded to betray his friend to the police.[2]

Unlike the civil rights issue, the antinuclear movements did not have stark real-life examples that the news media might have been coaxed to cover. They were limited to the by then iconic images of atmospheric test mushroom clouds and the grainy and silent newsreel footage of Hiroshima's slow-moving casualties. They also could not penetrate the multiple rings of security that conceal the immense firepower amassed over forty years of a nuclear arms race. The progressive concealment—first by national security, then by secret development, and finally by progressive mystification of arms control—made the issue difficult to dramatize in a realistic way that could summon the powers of moral suasion. Inevitably the issue was relinquished to the control of guardians, allowing them to make judgments about citizens interests and acting on these judgments without adequate accountability.

## What Does It Matter?

Of course one needs to make the case that citizen involvement on these issues makes a difference. It is absolutely clear that in both cases the antinuclear movements achieved the not inconsiderable success of placing on the national agenda a vitally important issue that none of the presidents could safely ignore (see Knopf 1991). The test ban movement pressed its case most successfully on the dangers of radiation, which preempted future resumption of atmospheric testing. No matter their editorial position, most newspapers and popular magazines during the fifties and sixties (the *New York Times* and *Time* magazine included) devoted a good deal of space to the issue, educating the public with the concepts and explanations needed to demonstrate the potential long-term dangers involved (Rosi 1964). On the larger issue of arms control, however, the movement had much less success, as is indicated most obviously by the partial nature of the test ban and by continued support for arms buildups to counter the Soviet threat, which Eisenhower, Kennedy, and others exaggerated for political advantage. Indeed, poll results showed the more educated public was willing to risk possible long-term effects of radiation for the sake of short-term gains in national security.

The freeze is credited with bringing the Reagan administration to heel, at least on its most jingoistic nuclear rhetoric (Waller 1987, 301), and with forcing some response on arms control. A closer look, however, reveals that these responses were small indeed. What might the outcome have been, for example, had the media framed the MX debate in the light of majority support for a nuclear weapons freeze? When the House voted in favor of the freeze and promptly followed with a contradictory vote in favor of the MX, the media hardly stirred. Nor did they vigorously pursue the fictive window of vulnerability even after the Scowcroft commission tepidly endorsed the MX and recommended that it be lowered into the allegedly vulnerable Minuteman silos. The absence of such critical reporting or more industrious examination of the window of vulnerability enabled an expensive arms program and helped Reagan to escape voter judgment on the freeze issue in the 1984 election.

Indeed, the freeze proposal's implications for ending the arms race were never fully and seriously explored; the media consistently failed to follow the proposal's simple statement of principle to its implied conclusion: a radical program of arresting the phenomenon of technology creep so as to change the system of arms control. The movement's strategy for keeping its message simple also played a part. The price was a partial and symbolic victory without any further policy implications.

On the larger issue of the significance of the Reagan arms control policy, it is tempting to work backward from the disintegration of the Soviet Union and credit the arms buildup as instrumental in that event. Indeed, this is the view of orthodox historians of the cold war, such as John Lewis Gaddis, who praises Reagan's policy for rebuilding American self-confidence, negotiating from strength, and "spooking" the Soviets. Gaddis argues that the Reagan arms buildup strained the Soviet economy to the breaking point, by then already weakened by economic stagnation and "strategic overstretch" due to the war in Afghanistan and open rebellion in Poland (Gaddis 1990, 203–4). The president who had been elected on a platform that rejected détente ironically had by the end of his term reinvigorated it and negotiated a 30 percent reduction in nuclear arms. Three years later the cold war ended, certifying, in Gaddis's view, George Kennan's doctrine of containment.

Another school of historians argues that the United States greatly exaggerated the threat of communist menace to lay a strategic rationale for expanding its global influence. H. W. Brands, for example, argues that the origins of the cold war lay in Truman's decision to replace Britain with the United States as the balance-keeper in European geopolitics. Withdrawal of British interest in maintaining the status quo in Turkey and American fears of Soviet influence there led to the rationale, which was articulated in a report written by the state, war, and navy departments that recommended American intervention. With Turkey representing (at best) an unknown for rallying American public opinion, the report identified the Greek civil war then taking place as the touchstone for the bogey of communist influence that would require U.S. response. At a stroke the report converted what under other circumstances would have been a questionable American interest in the outcome of an ambiguous civil war into a symbol of confidence building for noncommunist nations. In addition, it simplified the task of mobilizing public opinion against the Soviet Union by conflating communism with fascism: "If Stalin was simply Hitler with a better mustache, Americans had merely to transfer to the former their loathing for the latter." The logic of the Truman doctrine fed into the Manichaean worldview promoted by NSC-68 and shortly thereafter into the railings of Joe McCarthy (Brands 1993, 20–21, 32).

In Brands's view American innocence depended on the confirmation of a powerful Soviet devil, with evidence for the preposterous overstatement of its power lying in the swift and unremarkable collapse of the Soviet Union: "The most obvious question was whether it had been necessary for Americans to get so worked up over an enemy that proved to be a shell—a large country, to be sure, with formidable weapons, but one with a decrepit economy and a political will insufficient to keep it from breaking apart at the first wind of honest reform. Had the Soviet threat ever been very great? How much of the perceived threat had been genuine, and how much a figment of American imaginations?" (*Washington Post,* September 26, 1993, sec. X, p. 1).

In time the Soviet and American intelligence documents may add weight to one of these interpretations. The issue is not whether the peace movements were correct in their assessment (although there is much evidence, cited in this study, of the continuous exaggeration of Soviet force levels to justify huge defense budgets) but how they were treated by the mass media, which were no better equipped than these eminent historians to render a judgment. This, then, raises the familiar issue of citizen competence to judge the formidable complexities of arms policy.

In terms of the two superpowers' relative strength during the late fifties and early sixties, the United States enjoyed unquestioned superiority. As I have shown, the news media simply failed to illuminate the issue well enough for interested citizens to come to an informed opinion. Can one seriously claim that a wider circulation of the true state of the arms balance would not have affected public sentiment on bearing the burden of enormous defense budgets?

Even so, it might be replied, are we not better served by disinterested technocratic expertise? Are not these decisions better made by those who have the specialized training to assess the significance of throw-weight, launchers, nuclear war scenarios, and so on? One way to assess their success is to look at the record of the last fifty years. The evidence seems to support such a conclusion. We have, after all, avoided a nuclear conflict. But has that been the result of precisely calibrated arms policy?

After reviewing in great detail the record of changing nuclear strategies, Freedman (1989) concludes that the key to avoiding nuclear confrontation was not rational analysis of increasingly complex scenarios but the political will to avert conflict. Despite superficial appeals to a rational calculus, much uncertainty remains after the application of theories that model likely reactions to changing circumstances built, as Freedman points out, on conjecture and speculation (428–29). Indeed, in his analysis of both high- and low-risk nuclear crises (e.g., Korea, Berlin, and Cuba), Richard Betts found that leaders often made decisions after discussions that did not fully evaluate or speak to the full military consequences of their actions (Betts 1987, 9).

On the issue of instrumental knowledge, that necessary to make the calculations of cost and risk for nuclear strategy, there are both theoretical and historical reasons for questioning the practice of leaving the decisions to specialized elites. Decisions about cost and risk *are* formidably complex, as is indicated by the difficulty even technologically sophisticated reporters have in conveying the details of nuclear arms levels and their implications for strategy to the readers of the *New York Times*. But, as I have showed, even the most specialized elites disagreed about proper decision making.

In the end the most persuasive argument for increased citizen control of these issues rests on both pragmatic and moral grounds. On pragmatic grounds, the evidence shows that detailed technical understanding has not played the most important role in the making of arms policy. For example, Ronald Reagan conducted such policy with less than a nuanced understanding of Soviet force levels. In addition, Congress approved funding for the deployment of the MX even though the missile would have been no less vulnerable to a Soviet first strike than were existing systems, and Les Aspin formulated a successful strategy for congressional approval of the MX based on a materially irrelevant "balancing" rule used by legislators to determine the direction of their vote.

The moral case also rejects mere expertise. Arguments about nuclear issues are ultimately about the morality of judgments such as the justifiability of nuclear war and the moral permissibility of targeting population centers (Dahl 1989, 68). Since these decisions are about moral choices, they require the involvement of more citizens rather than fewer, because ultimately all are affected and because, as Dahl argues, each citizen is best equipped to understand his or her own interests (Dahl 1989, 70).

Here, then, I return to the media's special responsibility for creating publics, for making citizens aware of the issues that affect them. I have shown here that such responsibility lies less in providing a detailed account of increasingly complex facts than in contextualizing these in a moral universe. This contextualization is where the techniques of investigative journalism are most effective, namely, in establishing a deviation from the ideal (see Protess et al. 1991). In these accounts reporters shine their lights on unpleasant realities, be they corrupt public officials, unhealthy practices, or dangerous conditions. Certainly the facts of these are important, but more important for mobilizing citizen (and elite) reaction and response are the individual cases that illustrate the injustices and create the passion necessary for reform (Ettema and Glasser 1998). Political movements dwell in these same precincts and are most effective when they make their case on these grounds. This study supports the conclusion that their success depends on the media's recognition of their moral case and of the public discourse inspired by it. To date, however, the media have not fully engaged with the causes of the antinuclear movements and thus have helped to exclude nuclear weapons issues from the public agenda. In so doing, they have narrowed the scope of debate on an issue that has the gravest consequences for every living being.

## The Constricted Public Sphere

In the period bracketed by the two movements, the extremes of uncritical cold war ideology collapsed, only to be replaced by media deference to technical expertise. What is constant across both movements is the devaluation of citizen participation in politics. At the core of that devaluation is not a conspiracy of the wealthy or the powerful but a constricted notion regarding the proper ends of power. Media and citizens alike share in the suspicion of politics, especially as practiced by those who do not enjoy legitimacy, which apparently is restricted to officeholders and those certified as expert.

Political movements live in a space granted them by the mass media when government policy is in disarray or at odds with an aroused public opinion. A long view of the evidence shows that the media act as a counterbalance on government and antinuclear movements alike. The weight of media influence is ever poised, however, to restore legitimacy on the nuclear issue to government and its agents.

## Notes

1. In his memoirs Reston recounts how Kennedy had suggested that it might be helpful if Reston wrote a column on the United States' intention to go to war if the Soviets threatened Berlin. With the knowledge of the paper's "responsible" editors, the specific words used to communicate the threat were approved by Kennedy himself. In an elliptical statement of regret, Reston said he was unhappy with this "selective cooperation," suggesting that such "old secret diplomacy," now over, and the diplomacy of secret arrangements it had facilitated had not prevented and may have even contributed to the start of two world wars (Reston 1991, 469–70).

2. I would like to thank Alexander Kantas (1974) for this insight and example.

# REFERENCES CITED


Aldrich, John H., John L. Sullivan, and Eugene Borgada. 1989. "Foreign Affairs and Issue Voting: Do Presidential Candidates 'Waltz before a Blind Audience'?" *American Political Science Review* 83:123–41.

Almond, Gabriel A. 1960. *The American People and Foreign Policy.* New York: Praeger.

Althaus, Scott L. 1998. "Information Effects in Collective Preferences." *American Political Science Review* 92:545–58.

Ambrose, Stephen E. 1984. *Eisenhower: The President.* New York: Simon and Schuster.

———. 1988. *Rise to Globalism: American Foreign Policy since 1938.* New York: Penguin.

Baldasty, Gerald J. 1976. "Toward an Understanding of the First Amendment: Boston Newspapers, 1782–1791." *Journalism History* 3:25–32.

Barber, Benjamin. 1984. *Strong Democracy.* Berkeley: University of California Press.

Bartels, Larry M. 1991. "Constituency Opinion and Congressional Policy Making: The Reagan Defense Buildup." *American Political Science Review* 85:457–74.

Bennett, W. Lance. 1990. "Toward a Theory of Press-State Relations in the United States." *Journal of Communication* 40:103–26.

Berlin, Isaiah. 1969. "Two Concepts of Liberty." *Four Essays on Liberty.* Oxford: Oxford University Press.

Beschloss, Michael R. 1986. *MAYDAY: Eisenhower, Khrushchev and the U2 Affair.* New York: Harper and Row.

———. 1991. *The Crisis Years: Kennedy and Khrushchev, 1961–1963.* New York: Burlingame.

Betts, Richard K. 1987. *Nuclear Blackmail and Nuclear Balance.* Washington, D.C.: The Brookings Institution.

Bjork, Rebecca S. 1989. "The Strategic Defense Initiative: Symbolic Containment of the Nuclear Threat." Ph.D. diss., University of Southern California, Los Angeles.

Blechman, Barry M., and Stephen S. Kaplan. 1978. *Force without War: U.S. Armed Forces as a Political Instrument.* Washington: The Brookings Institution.

Bourdieu, Pierre. 1979. "Public Opinion Does Not Exist." In *Communication and Class Struggle,* ed. Armand Mattelart and Seth Siegelaub. London: International General.

Bower, Gordon H., John B. Black, and Terence J. Turner. 1979. "Scripts in Memory for Text." *Cognitive Psychology* 11:177–220.

Boyer, Paul. 1984. "From Activism to Apathy: The American People and Nuclear Weapons, 1953–1980." *Journal of American History* 70:821–44.

———. 1985. *By the Bomb's Early Light.* New York: Pantheon.

Brands, H. W. 1993. *The Devil We Knew: Americans and the Cold War.* New York: Oxford University Press.

Brown, Richard D. 1996. *The Strength of a People: The Idea of an Informed Citizenry, 1650–1870.* Chapel Hill: University of North Carolina Press.

Brzezinski, Zbigniew. 1983. *Power and Principle: Memoirs of the National Security Adviser, 1977–1981.* New York: Farrar, Straus, Giroux.

Cannon, Lou. 1991. *President Reagan: The Role of a Lifetime.* New York: Simon and Schuster.

Chilton, Paul. 1987. "Metaphor, Euphemism, and the Militarization of Language." *Current Research on Peace and Violence* 10:7–19.

Chong, Dennis. 1991. *Collective Action and the Civil Rights Movement.* Chicago: University of Chicago Press.

Cohen, Bernard C. 1973. *The Public's Impact on Foreign Policy.* Boston: Little, Brown.

Cortright, David. 1993. *Peace Works: The Citizen's Role in Ending the Cold War.* Boulder, Colo.: Westview.

Cousins, Norman. 1972. *The Improbable Triumvirate: John F. Kennedy, Pope John, Nikita Khrushchev.* New York: Norton.

Dahl, Robert A. 1985. *Controlling Nuclear Weapons: Democracy versus Guardianship.* Syracuse, N.Y.: Syracuse University Press.

———. 1989. *Democracy and Its Critics.* New Haven, Conn.: Yale University Press.

DeBenedetti, Charles. 1980. *The Peace Reform in American History.* Bloomington: Indiana University Press.

Deming, Barbara. 1961. "The Ordeal of SANE." *The Nation,* March 11, pp. 200–205.

Divine, Robert A. 1978. *Blowing on the Wind: The Nuclear Test Debate, 1954–1960.* New York: Oxford University Press.

Doty, Paul. 1984. "What Now for Arms Control?" In *The Nuclear Weapons Freeze and Arms Control,* ed. Steven E. Miller. Cambridge, Mass.: Ballinger.

Drew, Elizabeth. 1983. "A Political Journal." *New Yorker,* June 20, pp. 39–63.

Edelman, Murray. 1988. *Constructing the Political Spectacle*. Chicago: University of Chicago Press.

Eisinger, Peter K. 1973. "The Conditions of Protest Behavior in American Cities." *American Political Science Review* 67:11–28.

Elster, Jon. 1983. *Sour Grapes: Studies in the Subversion of Rationality*. Cambridge: Cambridge University Press.

Entman, Robert M. 1989. *Democracy without Citizens*. New York: Oxford University Press.

———. 1991. "Framing U.S. Coverage of International News: Contrasts in Narratives of the KAL and Iran Air Incidents." *Journal of Communication* 41:6–27.

———. 1993. "Framing: Toward Clarification of a Fractured Paradigm." *Journal of Communication* 43:51–58.

Entman, Robert M., and Benjamin I. Page. 1992. "The News before the Storm." Paper presented at the annual meeting of the American Political Science Association, Chicago.

Entman, Robert M., and Andrew Rojecki. 1993. "Freezing Out the Public: Elite and Media Framing of the U.S. Anti-Nuclear Movement." *Political Communication* 10:155–73.

Entman, Robert M., and Steven S. Wildman. 1992. "Reconciling Economic and Non-economic Perspectives on Media Policy: Transcending the Marketplace of Ideas." *Journal of Communication* 42:5–19.

Ettema, James, and Theodore L. Glasser. 1998. *Custodians of Conscience: Investigative Journalism and Public Virtue*. New York: Columbia University Press.

Ferguson, Thomas, and Joel Rogers. 1986. *Right Turn*. New York: Hill and Wang.

Fischer, Gregory W. 1983. "Conceptual Models, Judgment, and the Treatment of Uncertainty in Nuclear Threat Assessment." *Journal of Social Issues* 39:87–116.

Fishman, Mark. 1982. "News and Nonevents: Making the Visible Invisible." In *Individuals in Mass Media Organizations: Creativity and Constraint*, ed. James S. Ettema and D. Charles Whitney. Beverly Hills, Calif.: Sage.

Fiske, Susan T., and Shelley E. Taylor. 1991. *Social Cognition*. New York: McGraw-Hill.

Fowler, Roger. 1991. *Language in the News*. London: Routledge.

Freedman, Lawrence. 1989. *The Evolution of Nuclear Strategy*. New York: St. Martin's.

Fussell, Paul. 1975. *The Great War and Modern Memory*. New York: Oxford University Press.

Gaddis, John Lewis. 1990. "Arms Control: Hanging Tough Paid Off." In *Reagan as President*, ed. Paul Boyer. Chicago: Ivan R. Dee.

Gallup, George H. 1984. *Public Opinion 1983*. Wilmington, Del.: Scholarly Resources.

Gamson, William A., and David S. Meyer. 1996. "Framing Political Opportunity."

In *Comparative Perspectives on Social Movements,* ed. Doug McAdam, John D. McCarthy, and Mayer N. Zald. Cambridge: Cambridge University Press.

Gamson, William A., and André Modigliani. 1966. "Knowledge and Foreign Policy Opinions: Some Models for Consideration." *Public Opinion Quarterly* 30:187–99.

———. 1989. "Media Discourse and Public Opinion on Nuclear Power: A Constructionist Approach." *American Journal of Sociology* 95:1–37.

Gans, Herbert J. 1979. *Deciding What's News.* New York: Vintage.

Garrow, David. 1978. *Protest at Selma: Martin Luther King, Jr., and the Voting Rights Act of 1965.* New Haven, Conn.: Yale University Press.

Garthoff, Raymond L. 1985. *Détente and Confrontation: American-Soviet Relations from Nixon to Reagan.* Washington, D.C.: The Brookings Institution.

———. 1994. *The Great Transition: American-Soviet Relations and the End of the Cold War.* Washington, D.C.: The Brookings Institution.

Giglio, James N. 1991. *The Presidency of John F. Kennedy.* Lawrence: University Press of Kansas.

Ginsberg, Benjamin. 1986. *The Captive Public: How Mass Opinion Promotes State Power.* New York: Basic Books.

Gitlin, Todd. 1980. *The Whole World Is Watching.* Berkeley: University of California Press.

Graham, Thomas W. 1988. "The Pattern and Importance of Public Knowledge in the Nuclear Age." *Journal of Conflict Resolution* 32:319–34.

———. 1989. "The Politics of Failure: Strategic Nuclear Arms Control, Public Opinion, and Domestic Politics in the United States—1945–1980." Ph.D. diss., Massachusetts Institute of Technology, Cambridge.

Gurevitch, Michael, and Mark R. Levy, eds. 1985. *Mass Communication Review Yearbook.* Vol. 5. Beverly Hills, Calif.: Sage.

Haig, Alexander. 1984. *Caveat: Realism, Reagan, and Foreign Policy.* New York: Macmillan.

Halberstam, David. 1979. *The Powers That Be.* New York: Knopf.

Hallin, Daniel C. 1986. *The Uncensored War.* New York: Oxford University Press.

———. 1992. "The Passing of the 'High Modernism' of American Journalism." *Journal of Communication* 42:14–25.

Hartley, Thomas, and Bruce Russett. 1992. "Public Opinion and the Common Defense: Who Governs Military Spending in the United States?" *American Political Science Review* 86:905–15.

Hastie, Reid. 1987. "Information Processing Theory for the Survey Researcher." In *Social Information Processing and Survey Methodology,* ed. Hans-J. Hippler, Norbert Schwarz, and Seymour Sudman. New York: Springer-Verlag.

Hayek, Friedrich A. von. 1944. *The Road to Serfdom.* Chicago: University of Chicago Press.

Herbst, Susan. 1993. *Numbered Voices.* Chicago: University of Chicago Press.

Herken, Gregg. 1985. *Counsels of War.* New York: Knopf.

Hirschman, Albert O. 1991. *The Rhetoric of Reaction.* Cambridge, Mass.: Belknap/Harvard University Press.

Hogan, Michael J. 1994. *The Nuclear Freeze Campaign: Rhetoric and Foreign Policy in the Telepolitical Age.* East Lansing: Michigan State University Press.

Hogan, Michael, and Ted J. Smith III. 1991. "Public Opinion and the Freeze." *Public Opinion Quarterly* 55:554–69.

Holmes, Stephen. 1990. "Liberal Constraints on Private Power: Reflections on the Origins of Access Regulation." In *Democracy and the Mass Media,* ed. Judith Lichtenberg. Cambridge: Cambridge University Press.

Jacoby, Russell. 1987. *The Last Intellectuals: American Culture in the Age of Academe.* New York: Basic Books.

Janis, Irving. 1972. *Victims of Group-Think.* Boston: Houghton-Mifflin.

Kantas, Alexander A. 1974. "Enigmas of Justice: Marlowe to Ford." Ph.D. diss., University of Illinois, Urbana-Champaign.

Karp, Walter. 1992. *Buried Alive: Essays on Our Endangered Republic.* New York: Franklin Square.

Katz, Milton S. 1986. *Ban the Bomb: A History of SANE, the Committee for a Sane Nuclear Policy, 1957–1985.* New York: Greenwood.

Kern, Montague, Patricia W. Levering, and Ralph B. Levering. 1983. *The Kennedy Crises: The Press, the Presidency, and Foreign Policy.* Chapel Hill: University of North Carolina Press.

Kertzer, David I. 1988. *Ritual, Politics, and Power.* New Haven, Conn.: Yale University Press.

Kingdon, John W. 1984. *Agendas, Alternatives, and Public Policies.* Boston: Little, Brown.

Klandermans, Bert. 1984. "Mobilization and Participation: Social-Psychological Expansions of Resource Mobilization Theory." *American Sociological Review* 49:583–600.

Kleidman, Robert. 1993. *Organizing for Peace: Neutrality, the Test Ban, and the Freeze.* Syracuse, N.Y.: Syracuse University Press.

Knopf, Jeffrey W. 1991. "Domestic Politics, Citizen Activism, and U.S. Nuclear Arms Control Policy." Ph.D. diss., Stanford University, Palo Alto, Calif.

Kohut, Andrew. 1989. "Stability and Change in Opinions about Nuclear Weapons Policy, 1945–1987." *Deep Cuts and the Future of Nuclear Deterrence.* Lanham, Md.: University Press of America.

Leavitt, Robert. 1983. "Freezing the Arms Race: The Genesis of a Mass Movement." Unpublished study, Kennedy School of Government, Harvard University, Cambridge, Mass.

Levy, Leonard W. 1988. *Original Intent and the Framers' Constitution.* New York: Macmillan.

*Liberation.* 1956. "Tract for the Times," 1 (March): 3–6.

———. 1959a. "A Sign of the Times," 4 (May): 10.

———. 1959b. "The Times Replies," 4 (June): 3–4.

———. 1963a. "SANE Repudiates Unilateralists, Pacifists," 8 (Summer): 11.

———. 1963b. "Uncle Tom-ism in the Peace Movement," 8 (June): 3.

Lipsky, Michael. 1968. "Protest as a Political Resource." *American Political Science Review* 62:1145–58.

Lodge, Milton, and Kathleen M. McGraw. 1991. Response to Kuklinski et al., "Where Is the Schema? Critiques." *American Political Science Review* 85:1357–64.

Lowi, Theodore. 1973. *The Politics of Disorder.* New York: Basic Books.

Madison, James. [1788] 1981. *The Federalist,* no. 10. In *The Mind of the Founder,* ed. Marvin Meyers. Hanover, N.H.: University Press of New England.

Mansbridge, Jane J. 1980. *Beyond Adversary Democracy.* Chicago: University of Chicago Press.

Mayer, William G. 1993. "Poll Trends: Trends in Media Usage." *Public Opinion Quarterly* 57:593–611.

McAdam, Doug. 1982. *Political Process and the Development of Black Insurgency.* Chicago: University of Chicago Press.

McAdam, Doug, John D. McCarthy, and Mayer N. Zald. 1988. "Social Movements." In *Handbook of Sociology,* ed. Neil J. Smelser. Newbury Park, Calif.: Sage.

McClosky, Herbert, and John Zaller. 1984. *The American Ethos.* Cambridge, Mass.: Harvard University Press.

McCombs, Maxwell E., and Donald L. Shaw. 1972. "The Agenda-Setting Function of the Mass Media." *Public Opinion Quarterly* 36:176–87.

Megill, Allan. 1994. "Four Senses of Objectivity." In *Rethinking Objectivity,* ed. Allan Megill. Durham, N.C.: Duke University Press.

Meyer, David S. 1990. *A Winter of Discontent: The Nuclear Freeze and American Politics.* New York: Praeger.

Mill, John Stuart. [1859] 1974. *On Liberty.* London: Penguin.

Miller, Warren, and J. Merrill Shanks. 1982. "Policy Direction and Presidential Leadership—Alternative Interpretations of the 1980 Election." *British Journal of Political Science* 12:299–356.

Nacos, Brigitte L. 1990. *The Press, Presidents, and Crises.* New York: Columbia University Press.

Nagel, Thomas. 1986. *The View from Nowhere.* New York: Oxford University Press.

Neuman, W. Russell, Marion R. Just, and Ann N. Crigler. 1992. *Common Knowledge: News and the Construction of Political Meaning.* Chicago: University of Chicago Press.

Newhouse, John. 1989. *War and Peace in the Nuclear Age.* New York: Knopf.

Noelle-Neumann, Elisabeth. 1974. "The Spiral of Silence: A Theory of Public Opinion." *Journal of Communication* 24:43–51.

Osgood, Charles E. 1962. *An Alternative to War or Surrender.* Urbana: University of Illinois Press.

Pach, Chester J., Jr., and Elmo Richardson. 1991. *The Presidency of Dwight D. Eisenhower.* Lawrence: University Press of Kansas.

Page, Benjamin I. 1978. *Choices and Echoes in Presidential Elections.* Chicago: University of Chicago Press.

———. 1996. *Who Deliberates?* Chicago: University of Chicago Press.

Page, Benjamin I., and Robert Y. Shapiro. 1992. *The Rational Public.* Chicago: University of Chicago Press.

Page, Benjamin I., Robert Y. Shapiro, and Glenn R. Dempsey. 1990. "What Moves Public Opinion." *American Political Science Review* 81:23–43.

Paletz, David L., and Robert M. Entman. 1981. *Media Power Politics.* New York: Free Press.

Paterson, Thomas G., ed. 1989. *Kennedy's Quest for Victory: American Foreign Policy, 1961–1963.* New York: Oxford University Press.

Porter, Theodore. 1994. "Objectivity as Standardization." In *Rethinking Objectivity,* ed. Allan Megill. Durham, N.C.: Duke University Press.

———. 1995. *Trust in Numbers: The Pursuit of Objectivity in Science and Public Life.* Princeton, N.J.: Princeton University Press.

Protess, David L., Fay L. Cook, Jack C. Doppelt, James S. Ettema, Margaret T. Gordon, Donna R. Leff, and Peter Miller. 1991. *The Journalism of Outrage: Investigative Reporting and Agenda Building in America.* New York: Guilford.

Reston, James. 1991. *Deadline: A Memoir.* New York: Random House.

Rosenau, James N. 1961. *Public Opinion and Foreign Policy.* New York: Random House.

Rosi, Eugene J. 1964. "How 50 Periodicals and the *Times* Interpreted the Test Ban Controversy." *Journalism Quarterly* 41:545–56.

———. 1965. "Mass and Attentive Opinion on Nuclear Weapons Tests and Fallout, 1965–1963." *Public Opinion Quarterly* 29:280–97.

Russell, George. 1983. "Cooling off the Nuclear Debate." *Time,* May 30, p. 16.

Russett, Bruce. 1990. *Controlling the Sword.* Cambridge, Mass.: Harvard University Press.

Ryan, Charlotte. 1991. *Prime Time Activism: Media Strategies for Grassroots Organizing.* Boston: South End.

Sanders, Jerry W. 1983. *Peddlers of Crisis: The Committee on the Present Danger and the Politics of Containment.* Boston: South End.

Schattschneider, E. E. 1960. *The Semi-Sovereign People.* New York: Holt, Rinehart and Winston.

Schlesinger, Arthur M., Jr. 1965. *A Thousand Days.* Boston: Houghton-Mifflin.

Schultz, George P. 1993. *Triumph and Turmoil: My Years as Secretary of State.* New York: Macmillan.

Schutz, Alfred. 1962. *Collected Papers.* Vol. 1: *The Problem of Social Reality.* The Hague: Martinus Nijhoff.

Schwartz, Stephen I. 1998. *Atomic Audit: The Costs and Consequences of U.S. Nuclear Weapons since 1940.* Washington, D.C.: The Brookings Institution.

Seaborg, Glenn T. 1981. *Kennedy, Khrushchev, and the Test Ban.* Berkeley: University of California Press.

Sherry, Michael. 1995. *In the Shadow of War.* New Haven, Conn.: Yale University Press.

Shoemaker, Pamela J., and Stephen D. Reese. 1996. *Mediating the Message: Theories of Influence on Mass Media Content.* New York: Longman.

Smith, Jeffery A. 1986. "Legal Historians and the Press Cause." *Communications and the Law* 8:69–80.

Solo, Pam. 1988. *From Protest to Policy.* Cambridge, Mass.: Ballinger.

Spector, Malcom, and John I. Kitsuse. 1987. *Constructing Social Problems.* New York: Aldine De Gruyter.

Strodthoff, Glenn G., Robert P. Hawkins, and A. Clay Schoenfeld. 1985. "Media Roles in a Social Movement: A Model of Ideology Diffusion." *Journal of Communication* 35:134–53.

Stubbing, Richard A. 1986. *The Defense Game.* New York: Harper and Row.

Swerdlow, Amy. 1993. *Women Strike for Peace.* Chicago: University of Chicago Press.

Talbott, Strobe. 1985. *Deadly Gambits.* New York: Vintage.

Teeter, Dwight L. 1968. "Press Freedom and the Public Printing." *Journalism Quarterly* 45:445–51.

Terchek, Ronald J. 1970. *The Making of the Test Ban Treaty.* The Hague: Martinus Nijhoff.

Tetlock, Philip E. 1983. "Policy-Makers' Images of International Conflict." *Journal of Social Issues* 39:67–86.

Truman, David Bicknell. 1951. *The Governmental Process: Political Interests and Public Opinion.* New York: Knopf.

Tuchman, Gaye. 1972. "Objectivity as Strategic Ritual: An Examination of Newsmen's Notions of Objectivity." *American Journal of Sociology* 77:660–79.

———. 1978. *Making News.* New York: Free Press.

Tyler, Tom R., and Kathleen M. McGraw. 1983. "The Threat of Nuclear War: Risk Interpretation and Behavioral Response." *Journal of Social Issues* 39:25–40.

Tyroler, Charles, II. 1984. *Alerting America: The Papers of the Committee on the Present Danger.* Washington, D.C.: Pergamon-Brassey's.

Vance, Cyrus R. 1983. *Hard Choices: Critical Years in America's Foreign Policy.* New York: Simon and Schuster.

Waller, Douglas C. 1987. *Congress and the Nuclear Freeze.* Amherst: University of Massachusetts.

Weart, Spencer R. 1988. *Nuclear Fear: A History of Images.* Cambridge, Mass.: Harvard University Press.

White, Hayden V. 1987. *The Content of the Form.* Baltimore, Md.: Johns Hopkins University Press.

Wittner, Lawrence S. 1969. *Rebels against the War: The American Peace Movement, 1941–1960.* New York: Columbia University Press.

———. 1993. *One World or None: A History of the World Nuclear Disarmament Movement through 1953*. Vol. 1. Stanford, Calif.: Stanford University Press.

Wolfsfeld, Gadi. 1997. *Media and Political Conflict: News from the Middle East*. Cambridge: Cambridge University Press.

Zaller, John. 1992. *The Nature and Origins of Mass Opinion*. New York: Cambridge University Press.

Zelizer, Barbie. 1992. *Covering the Body*. Chicago: University of Chicago.

INDEX

ANDREW ROJECKI, an assistant professor in the School of Journalism at Indiana University at Bloomington, is the coauthor (with Robert Entman) of *The Black Image in the White Mind: Media and Race Relations in America*. His research interests are in political movements and political communication.

THE HISTORY OF COMMUNICATION

Selling Free Enterprise: The Business Assault on Labor and Liberalism, 1945–60 *Elizabeth A. Fones-Wolf*

Last Rights: Revisiting *Four Theories of the Press* *Edited by John C. Nerone*

"We Called Each Other Comrade": Charles H. Kerr & Company, Radical Publishers *Allen Ruff*

WCFL, Chicago's Voice of Labor, 1926–78 *Nathan Godfried*

Taking the Risk Out of Democracy: Corporate Propaganda versus Freedom and Liberty *Alex Carey; edited by Andrew Lohrey*

Media, Market, and Democracy in China: Between the Party Line and the Bottom Line *Yuezhi Zhao*

Print Culture in a Diverse America *Edited by James P. Danky and Wayne A. Wiegand*

The Newspaper Indian: Native American Identity in the Press, 1820–90 *John M. Coward*

E. W. Scripps and the Business of Newspapers *Gerald J. Baldasty*

Picturing the Past: Media, History, and Photography *Edited by Bonnie Brennen and Hanno Hardt*

Rich Media, Poor Democracy: Communication Politics in Dubious Times *Robert W. McChesney*

Silencing the Opposition: Antinuclear Movements and the Media in the Cold War *Andrew Rojecki*

Typeset in 10/13 Sabon
with Sabon display
Designed by Dennis Roberts
Composed by Jim Proefrock
at the University of Illinois Press
Manufactured by Versa Press, Inc.

University of Illinois Press
1325 South Oak Street
Champaign, IL 61820-6903
www.press.uillinois.edu